OUR PROMISED LAND

THE MACMILLAN COMPANY
NEW YORK · BOSTON · CHICAGO · DALLAS
ATLANTA · SAN FRANCISCO

MACMILLAN AND CO., Limited
LONDON · BOMBAY · CALCUTTA · MADRAS
MELBOURNE

THE MACMILLAN COMPANY
OF CANADA, Limited
TORONTO

Our
Promised Land

by
Richard L.
Neuberger

New York
The Macmillan Company
1938

TO

MY MOTHER

"I view a great, free, and independent empire on the Columbia River."   —Thomas Jefferson, 1813.

Foreword

SOME newspaper men have England for a beat. Others have Switzerland or Egypt or Japan. Still others have New York or Washington or Chicago. Mine is a frontier—a frontier so vast that France could be put into it twice and there yet would be many miles of forests and ravines and uplands left over.

I am indebted to a great many individuals for much of my information and material about this frontier. Some of their names, I do not know. To mention all whose names I do know would be to list hundreds of people living all the way from the continental divide to where the Columbia River rushes into the sea. Some of the men and women to whom I am appreciative are ranchers and homesteaders who never have been out of the backwoods. Others are those who either make or report the news along the thin strip of Western civilization that fringes the Pacific seaboard.

These people, I am sure, are amply thanked with the thought that they have been of some help in presenting to the nation at large a description of the inhabitants and land of the last great outpost region of our country.

I am grateful to the editors of *Harper's Magazine, Esquire, Collier's,* the *American Magazine, Current History, Country Home,* the New York *Times,* the *New Republic,* and the Portland *Oregonian* for their courteous permission to reprint, with some revision, a portion of the material and papers contained in this volume.

RICHARD L. NEUBERGER

PORTLAND, OREGON
August 30, 1938

Contents

OUR PROMISED LAND

1. Last Frontier

IN ALL that vast expanse of land and water and sky, the twin threads of the single-line railroad track, glistening in the morning sun, were the only indication of the presence of man.

Off on the distant horizon a thin wisp of smoke might have marked the campfire of a roving band of fishermen or a solitary trapper, but it might also have been the smouldering product of one of the lightning storms that periodically crackled in the mountains. Loneliness and solitude dominated the scene. It was a day's journey by horseback to the horizon, and yet all those level meadows and gently sloping valleys that would have to be crossed had never been touched by a farmer's plow.

The silence was broken only by the wind in the fir trees and by the subdued roar of white water breaking around a boulder in the center of the river. A heron waded gingerly in an eddy close to the shore, and high overhead an eagle flapped majestically across the sky. A muskrat scrambled through a clump of cottonwood. Beyond the meadows and plains, hills towered on every side. Only where the river poured turbulently into a deep-walled gorge was there a break in the slopes and uplands, rolling away to the horizon like the folds of a monstrous blanket. Here and there, patches of rich green grass and still darker rectangles of evergreen trees transformed the blanket into a vast quilt.

Except for the railroad twisting among hummocks of ground and clinging to the shore of the river, the vista was as primitive and wild as the frowning battlements of lava and granite which crowned the hills. The track seemed to represent an invader that had penetrated a strange land but never conquered it. Up to the edge of the right-of-way the wilderness reached, waiting in ominous silence to claim back the brief foothold man had won. Where the track circled around a forbidding bluff, the ribbons of steel looked far more ephemeral than the gnarled and wind-beaten hemlock trees that grew precariously from the lip of the precipice. A block signal, arm pointed toward the sky, stood at another sharp turn in the line—gaunt and weather-stained guardian of the people from distant cities who were whirled through this fastness of forest and meadow and mountain.

The sun had been in the sky only a few hours, and the dew of the August morning still wetted the grass and the rails. Far off—one hundred miles away—night clouds had not yet been blown from a towering snow-covered peak that loomed above the surrounding country. They clung to the lofty mass of rock and glaciers like a half-torn shroud. Below the mountain, undulating ridges and valleys rolled on as seemingly endless as the waves of the ocean. The scene might have been a new land, looked upon for the first time by argonauts bolder and more adventurous than the civilization they had left behind them. Only the winding railroad track told that the argonauts had already arrived—that, though they had not yet subdued and vanquished the wilderness, they had nevertheless entered its stronghold.

-2-

The great, black mountain locomotive came from the East, and through the spacious window of the dining car, all this vast, unpopulated grandeur was observed by a broad-shouldered, thirty-eight-year-old man in a thin tweed suit. He let his breakfast grow cold as he watched the region the train was traversing. While his scrambled eggs jelled into hard little lumps and his companions reminded him of his rapidly cooling meal, he gazed out of the window across the plains and hills and uplands to the mountains far beyond. Then he turned away, picked up a menu stuck between the cream pitcher and sugar bowl, and started to scribble on its back. As the Democratic party's 1920 nominee for the Vice Presidency of the United States, he had an important campaign speech to deliver that night, and he knew now what he would say. He wrote hastily:

Coming through today on the train has made me think pretty deeply. When you cross the mountain States and that portion of the coast States that lies well back from the ocean, you are impressed by those great stretches of physical territory, just land, territory now practically unused but destined some day to contain the homes of thousands and hundreds of thousands of citizens like us, a territory to be developed by the nation and for the nation. As we were coming down the river today, I could not help thinking, as everyone does, of all that water running down unchecked to the sea.

The big man put down his pencil for a moment, and looked out of the window again. The train was still rolling through a solitude of valleys and hills that, like some mammoth wall of defense, seemed to cut off the world without. He wrote on:

It is not a problem of the State of Washington; it is not a problem of the State of Idaho; it is a problem that touches all the other States in the Union. It is a problem that interests us way back in old New York State.

The train crashed on. It sped past the lonely butte where half a century before the Sioux had massacred Custer. It crossed the Clearwater and whizzed between long walls of fir and cedar trees. Into the basin of the Snake it clattered, and the hills became more formidable and the mountains higher. Over trestles with spindly-latticed legs and through tunnels that bisected ranges, the train roared. Mountain time became Pacific time and watches were set back an hour. Toward the sunset the big locomotive moved again. A saddle-like pass appeared in the ranges ahead, and the train began to climb. It jerked fitfully up the grade, and at a siding where the rails were red with rust a second engine was coupled to the long chain of passenger and baggage cars. Cliffs towered on either side of the line, and the train rolled with a dull roar through a rock-bound corridor of bluffs and crags. Above in the August sky the sun shone brightly, but in the gorge the dusk of twilight prevailed. Occasionally there was a deeper roar when the ledge supporting the track was gone altogether, and separating the train and the angry mountain river below were only girders of steel suspended from the wall of the canyon. Over the humpback summit of the pass the train finally puffed, and coasted easily down the other slope. Boulders and shale and pumice gave way to wind-blown hemlocks and sagebrush; and then tall timber hemmed in the right-of-way once more. Trees that had been growing when Columbus discovered the New World cast shadows on the roadbed. Wild flowers encircled their trunks with a pris-matic, gently swaying fringe. Firs as high as skyscrapers lifted needled tops toward the blue. In the wake of the train, an antlered deer bounded out of one forest wall, cleared the track in a mighty leap, and disappeared in the other curtain of green.

The train gathered speed. The line was straighter now. The timbered highlands merged with broad valleys that were measured by horizons rather than miles. For hours the hammering locomotive had been hauling the heavy, black cars through a limitless land of mountains and lowlands and rivers and plains, and yet the railroad itself remained virtually the only evidence of man's handiwork. The train had passed enough timber to house millions of people crowded in slums and rookeries on the other side of the continent. It had whizzed by pastures and ranges that could graze thousands of herds of sheep and cattle. It had penetrated plains sufficiently fertile and wide to give countless impoverished families a decent and adequate diet. It had crossed mountain ranges rich with copper and bauxite and silver and zinc. It had rolled along the shores of the great river of the West: the Columbia, crashing to the sea with the potential hydroelectric power of a score of Niagaras. And in this treasure-trove of undeveloped resources, miles and miles of solitude had separated every farm and settlement. Ranches were farther apart than the eye could see. The big engine stopped for water as often as it ground to a halt to let on and off passengers. Loneliness dominated each vista, whether it was one of smiling valleys or forbidding, rock-crowned hills.

The train pounded west. Smoke billowed back from the locomotive in a column parallel to the single line of telephone wires. Now and then double track would be seen momentarily; another train would crash by in the opposite direction; in a few minutes it would be a smudge of smoke in the distance; only the ominous red of the block signals would tell that it had passed, and again the landscape would be still and lonely. Grade crossings would be hours apart—over roads dusty and little used. Deep and mysterious draws in the increasingly distant hills would become thin and narrow slits.

And Franklin Delano Roosevelt, not quite forty and still a comparative newcomer in politics, sat and looked out on the last great frontier of his country, a frontier eight times as large as England and as untamed as Africa. The vastness of this frontier had held and astounded him when he let his breakfast grow cold while he scrawled on a dining-car menu the hope that some day the deep wilderness through which he was passing would contain the homes of hundreds of thousands of his fellow citizens.

The train hurtled on into the sundown.

-3-

It was Thomas Jefferson who started it all. The third President could not be content with his country confined to a narrow strip of land along the Atlantic coast. He wanted American sovereignty extended as far beyond as man could travel. Throughout his career Jefferson had been intrigued by the possibilities of going overland to the Pacific Ocean. A decade before he became President, he had given attention in Paris to the wild plans of John Ledyard, a madcap Connecticut Yankee who promised to sail from Siberia to the cape-bound Northwest coast. Every story that came from the hinterlands, Jefferson listened to eagerly. It was there he believed the future and hope of America lay. To scores of his contemporaries Jefferson wrote letters predicting a great, free, and independent empire on the Western seaboard beyond the Rocky Mountains. Particularly, he was interested in the tales of a vast waterway that cut through the ranges and emptied into the Pacific. At that time all the principal rivers of the continent—the Mississippi, the Missouri, the St. Lawrence, the Hudson, the Kennebec, the Rappahannock, the Potomac—were thought to flow mainly from north to south. But Jefferson had heard stories of a great, roaring river that bisected the uplands of the Pacific *from east to west*. Jonathan Carver, a soldier who had explored the country around the Great Lakes, had picked up whispers and gossip about this legendary stream and in his journals he called it the Oregon. Jefferson read Carver's reports, and so did the poet William Cullen Bryant, who wrote in "Thanatopsis":

> Or lose thyself in the continuous woods
> Where rolls the Oregon, and hears no sound,
> Save his own dashings . . .

The fuel of Jefferson's vivid imagination was fired by the stories of the river that carved its way through the massive mountains on the other side of the plains. He was not sure whether its correct name was Oregon or Columbia, but he knew it had a place in American destiny. Of that he was certain. He had the river in mind when he made the Louisiana Purchase from Napoleon, and he was thinking almost exclusively of it the day he announced the most important exploration in the history of the United States: the Lewis and Clark expedition.

Not alone the third President of the struggling young republic sought dominion over the mysterious waterway in the West. The British wanted it also. They hoped to extend the Canadian border to the southern bank of the stream's east-to-west traverse between the ramparts of the mountains. To the nation that first explored and claimed the region would go a vast prize—although how vast it actually was neither Jefferson nor the English realized. On the shoulders of a young man Jefferson, with characteristic daring, placed the responsibility of determining the future size of the country. He commissioned his private secretary, twenty-nine-year-old Captain Meriwether Lewis of Albemarle, Virginia, to lead an expedition that would map the Louisiana Purchase, go down the great river beyond the plains, and plant the Stars and Stripes on the shore of the Pacific Ocean. To share his command, Lewis selected his best friend, Lieutenant William Clark, with whom he had played as a boy. On May 14, 1804, the two young army officers turned their backs on civilization at St. Louis, and with twenty-nine companions set out to try to triple the area of their country. No other expedition has ever been so inextricably bound up with the fate of the United States as this one of lean and jut-jawed men carrying long rifles and wearing buckskin tunics—men who plunged into an unknown wilderness toward a goal at least a year's travel away.

They went hungry; they froze; they fled for their lives from hostile Indians; they suffered terribly beneath the scorching sun of the plains; they endured long and melancholy delays while the intrepid Captain Lewis sustained periodic spells of hypochondria; they forded icy rivers and climbed jagged ranges. But inexorably and relentlessly they forged westward. Across the prairie and over the continental divide they trekked. An Indian woman named Sacajawea guided them. Several times she saved the expedition from tragic and fatal failure. Had it not been for this squaw with her half-breed papoose on her back, the English trader Simon Fraser might have reached the Pacific ahead of Jefferson's emissaries, and the history of the North American continent would have been changed. In the autumn of 1805, from a towering, razorback ridge, Sacajawea pointed dramatically into the sunset. Lewis shaded his eyes, and his gaze followed her bony, brown forefinger. In the distance shimmered a river larger and more turbulent than any they yet had crossed—a river that flowed westward. The Indian woman, the slave-wife won in a gambling bout by a French interpreter named Charbonneau, had guided them to the great waterway of which President Jefferson had dreamed! Not far beyond was the Pacific, and American dominion over a limitless land of mountains and plains and forests and hills.

In long, slim canoes the frontiersmen swept down the foaming river. They referred to it not as the Oregon but as the Columbia, using the name given in 1792 by Captain Robert Gray of Boston, who called the stream after his schooner the *Columbia*. Both Lewis and Clark were amazed by the immensity and grandeur of the region the river drained. Continually in their journals they commented on the seemingly endless uplands and heights that marched away to the horizon. They saw mountains which lost their summits in the clouds, and they glimpsed waterfalls that fell so far they vanished in spray. They picked wild flowers within sight of eternal snows, and they stood at the base of overhanging cliffs man could never climb. Where the Columbia boiled angrily around tooth-edged boulders or dropped thunderously over precipitous ledges, they made laborious portages and tramped through forests as dense as darkness. Most of these scenes no white men had glimpsed before. Only near the mouth of the river had others of their race preceded them.

Early in November the waterway widened and, far off, the argonauts thought they heard a dull and rumbling roar. A few days later they swept around a bend in the river and there it was, breaking in white-capped splendor beyond the bar—the Pacific! They went ashore, unfurled the American flag, and Lewis walked to a towering fir tree and carved in a place he stripped clear of bark,

MERIWETHER LEWIS, ALBEMARLE, VIRGINIA
CAPTAIN U. S. ARMY, NOVEMBER 18, 1805

The tall explorer, thin and somber in tattered buckskins, later to die a suicide to his spells of melancholia, walked back to the canoes. He looked for a minute on the rugged, fir-studded hills, on the swiftly flowing river, and on the ocean that stretched across the world to the Orient. He laid his hand on the flagstaff and watched the red, white, and blue standard blowing in the breeze. Then he gave orders to camp.

Not many days afterwards, Clark carved with his hatchet on another lofty tree,

WM. CLARK DECEMBER 3D 1805 BY
LAND FROM THE U. STATES IN 1804 & 5

And so the little republic on the other side of the continent laid claim to the vast wilderness fastnesses of the Oregon Country.

Lewis and Clark struggled back to civilization, and Jefferson said their return brought him "unspeakable joy." From the time the expedition had vanished in the solitude, the President had been mercilessly attacked by the Federalists for sending thirty-one men to certain death. In language surprisingly similar to that applied to the more resourceful among his successors, Jefferson was accused of risking "life and property in a search for the mysteries of the unknown and the unknowable." So the reappearance of the ragged and weary frontiersmen solved a political as well as a territorial problem. The United States had beaten the British in the race to claim the Columbia River region, and Jefferson stood vindicated in his sending of an expedition to explore the wilderness of the West. The President had predicted that Lewis might see mastodons and mammoths in the unexplored fastnesses beyond the Missouri, but now he felt his young secretary had found something more important than prehistoric elephants—a vast river basin of limitless potentialities in timber, minerals, furs, and agricultural products. Until he died Jefferson believed that much of the future of the United States lay in the great region through which Lewis and Clark had trekked. During the remainder of his term in the Presidency and later at Monticello, he wrote enthusiastically about the territory Captain Lewis had described to him.

Among those with whom Jefferson carried on correspondence regarding the Far West was John Jacob Astor, who wanted to establish a post at the mouth of the Columbia River for the fur trade with the Orient. The reports of Lewis and Clark, and the letters of Jefferson, convinced Astor that this could be done. An essential part of his scheme was a route overland through the mountain barrier that extended from the Arctic Sea to Mexico—and the dauntless adventurers picked by America's third President had pioneered the trail. So Astor formed the Pacific Fur Company, guaranteed to put up $400,000 himself, and the first capitalistic venture in the history of the Columbia River was under way.

-4-

In this initial struggle between New York finance and the most primitive river basin of the continent, the forces of the wilderness almost triumphed. Astor's 290-ton ship the *Tonquin* sent the mate and seven men to find a channel through the breakers that crashed on the bar outside the mouth of the

Columbia. Ebenezer Fox, the mate, looked at the wild and angry maelstrom where the great river joined the sea, and shook his head. He said he did not want to leave his bones in the wilderness. Captain Jonathan Thorne was a thin-lipped commander who believed in naval discipline. "Push off!" he ordered. The mate and his men were never seen again. Neither was another boat that tried to cross the ominous bar. And the *Tonquin* itself disappeared forever a short time later. Captain Thorne disregarded the warnings that he was treating the Indians too brutally. He believed he had the savages thoroughly cowed. One morning he pushed aside a sailor who said the Indians were concealing weapons beneath the bundles of furs they brought on board to trade. Jonathan Thorne never pushed another seaman. A chief nodded his head in signal and the Indians pulled out tomahawks and spears and killed every white man on deck, save one. This nameless survivor they only wounded. While the savages looted the ship, he crawled painfully, unnoticed, down the companionway to the powder magazine. The Indians watching from the shore saw the *Tonquin* suddenly soar skyward in a thousand pieces and then settle on the ocean, a conglomeration of splintered wood and mangled bodies. One of the bodies was that of Alexander Mackay, Astor's partner. The first man hatcheted when the Indians attacked, his dream of wealth in the Northwest gained him only a grave in uncharted seas beside his red-skinned slayers.

Overland, along the route of Lewis and Clark, the Pacific Fur Company sent another expedition. Astor was determined to control a post where the Columbia flowed into the Pacific. The perils suffered by land were almost as dangerous as the fatal events encountered by the *Tonquin* at sea. In the cavernous Hell's Canyon of the Snake River, just above the juncture of that swirling stream with the Columbia, the adventurers nearly perished from starvation. Four boats were lost and two men were drowned. One man went mad. The party that finally reached the mouth of the Columbia was ragged and tattered and half crazed from privation. Astor sent another ship, the *Lark*, to the tiny settlement his men had whittled in the wilderness. But the *Lark* got snared in a brute of a storm and sank with a heavy loss of life. Astor's enterprise seemed cursed. Death and destruction accompanied each mile by land and each knot at sea. The financial failure of the project was inevitable. The post was abandoned. The white man had gained an insecure foothold where the great river of the West joined the Pacific, but the price in suffering and money had been too high. Probably the most significant results of the adventure were the mapping of what later became the Oregon Trail, and the writing of *Astoria* by Washington Irving. The vast territory beyond the Rocky Mountains this book described with the picturesqueness and fervor that the prosaic journals of Lewis and Clark had lacked.

The next year Irving published *The Adventures of Captain Bonneville*. The hero was a romantic, vagabonding army officer, Benjamin L. E. Bonneville, who explored and charted the Columbia River region. In crisp, colorful prose that stemmed from French birth and background, he kept an account of his westward wanderings which he turned over to Irving. Bonneville himself was of little importance. He had obtained an appointment to West Point through the influence of Thomas Paine, but his military career was undistinguished. He built posts in such unstrategic places that the fur trappers called them Fort Nonsense and Bonneville's Folly. His name is perpetuated in history because of two incidents: his opportune contact with Irving, and the fact that the settlement named after him was located exactly at tidewater on the Columbia, where a century later other army officers dis-

covered they could generate countless kilowatts of hydroelectric energy.

-5-

Men with plows started to cross the continent. Wagon
trains creaked laboriously over the continental divide. Missionaries, both Catholic and Protestant, risked their lives to
bring religion to the country's farthest-flung frontier. A Pres-
byterian minister named Marcus Whitman took his indom-
itable wife Narcissa with him into the wilderness. She was
the first white woman to make a home west of the Rocky
Mountains. And although Narcissa's blond scalp eventually
dangled against the greasy thigh of a Cayuse warrior, other
housewives followed her trail to the Pacific coast. In 1839 the
first large company made the journey overland from Missouri. Others arrived by sea and rocked and tossed in the
stormy waters off the tip of South America. "Did you come
the plains over, the Isthmus across, or the Horn around?"
was the singsong question that greeted newcomers.

Where once trappers had crept from windfall to windfall
under the mantle of night, fearful of the sinewy arms that
sped arrows and tomahawks on their deadly way, occasional
farms and ranches began to appear. Agriculture slowly supplanted trading as the dominant activity. The start made by
the massacred Whitman and the other pioneering missionaries
became the foundation of at least a desultory sort of civilization. The farms were lonely and far between, but they were
farms and not trappers' bivouacs. The settlements were small
and isolated, but they were actually settlements and no longer
trading posts. The plow and hoe were superseding the trap
and rifle. To the farms there was some permanence. They

might last only a year or so—until the water gave out, or a young wife from Ohio went mad from loneliness, or the Indians took to the warpath. Yet these shacks on their plots of crudely cultivated ground represented the genesis of a civilization, even if there was not enough fertility in some of the soil to grow a decent crop of weeds. When the Indians raided and attacked, the farmers died at the windows of their cabins or later at the torture stake. Unlike the trappers and traders, they did not flee silently along the forest trails and over another wall of ranges to a new abundance of furs. The farmers had homes to defend, and they stayed and defended them. They also built blockhouses and stockades, and they appealed to Washington for military assistance. Troops of blue-coated cavalry began to patrol the wilds of the Columbia basin, and one night a young lieutenant named Phil Sheridan made a wild ride at the head of a column of dragoons up the river canyon from Fort Vancouver and rescued a party of settlers besieged at The Dalles.

One of the pioneers from the Middle West had brought an Iowa statute book in the bottom of his covered wagon, and he took this with him in 1843 to a meeting at the Methodist mission in Champoeg. There, in the heart of the Columbia River region, the first provisional government on the continent's sundown seaboard was established. The constitution of Iowa was the pattern it followed, because the settler's volume had been the only authoritative precedent available. "We, the people of the Oregon Territory," proclaimed the preamble, "for the purposes of mutual protection and to secure peace and prosperity among ourselves agree to adopt the following laws and regulations until such time as the United States of America extend their jurisdiction over us."

Back across the country went the report of these first stirrings of the body *politic* on the Pacific coast. Talk even began

of building a railroad over the Rockies, although Senator
McDuffie of South Carolina shouted that such a proposal
"manifests a wild spirit of adventure which I never expected
to hear broached in the Senate of the United States." Thomas
H. Benton of Missouri roared him down and cried that
America's future was in the great area beyond the mountains.
But England had not yet relinquished all hope that it was
British future which rested in the vast river basin west of the
divide. Lewis and Clark had explored the region inland but,
after all, it had been an officer of His Majesty's navy, Captain
George Vancouver, who had cruised painstakingly along the
coast line a decade and a half before the American frontiersmen reached the mouth of the Columbia. Vancouver had
charted the navigable waters so carefully that his maps still
were used above all others. The British insisted the basin of
the Columbia was rightfully theirs.

The possession of the watershed of the great river of the
West suddenly became a national question. It was the issue of
the hour. "Fifty-four forty or fight!" challenged the Democrats in the election of 1844, and they were swept triumphantly into office. President Polk soon compromised on his
campaign demand that the United States control all the territory up to the line of 54° 40'. He accepted a boundary line
at the forty-ninth parallel. "Oh! mouse that was delivered of
a mountain," Benton taunted the members of his own party
in the Senate, "thy name shall be fifty-four forty." Secretary
of State Calhoun answered that boldness and precipitancy
might have lost the Columbia basin forever, whereas caution
and moderation assured at least partial success.

-6-

In 1859 approximately one hundred thousand square miles
of the Columbia River area was admitted to the Union as the
State of Oregon. The United States now had an actual as
well as a theoretical stake in the Pacific Northwest. The re-
placing of the ephemeral framework of the trading-post system with a more enduring civilization was accelerated. The
migration westward increased. Along the Oregon Trail hundreds of wagons rumbled where only a dozen had rolled
before. Yet the vast wilderness was not basically altered.
Here and there settlements of a more permanent variety expanded into towns, and the towns into cities—but the frontier
remained. The rest of the country, with the exception of the
arid Southwest, was at least relatively cultivated agricul-
turally and fairly well developed industrially. But the land
Lewis and Clark had explored was still almost as primeval as
when the adventurers had paddled down the turbulent river
in 1805. The same flag flew over the Battery in New York
and the blockhouse at Oregon City, but the halyards were
raised and lowered by men who literally lived in different
periods of civilization. Steamboats plowed the Mississippi
when only log rafts and Indian canoes rode the rapids of the
Columbia. The Brooklyn Bridge was already a familiar feature of the New York landscape when the reconnaissance
engineers of the newly organized Great Northern Railway
were desperately trying to persuade their superstitious Black-
feet guides to show them a hidden pass through the Rockies
that Indian legend said was haunted. Chicago was a tumultuous city and had survived the fire precipitated by Mrs.
O'Leary's cow when Indians, furious over the encroachment
of the white men on their last domain, were still terrorizing

settlers in the Oregon Country. Philadelphia and Cleveland
had assumed metropolitan stature long before the Northern
Pacific connected Seattle with the East by rail. A citizen in
Richmond could be run over by an electric car while his fellow citizens were having their scalps lifted on the opposite
side of the continent. In no other nation was there a contrast
any greater than that between the centers of population along
the Atlantic seaboard and the wilderness of the Columbia
River watershed. The life span of an aged man, at least,
separated them in development—a circumstance not surprising, for there had been a settlement at New York practically
two centuries before Sacajawea pointed her arm and Captain
Lewis saw the Columbia. Women in Baltimore and Boston
and Buffalo could walk placidly to church in Easter bonnets
and gay bustles, and other women three thousand miles away
worshiped in rustic, stockaded mission houses and thanked
God when they did not suffer the fate of their friends who
had been dragged from the same mission houses to die
instantly beneath a tomahawk or later, tied against a stunted
pine tree in some Indian village. The most humble individuals in Kansas City and New York were enjoying the early
results of technological skill when old Governor Elisha Ferry
of Washington Territory was traveling via cow ponies and
birchbark canoes through the land he ruled.

The Far Northwest for the first time became more than a
fringe on the carpet of the nation when the railroads, which
Senator McDuffie had predicted the wealth of the Indies
could not get to Oregon, were laid across the mountains.
Villard formed his famous "blind pool" and built the Northern Pacific. From the main track of the Union Pacific, the
Harrimans constructed the Oregon Short Line over the
ranges of Idaho and through the gorge of the Columbia.
Down the southern bank of the river the Short Line twisted.

Along the northern shore, James J. Hill's Great Northern grabbed a similar short cut through the bastions of the Cascades. Expansion-minded Congresses generously handed out the people's lands to the railroads, and the railroads launched intensive ballyhoo campaigns to persuade people to settle on acres fit only for coyotes and sagebrush. "Without Irrigation Western Progress Stops" is the present slogan of the National Reclamation Association. This little item did not bother the railroads in the nineties, and thousands of Americans were promised that a new Canaan awaited them on the rainless plateaus of Idaho and eastern Washington. For a year or so, the accumulated moisture in the soil would give a precarious support to dry farming. Then the water would be gone, and abandoned homesteads and crumbling barns would tell a story of blighted hopes and wasted effort.

Many of the farmers thus broken in spirit and body, by a combination of ruthless promoters and the grim wilderness, turned to the cities that were springing up at places strategic to rail and water transportation. They did not know there were other lands near by where grain and fruits and vegetables could grow in abundance. Nor were they aware of the irrigation and reclamation possibilities of the sections they had deserted. The Federal government had made no adequate soil and water surveys, and the State governments were new and inefficient. Frying hamburger steaks in a waterfront eating joint in Seattle or Portland was preferable to attempting to grow wheat on ground as dry as leather. The loneliness of even the fertile valleys and uplands also helped to drive people from the farms to the cities. There were no automobiles in those days, and frequently ranches were a hundred miles apart. Many of the newcomers to the Columbia basin had been agriculturalists in the Middle West and the South, but this solitude was not encompassed by their

experiences. In Iowa in 1880 there were twenty-nine persons
to every square mile, and in Kentucky there were forty-one.
In the Pacific Northwest each individual averaged a square
mile to himself. Men and women who could not stand the
loneliness turned their backs on their farms and moved to the
cities and towns. They became longshoremen and streetcar
conductors and waitresses and stenographers—anything to
escape from the isolation they were not psychologically
equipped to endure. The State of Washington increased
much more rapidly in population than Oregon or Idaho or
Montana. In 1880 it had fewer people per square mile than
Oregon, but a decade later it was far ahead of the other State.
This was because Washington, with the great harbor of Puget
Sound, contained the principal cities of the territory. When
scorched crops or unbearable solitude drove immigrants from
the soil, they generally wandered to Seattle or Spokane or
Tacoma. The only competition to these Washington cities
was from Portland, built where the tranquil Willamette
joined the foaming Columbia. Today, not all the abandoned
farms in the Columbia River country are on land that is arid
and dry. Just as the deserted homesteads of the sagebrush
plateau tell a mute story of seeds that never sprouted, so do
decaying ranch houses in remote but lush valleys describe
loneliness as unendurable as fruitless crops. A considerable
proportion of these discouraged and beaten farmers gave up
rural life for good.

So when most of the other cities of America had assumed
their full stature, the communities of the Pacific Northwest
were still draining the frontier. The region was also the
jumping-off place for the Klondike gold rush in '98; and
back to Tacoma, Seattle, and Portland came many of the adventurers who struggled over Chilkoot Pass—the lucky and
the luckless ones alike—to revive the frontier spirit in cities

civilization's furrow. Thick forests stand untouched by the logger's ax. Surging rivers flow to the Pacific unchecked by power penstocks. A limited train en route through the Northwest from the East clicks along, hour after hour, past slopes and wooded groves unchanged since Lewis and Clark. Rich prizes in timber, hydroelectricity, wheat, copper, bauxite, gold, and transportation rights are yet to be won by the groups that can gain the tightest grip on government. In Seattle and Portland exist all the complexities and social problems of modern civilization, but in the mountains that loom like a fortress battlement back of these cities are the resources about which centered the economic conflicts of the country's expansion period. More than two-fifths of the potential hydroelectric energy of the nation, one-fifth of the wheat, two-fifths of the forest reserves, one-fourth of the wool, one-third of the apples, the world's principal supply of Chinook salmon— these are trophies that have helped to merge the political eras of the New Deal and the Robber Barons and, in the struggle for governmental powers, have been used to justify either ruthless or garish tactics, as particular situations required.

Politics on the last great frontier of the United States is a snarled and uproarious hodgepodge. Many of the occurrences are almost incredible, savoring of scenes in a Gilbert and Sullivan operetta or a George S. Kaufman farce. Equally bizarre and fantastic are the individual participants in this chaotic political hurly-burly. Frequently they perform in ludicrous, Harpo Marx fashion and attempt to have themselves laughed into power; the State of Washington has a lieutenant governor who says: "I never wear a vest. I'm not going to let anybody accuse me of standing for the vested interests." On other occasions these *Of Thee I Sing* characters come to life, pose as statesmen of Olympian wisdom, and make public utterances that invariably lead to embarrassing consequences;

the governor of Oregon gained office as a 100 per cent bona fide New Dealer, and virtually his first official act was to veto a legislative act that later turned out to have been drafted by the President and Secretary Ickes.

The politicians of the Northwest use any and all techniques, and their political philosophy is as jumbled as confetti. Their strange antics have thoroughly insulated their constituents against virtually all political shocks. The voters of the Columbia Basin are prepared for anything. To them a seemingly shell-shocked public official is not unique. He is merely a typical ingredient in the weirdest political goulash ever stirred with the ladle of democracy. The struggle to control the treasure-trove of undeveloped natural resources of an area more than twice as large as Spain has become a *disjecta membra* of society women pickets, politically minded orchestra leaders, ambitious chiropractors and painless dentists, blustering army officers, crackpot initiative campaigns to increase the bounty on sage rats in Crook County in Oregon, or to make it a misdemeanor for anyone in the State to smoke a cigarette; pugilistic labor organizers, high public officials with assumed names, other public officials who alter their basic economic theories as casually as they change their underwear, and still others whose social behavior is approximately that of a troop of escaped lunatics.

The Pacific Northwest is still largely a frontier. Its politics have not yet been reduced to the comparatively smoothly working machine operations of the East and Middle West. It is not a one-party region like the South. Action in the open is a necessary prerequisite to domination of a State by either a power company or a labor union. The votes of the people of Puyallup, Washington, or New Meadows, Idaho, cannot be won by slipping the right word and a roll of currency to a potbellied gentleman in a checked vest and derby hat. Some-

thing different must be done, such as streamlining a reactionary Republican into a left-wing Democrat or promising to
solve the unemployment situation by putting a lightly clad
female hostess on every trolley car. And the stakes are big
and the game is desperately played—because the Northwest
is a new country.

The four States of the Columbia River section have 13 per
cent of the area of the United States, but only 2.8 per cent of
the population. It is one of the last stands of the American
wilderness, a relatively unsettled expanse of lofty mountains,
fertile valleys, swift-flowing rivers, and timbered uplands to
which two hundred thousand refugees from the scorched Dust
Bowl have turned for sanctuary in the past several years.

-8-

In the disarrayed scramble for power and dominance on
this far-flung frontier, a young man with a waxed mustache
can spend his time one week introducing chorus girls and
exotic dancers at a night club, and the next being second in
command of an area larger than England. A red-baiter in
March becomes a production-for-use advocate by April. Seattle society matrons picket the mayor's office, and he calls them
"fur-clad, perfumed hussies and scabherders." The State of
Washington sends to Congress the most radical delegation in
the country, and at the same election votes to kill a State
income tax, thus perpetuating an all-inclusive sales tax opposed vigorously by the victorious congressional candidates.
Oregon casts an overwhelming two-to-one mandate for a
New Deal, and gets the most reactionary administration of
any State in the Union; the self-styled New Dealers are
mainly right-wing Republicans who have opportunely changed

their party registrations. Seattle's representative in Congress
goes wading in the fountain at Rockefeller Center in New
York and throws his landlady bodily out of her own apartment house. His colleague, the junior senator from Washington, denounces Hearst, the Supreme Court, the Liberty
League, and big business—but back home a recall is launched
against him because he is allegedly too conservative.* In
Tacoma a radical is a threat to the incumbent congressman,
and on election day—for the first time in the city's history—
the streetcar system breaks down and the men who work in
the mills are unable to get to the polls in time to vote. This
incident the radical uses as the main plank in his platform a
few years later, and goes not to the House, but to the United
States Senate. A distinguished magazine editor comes to the
University of Oregon and delivers a scholarly commencement address in defense of democracy.† The next day the
governor of the State calls him an "educated idiot." The
Seattle Chamber of Commerce ceremoniously names a city
councilman up for reëlection "First Citizen." He is decisively
defeated. "We have passed the peak of misunderstanding,"
the Northwest's dominant labor leader sanctimoniously declares, as his union takes on as a new organizer a gentleman
known in pugilistic circles as the "Aberdeen Assassin." Business men band together to defend law and order, and they
hold target practice with revolvers in the basement of a fash-
ionable residence. The mayor of a large city personally stages
a diaper-pinning contest to publicize the community and incidentally win popularity for reëlection purposes. Whether a
snow-covered peak almost three miles high shall be called
"Mount Tacoma" or "Mount Rainier" becomes a burning

---

* A United States Senator is not legally subject to recall, but on a number of
occasions in the Northwest recalls have been started against members of Congress
for the purpose of humiliating and embarrassing them.

† Oswald Garrison Villard, contributing editor of the *Nation*.

political issue, and congressmen are sent to the national capital with specific instructions in this respect. Newspaper reporters on strike close Mr. Hearst's Seattle paper, and he
hires the son-in-law of the President of the United States to
get it open again. Idaho manifests its affection for Borah by
giving him a sixth senatorial term, and also presents him with
a colleague who takes a diametrically opposite position on
virtually all major questions. A gentleman, address unknown,
elected to the Washington legislature is found in jail for
raping a twelve-year-old girl. Democrats of the State of
Washington hold a convention so violently debated that the
delegates, although they condemn the capitalistic system, forget to endorse President Roosevelt for reëlection. A suspected stock swindler sought by the State of New York is
alleged to have taken an alias and gotten himself overwhelmingly elected boss of the Seattle county commissioners. The
girls who work in newspaper circulation offices and the men
who brew beer in Oregon breweries learn they must join the
truck drivers' union—or else! The dean of the Senate of the
United States secludes himself in the Bitterroot Mountains
so that he will not be politically embarrassed by meeting the
national chairman of his party. The minority leader of the
Republicans swings shut the gates of his farm and refuses to
say whom he will back for President. The Federal government constructs a huge dam to checkmate the power companies and finds that in the process it threatens to destroy the
salmon industry.

Political events treated as freakish and unbelievable elsewhere are commonplace in the Pacific Northwest. The people
have become accustomed to reading over their coffee and
cereal that a leading candidate for mayor has just trudged
through town dressed as Mahatma Gandhi, and they are not
surprised to learn there will be no evening newspaper to read

over their pot roast and noodles because the longshoreman have called out the reporters and cameramen on strike.

And so here is the Pacific Northwest, the greatest frontier remaining in our country. Here is more than 40 per cent of America's hydroelectric power, and here are people, according to Representative John E. Rankin, co-author of the TVA legislation, paying electric bills twice as high as they should be. Here is two-fifths of the timber and one-fifth of the wheat, and here are hungry men living in tar-paper shanties and standing in line at soup kitchens and relief depots. Here is an almost limitless region of undeveloped natural resources: hills and forests and valleys practically as ignored by man as when Drake sailed along the Pacific coast almost five hundred years ago. And here are many of the social and economic problems that harass the crowded and congested States of the East. Here are men out of work and men who are hungry and men who are bitter and desperate and men who are homeless. Here are some of the drought refugees, huddled miserably in auto camps waiting for a chance to do something—anything; and rolling away to where land and sky meet are fertile acres that have never known cultivation. Here is a great new country, a land of vast resources of which Jefferson dreamed when he sent Lewis and Clark to claim it for the Republic. And here are governors and mayors and sheriffs who wantonly disregard the freedom to which Jefferson devoted his life. Here is a labor boss who rules his community as ruthlessly as a Genghis Khan; and here is another labor chieftain who plans class warfare. Here is a mayor whose political philosophy changes with the morning mists. And here is a governor who has suspended the Bill of Rights. And here is a lieutenant governor who wins popular support by behaving like a buffoon. And here is a man sentenced to seven years in prison for making a speech. And here is a public official said to be holding high office under an assumed name. And here are politicians winning their way to power by promising impoverished old people great wealth they can never possibly obtain. And here are men and women in the richest treasure-trove of natural resources left in the nation, existing on *per capita* incomes shockingly below the national average. Here are farmers in the fertile valleys of Oregon with as thin wallets as their fellow agrarians in the blistering furnace of the Dust Bowl. Here are sufficient of the elementary comforts of life for everyone—enough to support twenty times the present population. And yet here is labor warfare as brutal and labor racketeering as shameful as anywhere in the land. Here are utility monopolies that pay off on watered stock by denying to thousands of rural people the basic technological advantages of the electric age. Here is the epitome of the tragic failure to use political democracy to develop and utilize great natural resources—and it is a region that believes, implicitly and faithfully, in the principles on which democracy is based.

Here, for example, is Oregon. Principally an agricultural State, it is located in the heart of the main electric power area of the continent. Yet 70 per cent of its farms are as devoid of electricity as the Indian wigwams which preceded them. Of Oregon's 55,000 farms, 38,500 have not a kilowatt of power.* In the face of these incontrovertible facts, the governor of Oregon informs a congressional committee: "We have all of our people filled with electricity now; they are just choked with it." This man was elected to office by the votes of farmers who for generations have pumped water by hand and read

---

* These are 1933 statistics made available by the Federal government. Since the establishment of the Rural Electrification Administration, the figures have changed somewhat but not materially. The majority of the State's farms are still without power.

their Bibles beneath flickering oil lamps—farmers whose wives have labored over washboards and hand churns and irons heated on rickety wood stoves.

A stone's throw from the dimly lit homesteads of these people, enough hydroelectric power surges unused to the sea to mechanize every farm between Oregon and the Great Lakes.

Wandering men in the Northwest huddle at night beneath railroad culverts and look out through the rain and sleet to the forests of which the National Resources Committee has stated: "The four Columbia Basin States have it in their power to become the permanent wood lot of the nation." There are bread lines in Seattle and Spokane and Portland, and the curtailment of WPA relief invariably brings angry men on the picket line with banners warning that they do not intend to starve. While these scenes occur in the cities, only 8 per cent of a potentially fertile region of 253,000,000 acres is devoted to agriculture.

The Pacific Limited enters Oregon from the east in the morning and has crossed the State by nightfall, and occasionally a traveler sits at the window of the swaying observation car and wonders at the incongruity of all this. From the break of day the train clatters for hours over sections that could grow millions of bushels of wheat and graze thousands of herds of cattle. The afternoon sees it crashing past dense stands of prime timber. As the sun begins to dip behind the hills, the big locomotive enters the river gorge where billions of kilowatt-hours of electricity are as undeveloped as if Franklin had never sent his kite into the thunderheads. On the last mile of this journey, a few hundred yards from the station at Portland, the train rolls through Sullivan's Gulch. The gulch is spanned by a viaduct with heavy steel pillars set in concrete foundations. Built against these bases are scores of shanties made from laths and tar-paper and discarded lumber. Fires flicker in the evening dusk, and over them men are cooking dinner in battered ten-pound tomato cans. The men are dirty and ragged. Their clothes are not made from the wool of the countless sheep that could graze on the hills the train passed in the morning. They are not eating the grain that might be grown on the uncultivated plains the train whizzed past at midday. They are not housed in homes that could be built from the millions of board feet of timber the Limited roared by in the late afternoon. They do not enjoy the benefit of the latent electric energy the travelers saw in the Columbia River at twilight.

This is life in a hundred shanty towns, in the nation's richest vault of natural resources, in the year 1938.

-9-

On the hills high above Portland stands a heroic statue of the Indian girl who guided the explorers to the Pacific. In enduring bronze, she points into the distance, as on the by-gone day Captain Lewis looked for the first time on the great river of the West. Forever, Sacajawea watches the land she helped a President whom she never saw add to his country. She gazes out over what Jefferson visioned as a "great, free and independent empire on the Columbia River." And she sees taking place political warfare that is simultaneously the grimmest and the most ludicrous in the United States. She looks out over a struggle to control a new and unde-veloped country—a struggle that has united, in a helter-skelter of confusion, the political trends of the present with the political exploits of the past.

Extremes of both the right and the left are not uncommon on America's last frontier. Many conservatives in the Pacific Northwest believe the only way to deal with their opponents is by prison sentences of manslaughter proportions. The radicals, in turn, support the most aggressive and venturesome labor organizers in the country. There is little neutral ground. A prominent Unitarian minister once observed that what the Columbia basin needs and does not have is a centrist party. The spokesman of the American Federation of Labor forces in the Northwest is considerably more business-minded and stubborn than William Green, and the leader of the Committee for Industrial Organization is so far to the left of John L. Lewis that the latter cannot communicate with him by smoke signals. Moderation is not in the lexicon of the public personages who perform in this majestic amphitheater.

Yet the Northwest's people themselves are not readily susceptible to tirades of bitterness and hate. They live with the characteristic zest and neighborliness of an outpost land. Their leaders and some of their spokesmen may urge them on to violence from either the right or the left, but they respond only fitfully to these exhortations. The incitements to mob action come largely from above rather than below. The people are essentially decent. A year or so ago Governor Martin of Oregon said the farmers of his State should seize their pitchforks and run the labor unions off the waterfront. The leading farm organizations were not influenced by this outburst; instead, they rebuked the Governor for it. The populace of the Northwest is level-headed and temperate. Lynchings and sustained vigilantism are practically unknown in the region. Extremes in radicalism or reaction, buffoonery or barbarity, may arise on America's last frontier; yet these propensities seldom pervade the thinking of the people. On the whole, the inhabitants of the Far West are stable and tolerant and dispassionate. The exceptions to this are spectacular but isolated.

The frontiersman of old calmly bit off a chew of tobacco while he waited with long rifle and powder horn for the Yakimas whose smoke signals hung on the horizon. With the same equanimity his descendants watch the longshoremen and the timber barons as they ominously eye each other across the barricades.

Manifest destiny is yet to take place in the Pacific Northwest. Historic events are certain to occur in a potentially wealthy territory that has 13 per cent of the nation's land, yet only 2.8 per cent of the people. It is a region which inspired President Roosevelt, after he had traveled through it not long ago, to declare that Horace Greeley's advice, "Go west, young man," might still live in another day. "Promised Land" is the President's definition of the region. The Northwest has not been an active force in the Republic's destiny to date. The future is another story. In this vast area of four hundred thousand square miles—today the lunatic asylum of the country, politically—history is sure to be written in bold strokes. The present disproportion between resources and population cannot long remain. This becomes increasingly evident as refugees from the Dust Bowl, their goods piled high in battered automobiles, roll along the roads of the Far West in caravans longer than the covered wagon trains that came a hundred years ago. Frederick Jackson Turner has analyzed the disappearance of the American frontier—and in some respects it has disappeared. Yet people live in Oregon who have never pressed a light button, and the Bureau of Reclamation estimates that in the West there is an arid area, needing only water to become a fertile countryside, which alone is larger than a whole cluster of European nations.

"We chose a broad, rich bottom, many miles in length, well-watered, and supplied with timber, oak, fir, cottonwood, white ash scattered along the borders of its grassy plains where hundreds of acres were ready for the plow," wrote one of the pioneering Methodist missionaries who struggled into the Willamette Valley in 1838.

A century has passed, but those acres are still ready—not hundreds but millions of them.

2. Promised Land

Across the plains and over the Rockies they come—the Americans whose farms in the Dust Bowl are no more.

It is the most significant westward migration since the covered wagons of the old pioneers creaked on the Oregon Trail. Practically two hundred thousand people, their rural homes ruined by the fiery blasts of 100 degrees of searing heat, have crossed the continental divide and driven down into the uplands and valleys of the Pacific seaboard. More thousands are still coming. Other thousands are yet to come. So many nomads have not paraded consecutively into the Far West since the line of rail locked the country from coast to coast.

"Drive out on any of the main highways of our State," Senator Borah of Idaho said one sunny afternoon, "and you will see cars, sometimes almost caravans, fleeing from the devastations of the drought."

The venerable Senator predicted that soon the hegira of the wandering Dust Bowl refugees would attain amazing proportions, involving millions of people. He got out of his big armchair and walked to the window of his Boise hotel suite. He pointed to the gaunt hills in the distance. "The importance of the present migration cannot be overestimated," he said. "The Americans now coming West seek to colonize and develop this vast region of ours."

It is no romantic fiction that Middle Westerners dispossessed by the drought are invading the sundown seaboard. Felix Belair, covering the dust storms and heat spells for the New York *Times,* wrote, "Farmers with their possessions and families loaded into trucks that normally would be carrying a second crop of hay were headed West to Oregon, Washington, and Idaho."

The Resettlement Administration dipped into a limited budget and printed *Suggestions to Prospective Settlers in Idaho, Washington, and Oregon.* Thousands of families have read this information. They have been families seeking a new start in life—families fifteen hundred miles from their abandoned homes and still on the search for a place to live. Over every highway between the plains and the coast, drive people who do not know how long it will be before they sleep again with their own roof over their heads. From rusty rods hang the dust-splattered license plates of Oklahoma, Arkansas, Kansas, Colorado, Iowa, and the Dakotas.

There have been sporadic westward treks before. Intermittently, large groups of people from the Central States have set out for the coast. The present pilgrimage is different. It is sustained and continuous. Real and tangible reasons justify it. Thousands of farmers have been scorched off their acres in the Dust Bowl. Other thousands watched their farms blown away in great billows of topsoil that shrouded the land for days. What more natural and logical than for these people to head toward the nation's last frontier?

The Far West is thoroughly conscious and aware of what is happening. Placards in wayside emporiums announce, "We cater to drought refugees." Everywhere along the route the wanderers stop to ask questions, particularly about the water. Concern over weather conditions and water is practically a mania with them. "Is there plenty of rain?" they ask intently. People on the main highways hear that question from sunrise to sundown. A grocer in a little town in Idaho finally hung a sign in the window of his store:

NOT ENOUGH RAIN HERE. IRRIGATION O.K. THOUGH!

In a village a hundred miles west of Spokane, a druggist tacked a neatly lettered sign to his wall beside a picture of the President:

SURE YOU'RE WELCOME! F. D. R. SAYS SO HIMSELF.

Beneath this was a newspaper clipping of a speech by Mr. Roosevelt, urging that people crowded in the slums of the East and sweltering in the Dust Bowl of the Middle West look for new homes on the far side of the Rockies. "The President Sees a 'Promised Land,'" the banner headline read.

That is what these nomads are seeking as they pilot their dilapidated automobiles over the tortuous roads that cross the mountains—a Promised Land. They want fertile acres where there is ample rainfall. And if there is not enough moisture from the air, they seek plenty of it in the ground. They hesitate to stop at any place that lacks either a whopping precipitation record or a network of bubbling irrigation canals. The drought refugees have been burned off their farms once. They could not stand it a second time. They ask about water with almost fanatical anxiety. Localities that are hopelessly arid, they shun like a wasteland.

Some of the Dust Bowl pilgrims are glum and despondent. Others can laugh at misfortune like the bearded farmer—at least he had the ruddy cheeks of a farmer—I saw driving along U.S. Highway 30 in the Idaho hills. At the wheel of an antiquated green roadster with a Kansas license, he jolted past the crossroads where I had stopped. Suitcases, jugs, and sacks were strapped to both running boards. I wondered if he had to unload each time he opened the door, or if he was still spry enough to vault over the top. He resembled a rustic version of Chief Justice Hughes. On the sloping back of the ancient pilgrim's car was a piece of white cardboard with a message in black paint:

> Thirty miles from water,
> Forty miles to wood,
> Life is hell in the Dust Bowl
> And I'm leaving for good.

Whether the nomads thus can smile in the grip of disaster or whether they are crushed by their homeless plight, their experiences have been mainly uniform and similar: years of struggle on practically submarginal farms, then heat and dust, and now the long trek west. Most of these wanderers tell the same story of how they happened to start to the coast. I met a lean and rangy fellow with a family and an old touring car who was particularly vivid and literate in his description of the catastrophe that had turned him out of his South Dakota ranch and sent him in quest of the will-o'-the wisp of a Promised Land beyond the Rockies. He said his name was Emmett.

-2-

The weather was scorching; it had long ceased to be merely hot. Drops of sweat as big as green peas trickled off Jim Emmett's forehead and splattered on his denim shirt. He did not bother to wipe them away. He had stopped doing that two weeks before, when the thermometer in the shade of the back porch hit 102 degrees for the first time. He just leaned against the wobbly fence, as motionless as the windmill that towered above the water hole in his pasture. There was not enough breeze to make the windmill even creak. And what was the use of wind, he thought. The water hole was dry— as dry as the dust of what had once been his cornfield.

He finally summoned enough energy to move his tall, overall-clad frame across the barnyard. The heat was so heavy it was almost like walking through the dust storms that frequently followed the hot spells. He remembered how during the first dust storms they had sat on the steps of Duncan's general store and joked about which counties of Wyoming or Montana were being blown past then.

They didn't joke any more—not since their own South Dakota topsoil had been added to the huge swirls of dust hurtling toward the Atlantic Ocean, two thousand miles away. Jim looked down at the ruins of his fields. The corn still standing was dry and brown. Most of the stalks were broken in the middle and bent over to the earth. What the searing heat had not withered the grasshoppers had chewed. Half of his cattle had died. The ones that survived stood at the arid water hole and lowed mournfully.

Jim trudged slowly up the steps of the gaunt, weather-beaten farmhouse. Inside, a layer of dust coated everything. They kept the windows closed continually, but still it seeped through. Jim's wife, Martha, had stopped trying to fight it. Even their food tasted of dust. Whether they ate lima beans or canned peaches, the bite and grit of dust was the predominant taste. A fuzz of dust covered the gilt-framed picture of Jim's grandfather on the mantel. Old Wilson Emmett had started for the Far West on the Oregon Trail, but the rich, loamy soil of the Great Plains had induced him to unload his prairie schooner in the Dakotas.

Jim wondered what Grandfather Emmett would say if he could see that soil either blown away by the wind or caked into crumbly lumps by the scorching sun. Upstairs one of the children coughed. Jim thought he recognized Marjorie. The cough came again and again. Jim moved nervously. He had not forgotten the death of the little Brooks boy down the road from dust pneumonia. Jim looked at his grandfather's picture again. Maybe the old argonaut's journey to the Pacific coast would be finished yet. Jim had heard there was plenty of water in Oregon; too much water, some one had told him. Too much water! Jim didn't believe it.

He went outside and began tinkering with the motor of the six-year-old touring car parked near the gate.

Three days later the Emmett family took a last look at their dried-up farm, entrusted the keys and deed to Clyde Duncan at the general store with instructions to sell for what he could get, and Jim headed the radiator cap of the automobile into the West. A thin roll of ten-dollar bills was tucked in his pinch-clasp purse: the proceeds of the sale of the remnant of his livestock. Martha sat at Jim's side in the front seat, holding the youngest child on her lap. The other three children shared the dilapidated but spacious tonneau with pillows, books, pots, dishes, jars of preserves and pickles, andirons, baskets, and sundry other indispensable articles of household equipment. From a cartlike trailer, jolting rockily along behind, protruded bedsprings, chairs, tables, lamps, and the spinning-wheel that had belonged to Martha's Aunt Ruth.

The trek which Grandfather Emmett had started to the Oregon Country in a covered wagon in 1849 was about to be completed almost a century later by his grandson in a battered touring car.

-3-

There have been a lot of Jim Emmetts in the past two years. Exactly how many, not even the government knows. No accurate census of the drought refugees is available. It is not easy to catalogue impoverished Middle Westerners huddled in third-class tourist camps in Oregon, begging for seasonal employment in Idaho, or scrambling desperately to get on crowded relief rolls in California. That there have been at least fifty thousand families in this plight is a conservative calculation. Most statements place the number of Dust Bowl emigrants at a minimum of two hundred thousand. Some estimates are as high as three times that number. In the San Joaquin valley of California thousands of ragged families from the heat-stricken plains are starving to death or dying of disease. The trek from the Dust Bowl to the West is of such proportions that President Roosevelt has told Congress it ranks with the rise in unemployment as the most important unforeseen factor to intrude into the compli-cated Federal relief situation.

As they head into the sundown, these modern pilgrims are following the Oregon Trail, the course blazed years ago by their predecessors of wagon train and long rifle. Up through the lofty passes of the Rockies in Montana and Wyoming, and down into the Sawtooth Range of Idaho the drought refugees rattle in their heavily laden automobiles. Some of them stop in Senator Borah's home State, but others motor on toward the upland plateau of eastern Washington, and then swing down the Columbia River canyon where it cuts through the Cascade Mountains and merges with the fertile lowlands of the Pacific seaboard. An historical map will show that this was the route Lewis and Clark traveled in 1804,

when they carried the flag from ocean to ocean. The drought
sufferers who rest their sputtering engines at the Bonneville
Dam picnic grounds in Oregon eat their ham sandwiches and
drink their coffee within a few rods of where once gleamed
the campfire of the first white men to travel westward across
the American continent.

There is ample evidence of the extensiveness of the present
trek. A glance through the nonresident automobile registra-
tion lists of the State of Oregon showed me numerous cars
from such places as Huron, South Dakota; Palisade, Nebraska; Coldwater, Kansas; Garrison, North Dakota, and
Keokuk, Iowa. Not all information must be gathered in such
colorless fashion. One need only park alongside a through
highway on the coast to see for oneself the caravans of these
modern pioneers. They roll westward almost like a parade.
In a single hour from a grassy meadow near an Idaho road
I counted thirty-four automobiles with the license plates of
States between Chicago and the mountains. Conversation with
the occupants of these cars is the best way to understand the
problems and complexities of a migration that may some day
parallel in historic significance the journey of the prairie
schooners that first rumbled on the Oregon Trail.

I talked to seven bronzed young men, grouped around an
aged Oldsmobile truck parked above a clear creek which the
highway bridged. The license was from Oklahoma. "Had to
let the old crate cool," the tall driver said, and pointed to
the radiator from which steam and water were escaping in a
miniature geyser.

All seven lads, I learned, were from different families.
The drought had put their fathers on WPA rolls, and the
boys had driven West to see what opportunities there were
on the coast. They intended to stay a few months, hiring out
as farm hands to get their information about soil and crop

conditions direct. Then they would meet at Seattle or Boise or Portland, or some other prearranged point, and drive back to Oklahoma to report to their folks. If their verdict of the farming possibilities in the Pacific Northwest was favorable, their families would join the westward procession.

The boys told me they were camping along the way and they were getting harvest work in wayside fields and orchards to pay for their food. "We take our time slips out in grub," one of the youths confided. "We get 'bout twice as much that way." He showed me three or four sacks of fruits and vegetables on the floor of the truck. The oldest lad boiled some turnips and fried a big slab of bacon and a pan of potatoes. He and his friends ate like hungry lumberjacks.

"The drought fried out farms just like that," remarked the tall driver, nodding at the skillet of sizzling potatoes.

Another lad chimed in: "I sure hope we get a chance to get new farms here or in Oregon. Farming's all our folks have ever done." The driver told me that the fathers of several of his companions were anticipating bumper fruit or wheat crops before the drought struck. "The sun nearly baked their apples right on the trees," he explained. "My golly! We've just got to find somewhere our folks can start over again." For a moment his good humor vanished, and his calm gray eyes were worried and anxious as he gazed into the West.

I remember thinking that perhaps some pioneer boy of almost a century earlier had looked with the same troubled expression—possibly from the very meadow where we were standing—for signal smoke on the horizon. The specter of poverty, I thought, was no less real than the peril of painted savages on the warpath.

The last I saw of the lads from the Dust Bowl, they were sitting in the rear of the truck as it swayed around a bend in the road. Their truck once had carted wheat and other prod-

uce to market from the ranch of the tall boy's father. Now
the ranch was arid and withered, and the truck was the covered wagon for a modern reconnoitering expedition into the
Far Northwest. Probably it was such peregrination as that of
the Oklahoma lads which prompted President Roosevelt, on
one of his trips across the country, to declare that a wholesale
population drift westward was under way.

The speeches of the President have been an astonishingly
important factor in deciding people to turn toward the coast
in quest of new lands. Farm families, uncertain whether to
struggle along in the Dust Bowl or to pile their goods in a
trailer and go west, have been swayed by the rich, cultured
voice that comes over the radio sounding a modern "Westward ho!"

High on the uplands of the State of Washington I met a
rangy, taciturn farmer who acquainted me directly with the
tremendous influence Mr. Roosevelt has had in spurring on
this trek over the Rockies. The farmer was from South Dakota. Out of a worn wallet he pulled a frayed newspaper
clipping. He handed it to me and gestured at the dozen
dilapidated automobiles parked at a crossroads on U.S. Highway 97. All the cars were either heaped high with household
goods or coupled to heavily loaded trailers.

"We been followin' that newspaper piece there ever since
we left the Dakotas," the farmer said.

I looked at the clipping. It was the story of an address delivered several hours' drive from where we stood by the
President in the summer of 1934. The occasion of the speech
had been the start of actual construction on the great Bonneville and Grand Coulee dams.

"The piece was in the newspaper 'bout the time the first
drought hit us," my friend from South Dakota said. "I cut
it out and tacked it in the kitchen. We used to read it when-

ever the dust trickled in at the windows and the sun and heat gave our wheat another scorching."

I looked again to see what the President had said in the rugged fastnesses of the Columbia River region that held such significance for people caught in the furnace of the Dust Bowl, almost two days' travel eastward on a limited train. Here is what I read:

In this Northwestern section of the land, we still have an opportunity for a vastly increased population. There are many sections of the country, as you know, where conditions are crowded. There are many sections of the country where land has run out or been put to the wrong kind of use. America is growing. There are many people who want to go to a section of the country where they will have a better chance for themselves and their children—and there are a great many people who have children and need room for growing families.

Out here you have not just space, you have space that can be used by human beings—a wonderful land—a land of opportunity.

I returned the clipping to the farmer who had abandoned his parched acres in South Dakota to search for a new home in the vast basin of the Columbia River. He trudged back to his old touring car, stepped on a starter that whined protestingly and finally worked, and then drove off up the road. The other automobiles followed him, until they were rolling like a caravan over the sagebrush plateau of eastern Washington. I noticed that the majority of the cars had North or South Dakota license plates, although one or two were from Oklahoma and Kansas. To the running boards and fenders of all of them were strapped lamps, kettles, quilts, pictures, and other domestic articles. In most of the back seats could be seen the chubby faces and waving arms of little children. It was evident that the cars belonged to families who had pulled up the roots they had sunk in the scorched soil of the Middle

West drought areas and headed into the sunset, seeking another start in life. These people were not traveling west to
see Mount Rainier or Yellowstone National Park. They were
not on a camping trip. They had come to stay.

The automobiles of the wandering farmers from the Dust
Bowl dwindled in the distance. I watched them becoming
specks against the grim lava cliffs towering above the highway. Probably the wagons of the forty-niners had looked exactly like that against the same cliffs.

-4-

"A land of opportunity"—that was what the President had
said.

Opportunity? For some, but not for everyone.

A field secretary of the Gospel Army has reported that the
most shocking conditions of squalor and filth he has ever
observed exist among poverty-harassed drought refugees in
California. School districts in Oregon have faced bankruptcy
because of the increased strain placed on their budgets by the
additional teachers and facilities needed for the children of
the Dust Bowl emigrants. A considerable portion of the
drought families in Washington and Idaho are destitute and
would starve were it not for the subsistence doles they receive
from Federal and State relief.

The plight of these pilgrims takes many forms. A taxi
dancer in a shanty town near a big construction project asked
me if I wanted to go to her cabin. It would only cost a dollar,
she promised. She had tawny hair and a slender figure. She
had not camouflaged her face beneath as much lipstick and
rouge as the other girls, nor was she as hardboiled as her
contemporaries. Over a glass of beer—for which she earned

a few pennies' commission from the dance-hall management for persuading me to drink—I asked how she happened to be at her present occupation.

Her family had driven west from Nebraska when their farm dried up and the wind blew away what the sun had not shriveled. At Oregon City they had tried to find a farm in the Promised Land. But the $130 they had left from the sale of their Nebraska tract to the government at $4 an acre was not enough for even a down payment. Her father, she explained, had been unable to get work at either the pulp or the woolen mill which stood on the outskirts of town. "Plenty of our local people out of jobs, as it is," the foremen had said. When the $130 was gone and she had lost her part-time job in a novelty shop, they had been forced to go on relief.

The investigators and relief officials had been tough. There were enough Oregon citizens unemployed without these jobless invaders, the WPA office said. "Alien paupers," was what the Governor of the State called them. After a few weeks the relief headquarters had given them enough money to get back to Nebraska, and warned them that was all they would get. They used this money to live on for a short time, and then found the relief people had been in earnest. No more assistance; even the pittance on which they had been existing was gone.

They drove south along the coast, through the lush Willamette Valley. To buy gasoline and get food they picked hops. The wages were terrible, the food filthy. She remembered that a lot of the pickers had what a doctor in a near-by town called *Ascaris lumbricoides*, which was a long name for worms. She had stood that as long as she could, then had borrowed dimes and nickels from a lot of the other workers and taken a bus to Portland. Her family stayed on in the hop-pickers' camp. Her story of what had occurred in Portland was pretty melodramatic. She had needed money badly and found only temporary employment. Finally she had lived with a man for a while, and later had made good money dancing naked at stag parties. She had drifted around a lot, writing letters to her family now and then. They found work only at seasonal agricultural employment and nearly starved between jobs. They did not know what she was doing, however.

The girl looked around the ramshackle dance hall, built from laths and tar paper and discarded lumber. "So here I am," she said. The men paid her ten cents a dance; she kept five, and the management took the other nickel. She also earned a commission on any beer and sandwiches she could induce her acquaintances to buy. These pickings were slim, indeed; occasionally she augmented them when she shared the bed in her cabin with some man she had met on the dusty street or in the smoke-filled dance hall. She wore neither a brassière nor stockings, and learned that this commercial foresight helped all phases of her business. Her greatest fear was venereal disease. The town was full of it, and only a few of the men used the prophylactic stations in the construction camp.

Whether her highly theatrical tale was true, I cannot say. I only know she was one of the wanderers who traveled the Oregon Trail in 1937—and whatever opportunity she found was of a strange and dubious sort.

Other drought refugees have failed to find the Promised Land. This advertisement appeared in a number of Middle Western newspapers:

WANTED, 40 men to work in wood-cutting camp in Oregon. No experience necessary. Cabins and bedding provided, wood and water free. Tools and groceries obtainable at local prices on credit. Earn from $3 to $4 a day. Five years work available.

The end of this rainbow turned out to be a squalid lumber camp, where men toiled in the rain and sleet, and slept in leaky shacks. Three boys from Kansas worked there two months, and had a profit of exactly $3.80 to show for their combined efforts. They said they were fortunate. Most of their fellow workers were in debt to the company, which charged outrageous prices for third-class accommodations.

"Cutters from the drought area are very satisfactory workers," the owner of the camp sanctimoniously wrote the Federal employment service in Kansas. He asked that a whole caravan of families be sent him, adding, "Have them bring camping equipment only, as the winters are so open people can live in tents all winter."

The camp was on the Oregon coast, which has the heaviest precipitation record of any place in continental United States!

Unscrupulous land agents and real-estate salesmen wait for the Dust Bowl nomads as grimly as the Sioux and Cheyennes once lay in ambush for their bygone predecessors. Any farm in the Far West looks desirable to the people from the drought region. Generally, fuel and water are plentiful. Both were costly items back on the plains. The wanderers part with the four or five hundred dollars they may have left. They erect buildings, clear away stumps and trees, and till the land for crops. Then they harvest—weeds and sagebrush. When they have found they are on nonproductive soil, it is too late. Their money is gone, and so is their hard work. There is nothing they can do now except seek relief. The "farm" reverts to the mortgage company or real-estate firm, which can sell it in its improved form to another inexperienced and gullible family of wayfarers at a higher price per acre.

Tragic frauds of this sort occur frequently. The drought refugees want desperately to return to farming. It is all most of them have ever done. It is all they can do. When they see what appears to be a desirable chance to farm again, they grab at it. They are unfamiliar with local conditions and investigate only superficially. Not until afterwards—when their work and money are gone—do they consult the reports on soil and crops and weather. Unlike Davy Crockett, they do not make sure they are right before going ahead.

Yet not all the drought refugees have encountered failure and disappointment. Many of them have prospered in the great land beyond the mountains. Those fleeced by real-estate sharks or stricken in filthy camps are only part of the story. The rest of it is the account of families who have found better farms and a new chance. The Pacific Northwest is seven times as large as Illinois; at the same time it has fewer people than Chicago. In this sparsely settled region of fertile lowlands and green hills, thousands of people from the Dust Bowl are getting an opportunity to start over again. The families who have been rehabilitated provide a happy contrast to those who are still homeless wanderers.

-5-

Flaxen-haired Patsy Carlson is four years old. She is too young to know much about the hardy pioneers who braved a hostile wilderness to settle the Oregon Country. She does not realize, for example, that she is part of America's most important westward migration since those frontier families of long ago trudged and jolted across the plains.

With her father and mother and big sister Jane, aged ten, Patsy traveled toward the sunset last year. Their farm on the Kansas prairie lay behind them, bleak and desolate after the scourge of the drought. Patsy and her family had to find another place to live. So they were setting out for the Pacific coast, two thousand weary miles away.

Near the little Oregon village of Troutdale their old touring car broke down. Patsy looked out through the isinglass curtains at a big celery field while her father tinkered with the engine. Her father saw the celery field, too. It looked lush and loamy to his practiced farmer's eye, and in the distance a twisting river shimmered merrily. The river made up his mind. Deep-throated even from far away as it swirled around boulders along its edge, it did not look like a stream that would dry up in the heat of the most scorching summer. Patsy's father decided Troutdale, Oregon, was the place for the Carlson family to start over again.

That was about a year ago. Now, Patsy and her father and mother and sister live in a shingled little house over which the roses creep in the summer. Their neighbors told them to be sure to put up trellises for the roses. The celery in the fields below the house won honorable mention at the county fair and is helping pay off the debt on the farm. Patsy does not remember much about those gloomy days in the Dust Bowl. She is too busy playing with the other children whose parents cultivate and harvest the vast basin of the Columbia River.

"Patsy likes it here," her tall, blue-eyed father told me, as Patsy nestled in his arms after he had plodded home from a day's work heaping soil around the fibrous celery stalks.

"Don't you, Patsy?" he asked.

Patsy cuddled against her father's earth-stained overalls. "Um-hum," she said.

"A splendid crowd of people," is President Roosevelt's description of Patsy Carlson and the other westward wanderers from the Dust Bowl.

"It is up to us," he told the Northwest last autumn, "to help them to live better than they are living now."

That help was forthcoming even as the President spoke; it is still forthcoming today; the citizens of the majestic Columbia River basin insist it will continue to be forthcoming as long as one victim of the drought is homeless in their midst.

When the first dusty automobiles from the heat-ravaged prairies groaned over the continental divide and clattered down the Pacific slope, the people of the Northwest looked at the trek with suspicion and dismay. They had all sorts of apprehensions about this great stream of migratory population flowing into their land. Farmers feared a new source of competition to undercut agricultural prices. Sawmill workers and lumberjacks worried about a vast group of idle men to lower wage scales. Property owners foresaw an already staggering tax burden increased because of new school and relief requirements.

With the exception of the tax alarm, these fears proved false. The people from the Dust Bowl turned out to be solid, substantial Americans. For years they had farmed the plains, enduring hard times, bitter-cold winters, and choking-hot summers. It had taken the worst series of droughts in history to make them quit. They had not moved on until their farms dried up or blew away. People of this sort would not be liabilities to any community. Gradually the Northwest found that out. Whenever a Dust Bowl pilgrim got a chance to cultivate and harvest again, he almost invariably made good—and he did so without slashing farm prices or otherwise chiseling on his neighbors. The suspicions and fears slowly died. The Northwest began to take the nomads to its ample bosom.

Dan Whitaker was one of those embraced.

Seven or eight miles out of a little town in central Washington, Dan's heavily loaded old sedan from Iowa coasted to a standstill. He pulled a nickel and two or three pennies out of his pocket and looked at them forlornly. He turned to his wife, who had their small daughter on her lap.

"We're out of gas and money," he said. "Here is where we stop."

He started to push the unwieldy car off the highway and along a rutted country road. It moved creakingly. He strained like a tug-o'-war man. A streak of pain burned through his side. He slumped to the ground, moaning in anguish. His wife bent over him, then ran frantically to the highway. The little girl was still in her arms.

Three weeks later a graying man with horn-rimmed glasses sat at Dan's bedside in the ward of the county hospital. "Young man," he said, "that was a bad rupture. You had a narrow escape. And no wonder—you say you lived on potato soup for a week to save all your money for gas."

Dan nodded weakly. "Listen, doc, I must owe you folks a barrel of money. Get me a chance to pay it back. This is a wheat country. What I don't know about wheat wouldn't fill a salt-shaker—specialized in it at Iowa State."

"You're in no condition to do farm work."

"I know that. But I can help one of these farmers increase his production in six months. I know I can. Doc, we were making a go of it back there. It was the dust storms and crickets that licked me—nothing else."

The doctor stood up. He looked at the pale countenance and burning eyes of his young patient. "Young man," he said, "I think I have a friend to whom you might be a god-send."

Dan Whitaker is paying his debt to the doctor—and to the little hospital, too. He and his family have been living with an old wheat rancher, and Dan has shown him that scientific knowledge and methods learned on the plains of Iowa will help increase yield two thousand miles westward in the hills of Washington.

Pretty soon all the bills for the rupture will be paid. Then Dan intends to put the salary he gets from the rancher into a share in the ranch.

Along with little Patsy Carlson in Troutdale, Dan Whitaker has many counterparts. The hospitality and neighborliness of the Northwest have given encouragement and new chances to thousands of farmers. Long years ago, when savage war whoops still sounded in the canyon the Columbia cuts through the mountains, the early settlers used to chant their familiar greeting to late arrivals: "Did you come the plains over, the Isthmus across, or the Horn around?" Then they would show the newcomers where the good spring water bubbled from the ground, how to get to the stockade in case of Indian attacks, and what trees to cut down for cabins and corrals.

This pioneer friendliness lives again as the drought refugees complete their weary hegira. After the first touch of suspicion and resentment had worn away, the farmers of the Northwest began to outdo one another in assisting and advising the travelers from the Middle West. The hospitality to these twentieth century pilgrims has taken many forms. Granges and farmers' unions and other organizations hold special meetings to acquaint the Dust Bowl nomads with local crop conditions, weather problems, and marketing arrangements. Picnics, dinners, and sewing bees are planned in order that the women and children from beyond the Rockies may find new friends and companions in a strange land.

Other sorts of kindness are shown. In an Oregon town out on the electric line from Portland, a regular colony of drought victims was camped. Most of these families were without fruits and vegetables. They were keeping their wallets closed, saving their money for the farms they hoped to buy. They lived mainly on starches. So the Grange held a canning festival. Jars of tomatoes, pickles, pears, plums, jams, peaches, peas, and strawberries stacked the hall to the ceiling. A year later another such event took place. The Dust Bowl refugees who only twelve months earlier themselves had been helped were on hand with fruits and vegetables from their own farms to feed the latest influx of homeless nomads.

Some rural merchants even have provided "special information for drought people" at the bottom of their mimeographed bargain-day bulletins, and in a tiny grocery a bustling little Idaho storekeeper with rimless bifocals had paraphrased the greeting of the old pioneers and hung the result on the wall in crude lettering: "Did you come in a jallopie old, a trailer new, or a wagon rickety?"

The last part of his question was not as facetious as it might seem. A farmer near Acadia, Nebraska, set out for the West in a hay wagon pulled by a white-faced bull and a black draft-horse harnessed together!

Gradually, the people from the drought-blighted section of the nation are getting established anew on the Pacific coast. The day-to-day items in the newspapers of the region tell a saga of American history—a story of men and women, driven from their farms by dust and heat, starting over again in the Far West. This item, from the Portland *Oregonian*, is a typical one:

CENTRALIA, Feb. 2 (Special)—Five families from the drought area have recently been placed on farms in this vicinity, it was announced yesterday.

Mr. and Mrs. Byron Hoxsie of Salix, Nebraska, have taken over the R. Willrich 20-acre place at Rochester; Magnus Garthe of Lafayette, Colorado, has purchased the Elmer Hastings property at Rochester; Roland Bethune of Mountain Grove, Missouri, has acquired five acres at Rochester to raise poultry and fruit; Mrs. R. Trimble has brought two sons and a daughter from Stanley, Iowa, to specialize in poultry and truck-farming on an eight-acre place at Toledo, and a new home, chicken house and barn have been built by Robert Abshire of Octavia, Nebraska, on his 40-acre plot near Napavine.

Not far from Centralia, Paul Braxton and his wife are trying to build a new life for their three little daughters. They owned a 440-acre wheat and stock farm on the eastern edge of Montana, but the 1934 drought and a moving blanket of Mormon crickets stripped it nearly bare. Dust hung heavy in the air and seeped through the doors and windows. The little girls were threatened with dust pneumonia, so the Braxtons started west. Paul worked for a while in a CCC camp, then quit. He and his wife had their hearts in farming; it was their whole life. They had met in Chicago at a Four-H club meeting. They called their marriage "a typical Four-H romance." With the help of the Farm Security Administration they obtained a fertile 100-acre farm near Centralia.

"We just couldn't have gone on any longer without a farm," Paul said. "We were like sailors without a ship."

Now, the Braxtons have fifteen sheep, a few chickens, and thirty-seven head of fine, blooded Jerseys, including a pure-bred bull Paul was able to acquire from a friendly rancher near by. Paul sells B-grade milk and last month took second place in a Cowlitz County contest for butterfat content. He celebrated by putting in electric lights in the house and barn.

"We're coming along fast," Paul said with a grin. "All I need is a little better luck and we'll be as firmly rooted here as the fir trees. Right now, all I have is girls, and all my cows have bull-calves. I wish we could change that around!"

And he extended the grin into a big smile.

The people from the plains manifest an insatiable desire for information on farming in the Northwest. I went to a Grange dinner given for some of the latest Dust Bowl arrivals. During the meal I noticed a great gap at one of the tables. "Look," said some one next to me, pointing out through the window. On the lawn in front of the hall stood a whole line of drought refugees, eating their chicken fricassee and biscuits while the master of the Grange squatted on his haunches, showing them the consistency of the soil.

Yet it is neither their curiosity nor their wish to start farming again that most characterizes these modern argonauts. It is their courage. Senator Borah did not exaggerate when he once referred to the fortitude with which they face all sorts of misfortune and adversity. Most of the drought refugees are farmers who have been independent practically all their lives. Now, they find themselves dispossessed by heat and wind, and forced to travel two thousand miles to seek another farm home. Yet a field man for the Farm Security Administration assured me: "Those people from the Dust Bowl never complain or whimper. I haven't heard a squawk from them. All they ask for is a chance. Give it to them, and they'll make good."

A drought pilgrim near Moscow, Idaho, did not get a chance until his three children were starving—but he is a successful farmer today. The man entered a country store and made a five-cent purchase. As he went out, the storekeeper saw him snatch up a five-pound sack of flour and conceal it under his coat. The storekeeper sent for the sheriff, who followed the man to a squatter's shack he was temporarily occupying. When the Dust Bowl farmer opened the door, he set the sack down on the dirt floor. The children immediately pounced on it and began to eat the raw flour with their hands.

The sheriff was moved and horrified. He returned to the

proprietor of the store and said: "I'm not going to arrest that man. His children are starving to death. I think we had better take up a collection." So that drought wanderer got an opportunity to till the soil once more. Now he is making a go of a farm in the Idaho uplands.

There have been many episodes in the drought migration where Far Western hospitality and Middle Western courage have combined to rehabilitate families.

Mat Hutch from Morristown, South Dakota, lived with his wife and their five children in an eastern Oregon tourist camp for three months. Then he had an opportunity at the farm he wanted. The down payment of $600 took the last cent left from the sale of his Dakota equipment. Mat toiled fifteen hours a day, but it wasn't enough. The tractor missed fire, and he needed another irrigation ditch. He also needed a good crop if he was to hang onto the farm. Some of his neighbors knew about his predicament; they also knew about Mat's five youngsters.

One day five or six rugged Oregon ranchers came over, fixed the tractor, and nearly finished the irrigation ditch. Mat still has his farm. He is sure he will not lose it now.

If all these migrants are to be adequately cared for, Vernon A. Mund, professor of economics at the University of Washington, contends four things are necessary:

(1) Continued Federal spending for public works.
(2) Extensive reclamation programs.
(3) Classification of all idle land in the Northwest.
(4) Planning agencies for industrial and manufacturing development in the region.

Long-term loans, neighborly generosity, and help from various Federal agencies have made it possible for thousands of wandering families to get farms. But there are others still to be settled. The bright success in the watershed of the Columbia of many of the drought wanderers makes all the more tragic and incongruous the plight of those yet on the road. The great migration is a problem still. The State of Washington alone, says Dr. Mund, has more than 100,000 settlers from the Dust Bowl. That is a number to reckon with. It took a generation for that many pioneers to come West in the days of ox team and long rifle.

-6-

The people who have traveled west from the Dust Bowl present a national problem. They are as much a concern of the whole country as were the Americans whose ox teams pulled covered wagons across the Rockies before the sovereignty of the United States on the coast was definitely established. Blue-coated troops were sent to protect the pioneers of a century ago. Now, the frontiers are not only physical. They are also economic. The men who own the fertile lands of the Far West, regardless of whether those lands are under cultivation, cannot be pried away from their domain by force. Not for mortgage companies and nonresident investors and powerful ranch combines the treatment suffered by the Indians! Courts and deeds and land titles are better defenses of property than were spears and tomahawks and arrows. When settlers from the plains want rich land to till, they cannot shoulder rifles and call out the cavalry to help them take it. Those days passed into limbo when the railroad brought civilization West. The pioneers of old braved only the wilderness. The pilgrims of today encounter more than physical barriers; they also face the economics and conventions of modern society.

The worst conditions among the drought refugees still nomadic exist in California. It was California that was the goal of the covered-wagon party led by George Donner in 1846. Most of his followers starved to death in the grim mountains that hem in the Pacific seaboard. As I read from a chronicle of the West of that terrible experience which claimed so many lives, an Associated Press dispatch of a few days ago describes what is happening to part of the people who have followed the trail Donner pioneered. I quote:

. . . At least 70,000 persons, mostly families from the dust-ridden areas of the Southwest, are in desperate straits in San Joaquin Valley to the North—many starving and dying of disease. . . .

The situation is "shocking," said Harold H. Robertson, field secretary of the Gospel Army, national social and relief body.

He told of homeless, jobless families from Texas, Oklahoma, Arkansas, and Kansas and their ragged, hungry children camping out along the highways and in fields under "unbelievably" squalid conditions. They are beset by tuberculosis, typhoid, pneumonia, and various social diseases, and county hospitals, as well as relief agencies, are overtaxed, he said.

Will some of these men and women whose back-breaking toil brought wheat out of the Great Plains be relegated to the status of a permanent pauper class in the Far West? This question is made particularly important by the fact that the trek to the coast is still under way. Eventually the migration will move at least a million people two thousand miles farther westward. Stuart Chase says ten million is not a far-fetched impossibility. The United States as a whole looks upon the sundown seaboard as the Promised Land. A recent survey by *Fortune* showed that of all the great national regions, the country at large prefers the Pacific coast as a place to live.

3. The Biggest Thing on Earth

FIVE years ago Sam Seaton and Charlie Osborne and their families were the only people living in the rocky canyon where the Columbia River turns a horseshoe bend and swings north for several miles on its southward course through the State of Washington. Charlie's principal occupation was coaxing a tiny peach crop up through the arid ground each summer. Sam operated the crude, lumber-built ferry which provided the only means of crossing the stream. Occasionally a dust-splattered automobile jolted down the winding road from the rim of the cliff, but the most regular passengers on Sam's homemade conveyance were sheep being herded to their upland pastures. The bleating animals were taken across the river in relays, Sam and his son guiding the ferry along the taut cables which kept it from being swept downstream like a cigar box by the surging waters of the Columbia.

The two families dwelt ten or twelve miles from any settlement and nearly ninety miles from the nearest city. It was lonely in the canyon, and while Charlie cultivated his peaches Sam sometimes read to pass away the hours. Among the books in his cabin was a bent and tattered *World Almanac,* in which were to be found such salient facts as that the Panama Canal was the greatest of all engineering enterprises, and that the Great Pyramid of Gizeh in Egypt was the most massive single structure ever made by man.

Those facts are outdated now—and so is Sam Seaton's improvised ferry. Where he and Charlie once lived, sixty-eight hundred men are engaged in an undertaking more costly than the Panama Canal and larger than the ancient Pyramid of the Pharaohs. Since 1933 the site of the Osborne ranch has been occupied by a low, Colonial-style building from which engineers of the United States Bureau of Reclamation have supervised the construction of Grand Coulee Dam, a barrier across the Columbia River which will make other dams look like toys or models.

To most Americans, Grand Coulee is merely another of the ten or fifteen dams Mr. Roosevelt is building about the country to confound the private power companies and relieve unemployment. Completely lost in the five-year political hurly-burly between the New Deal and its antagonists has been the fact that Grand Coulee is the most elaborate and expensive engineering development ever undertaken by any government. When the Panama Canal was dug, the world marveled at the magnitude of the enterprise. Grand Coulee will cost approximately $25,000,000 more than the Panama Canal. All of us have heard a good deal about the hugeness of Boulder Dam; Grand Coulee will contain more than three times as much concrete. Yet the average citizen is not even certain of its location, or for what purpose it is being constructed. Persons entirely familiar with the Tennessee Valley Authority are unaware that Grand Coulee will produce more hydroelectric power than all seven dams in the TVA combined. The Passamaquoddy fiasco in Maine has been a *bête noire* of Republican budget balancers; yet the total proposed Passamaquoddy appropriation would scarcely finance the cement plant at Grand Coulee. The undertaking is so Brobdingnagian that Waldemar Borquist, the director of Sweden's Royal Board of Waterfalls, was astounded. "Our projects in

Sweden are only one-tenth or one-twentieth as large as this one," he said. "I am amazed by Grand Coulee. It is gigantic."

Let us clear away a little of the obfuscation surrounding this most stupendous of all Mr. Roosevelt's Public Works projects—and also, incidentally, the most stupendous construction undertaking in the history of mankind—by setting down some plain facts about it.

The site of Grand Coulee Dam is somewhat northeast of the exact center of the State of Washington. It is being constructed where the Columbia River doubles back on itself and flows north for a few miles. Approximately one hundred fifty miles upstream from the dam is the Canadian border; three times that distance down the river, the Columbia empties into the Pacific Ocean at Astoria, Oregon. Spokane is ninety miles away, and it is two hundred forty miles over the Cascade Mountains to Seattle. Although Grand Coulee will provide the world's largest supply of electric energy—producing, for example, six times as many kilowatts as the giant Dnieper Dam in Russia—it is regarded by the Federal Power Commission as primarily an irrigation project. The late Dr. Elwood Mead, United States Commissioner of Reclamation, stated that the undertaking would bring water to "the largest compact body of undeveloped land remaining in the United States and the most fertile."

It is the irrigation phase of Grand Coulee which raises social and economic questions transcending in significance those identified with any other Public Works enterprise of the Roosevelt Administration, except possibly the TVA. The completion of the dam will add more than a million and a half acres to the productive capacity of the nation. This land can be used and developed only if the Federal Government enters into an extensive program of assisting people in the slums and tenements of the East and in the Dust Bowl of the

Middle West to settle and cultivate a great chunk of fertile
soil almost a continent removed from their homes. Perhaps it
was such a program which President Roosevelt had in mind
when, standing beneath the lofty cliffs and overhanging crags
near Grand Coulee, he said in the summer of 1934:

You have acreage capable of supporting a much larger population than you now have. And we believe that by proceeding with
these great projects it will not only develop the well-being of the
Far West and the coast, but will also give an opportunity to many
individuals and many families back in the older, settled parts of
the nation to come out here and distribute some of the burdens
which fall on them more heavily than fall on the West. . . .

A great many years ago, seventy-five or eighty, an editor in
New York said, "Go West, young man, go West." Horace Greeley is supposed to be out of date today, but there is a great opportunity for the people of the East, people of the South, and in some
overcrowded parts of the Middle West. . . . You shall have the
opportunity of still going West. . . .

I know that this country is going to be filled with the homes not
only of a great many people from this State, but a great many
families from other States of the Union.

-2-

To understand the purpose of Grand Coulee Dam in general and the operation of its irrigation features in particular,
it is necessary to go back ages before the New Deal—to the
Pleistocene epoch, when Mr. Roosevelt's farthest-removed
progenitors were just coming upon the earth.

During that period the Cordilleran ice sheets spread over
North America. At the precise point of the present construction of Grand Coulee Dam, an ice obstruction completely
blocked the deeply canyoned Columbia River. Behind the

wedge of mobile ice the river quickly formed a huge lake, and then flowed over the rim of the canyon and started cutting a new channel directly at right angles to its former course. Augmented by an enormous inflow of glacial waters, the Columbia gouged out a new canyon fifty miles long, from five hundred to one thousand feet deep, and from two to five miles wide. At one point it poured over a four-hundred-foot precipice in the greatest cataract known to man, a plunge three miles across and possessing the volume of fifty Niagaras.

For thousands of years the river hewed this gash out of rock and shale. Then the ice sheet receded. The wall blocking the Columbia melted and dwindled away. The river returned to its original course. The cleft formed by the overflow behind the Cordilleran ice dam was left dry and barren, high above the stream which had once poured through it. Only a few scattered lakes indicated where the Columbia, swollen to many times its normal size, had previously flowed. The giant cataract was stranded as silent as the ages, its water-eroded walls telling, in the words of Dr. J Harlen Bretz of the University of Chicago, "a heroic tale of vanished power and glory far transcending that of Niagara, and beggaring the leisurely story of the Yellowstone, the Yosemite, or even the Grand Canyon of the Colorado."

The great cleft carved centuries ago by the antediluvian waters is known today as the Grand Coulee of the Columbia River. The Grand Coulee Dam is being built at the point where the dry bed of the prehistoric river diverged from the present course of the Columbia. Nearly seven thousand workmen and engineers are building a bulwark of concrete where once a migratory prong of the Cordilleran glacial sheet formed a barrier of ice. The dam will accomplish intentionally the result achieved capriciously by the rampant natural forces of the Pleistocene period. It will raise a portion of the Columbia back into the Coulee, and again the floor of the ancient gorge will be inundated. After being dry and arid throughout most of the history of mankind, the Grand Coulee once more will be a waterway. It is for this primary purpose that the government is constructing the most massive dam ever built, a dam which will contain enough concrete to make a monument as long and broad as a city block and three times as high as the Empire State Building.

At its crest Grand Coulee Dam will tower five hundred fifty feet above bedrock, and will raise the level of the Columbia three hundred fifty-five feet. An elaborate pumping apparatus, operated by power generated at the project, will elevate the water another two hundred eighty feet into the Coulee through a system of pipe lines and canals. Within three weeks after the pumping plant has started to function, the upper half of the Coulee—that above the site of the prehistoric waterfall—will be an enormous reservoir twenty-three miles long, three times as deep as the gorge below Niagara Falls, and covering twenty-three hundred acres. Efficient irrigation requires balancing reservoirs; they give a uniform flow, provide a steady volume during the low-water season, and forestall the need of diverting entire streams. Stuart Chase has pointed out that sometimes the original sources of water fail when a whole river is moved from its course for irrigation purposes. At Grand Coulee only one-tenth the total volume of the Columbia will have to be diverted. The twenty-three-mile storage pool, hewn by Nature almost a sixth of a mile deep in volcanic lava, will obviate the necessity of using more than a fraction of the river's flow. Ninety-foot earthen dikes at the ends of the Coulee will convert the cliff-bordered ditch into a lake.

From the vast balancing reservoir thus formed, gravity

canals will coast the water downhill to irrigate the Columbia basin project, a tract of land twice as large as the State of Rhode Island.

The Grand Coulee and the potentially fertile land below it were examined in 1922 by Major General George W. Goethals, the chief engineer of the Panama Canal during its construction. He tramped over the entire scene; he examined the surrounding topography. He noted that the land of the Columbia basin project was slightly below the level of the Coulee but far above the surface of the river, and agreed that the one method of irrigating the area efficiently was to run the water through the dry gorge. After completing his survey, General Goethals said the enterprise not only was as important as the Panama Canal, but would add more to the national wealth of the United States than either the Canal or the Alaskan Railroad.

Before analyzing in detail the territory to be irrigated and developed at Grand Coulee, let us ride up the floor of the prehistoric canyon on the special government railroad built twenty-nine miles from a spur of the Northern Pacific at Odair, Washington. The caboose at the end of the nineteen-car work train clicks along rockily as the right-of-way twists down a side gorge and enters the Grand Coulee itself. The bottom of the deep declivity is as smooth as a counterpane. Here and there a sparsely coned fir tree dots the flat waste, but mainly the landscape is barren and arid. Moving up the bottom of the Coulee is like rolling through a monstrous trough. The walls of the giant ditch are symmetrical and even; from the platform of the clattering caboose the cliffs on either side appear as sharp as shoe-box edges. Near the head of the Coulee the railway swings around a towering basalt formation appropriately described as Steamboat Rock, and emerges at the upper end of the vast conduit. There the train grinds to a stop; and we find ourselves looking down into the gorge where, five hundred feet below us, the Columbia River now runs—at right angles to the dry trough up which we have been traveling. This is the site of the dam.

The cliff walls do not rise abruptly from the river. On each side of the Columbia there is a gradual slope before the canyon becomes precipitous, and on these slopes are the buildings incidental to the enterprise. Directly below our slowly moving train, as it resumes its journey into the canyon, is a village of Colonial-style bungalows. The compact, uniform-sized houses, separated by patches of grass as carefully tended as golf greens, look to us on our height like toys or models. Two or three larger buildings are the school, several dormitories, and the general headquarters—the last-named almost on the exact site of Charlie Osborne's homestead. Squarely behind the school, in which Charlie himself is the janitor, frowns a granite bluff four hundred feet high. This community is listed in the office of the Postmaster General as "Coulee Dam, Washington." It is the government village which houses the Bureau of Reclamation engineers and employees supervising the work on the dam. There are some minor variations in the buildings, but largely the cottages appear to have been poured from a single mold. Even the porch lights, mailboxes, chandeliers, and clotheslines are the same.

Across the river is a compound of long halls and small cracker-box houses, with ten or twelve times as many buildings as the bungalow village. This is Mason City, the town plotted by the private contractors performing the actual construction work on the dam. The Grand Coulee bid was too staggering for one company to handle alone, and so three firms consolidated to build the structure—the Silas Mason Company of New York, the Walsh Construction Company of Iowa, and the Atkinson-Kier Company of California. This combine, known as the "M.W.A.K. Company," is building the dam; the Bureau of Reclamation engineers act only in a supervisory capacity. After the undertaking is completed, the dam will be operated by the government. Thus Coulee Dam is a permanent community; Mason City, by contrast, is relatively temporary, destined merely to meet the construction needs of the six or seven years required to build the project. When the dam is completed, it will be razed.

Not a chimney pokes through a roof in Mason City. The entire town is heated by electricity. This is an experiment to determine if the rickety wood stoves in the farm homes of the Pacific Northwest cannot be supplanted by transmission wires when the turbines of Grand Coulee begin grinding out two and a half million horsepower of hydroelectric energy. In the winter of 1935, when blizzards held the gorge in a grip of ice, Mason City was as warm and uniformly heated as near-by Coulee Dam with its orthodox oil furnaces and hearth fires. Aside from its complete electrification, Mason City is a typical company town. The contractors operate the theater, the pool hall, the barber shop, the general store, and virtually all other concessions. Prices are fairly high, and the workers grumble that most of their earnings are spent with the company. "They get us going and coming. By golly! President Roosevelt wouldn't stand for that if he knew about it," a number of them told me. The President is definitely the hero of at least three-fourths of the laborers on the dam, and over a majority of the bunks are pasted "F. D. R." stickers or newspaper photographs of Mr. Roosevelt.

A surprising feature is the preponderant number of young men employed at Grand Coulee. Waiting in line to eat in the mess hall, I noticed dozens of tall lads wearing football sweaters from near-by colleges and universities. The work is dangerous, and scarcely a day passes without some one's being

injured; fifty-four men have already been killed. I talked
with some of the older men engaged in specialized tasks,
and discovered that a considerable proportion of them had
drifted to Coulee after the completion of the giant Boulder
Dam on the Colorado River. They were unanimous in
agreeing there was no comparison between the magnitude
of the undertakings. "I thought Boulder Dam was the biggest thing on earth," one stoop-shouldered steel riveter said.
"Hell! This outfit makes it look like nothin' at all." He
swept a long arm down to where a temporary cofferdam as
long as Muscle Shoals was beginning to hold back the hitherto unshackled fury of the Columbia. White water breaking
with a subdued roar around the pier of the bridge connecting
Coulee Dam and Mason City indicated the speed and force
of the stream.

-3-

The best way to appreciate the vastness of this engineering
enterprise is to look at it from the river itself—from a motorboat, riding downstream on the Columbia. The motorboat
sticks its prow round a bluff at the water's edge. And there it
is—Grand Coulee! Between cliffs nearly a mile apart, steam
shovels scrape down to bedrock. From these cliffs protrude
trestles almost two hundred feet high. Along the trestles
move chains of flatcars carrying buckets of concrete. Cranes
reach out slowly like stork bills to empty the buckets into pits
far below the trestles. Hard against the granite walls of the
canyon are peaked cement silos which suggest the sentry
towers on the battlements of some medieval fortress. Cofferdams—steel cells backed by earth and lumber—flank each
side of the river. They have diverted the second largest

waterway in the United States from its course—an engineering feat never before attempted. On the summit of the cliffs above Mason City the pointed roofs of the world's largest gravel plant look no bigger than chalets clinging to a crag in the Alps.

On every side of the Columbia's horseshoe bend, naked escarpments of rock and shale tower against the sky. The only break is above the Bureau of Reclamation's bungalow village, where the cliffs part at the head of the Coulee. Far up the canyon wall is a sign "SAFETY PAYS." This marks where the crest of the dam will be. One looks from cliff to cliff. The granite bluffs are separated by nearly a mile of slope and water, yet in the not distant future they will be connected by a bulwark of concrete forty-three hundred feet long, five hundred fifty feet high, and five hundred feet thick at the base. Knock off the tower of the Empire State Building, chink up the windows, lengthen the structure almost three-fourths of a mile, pour over its center a waterfall more than twice as high as Niagara, and you have an improvised conception of the government's greatest construction undertaking.

When it is completed, the dam at Grand Coulee will be in a number of respects a large-scale reproduction of Norris Dam in the TVA. It will stretch in a straight line between the two bluffs like Norris Dam, and will not be curved at the crest like the giant Boulder Dam on the Colorado River. In several other features Grand Coulee will resemble the Norris project. It will be vertical on its upstream face, and the downstream face will slant to receive the spillway. Several visitors from the TVA, on observing the foundation for Grand Coulee and looking over the engineers' drafts of its completed appearance, have remarked that it will be a vast replica of Norris Dam. On each side of the spillway, powerhouses and pumping plants will partially cover the front of the Grand Coulee structure.

The Columbia River offers the biggest potential hydro-electric supply in the United States, and some surveys have estimated its power possibility as more than five times that of the Tennessee River, the key waterway of the TVA. Territory six times the size of England is drained by the Columbia, and this territory will be studded by towering transmission poles when Grand Coulee is completed. The drainage area extends into British Columbia and seven American States: Washington, Idaho, Oregon, Montana, Nevada, Utah, and Wyoming. The late Colonel Hugh L. Cooper, the builder of Europe's largest river barrier, the Dnieper Dam, declared that the horseshoe bend below the bed of the Coulee offered an opportunity for generating electricity at the lowest rate available in North America.

Most of the nation's great streams—the Mississippi, the Hudson, the St. Lawrence, the Colorado, and the Tennessee—have been put to work. Until three years ago the Columbia was virtually an unshackled liquid giant, even for navigation being useful only about one hundred fifty miles from the sea. Grand Coulee represents one of the first attempts of any magnitude to utilize the resources of the principal river on the Pacific seaboard and the second largest waterway of the United States.

The fury and volume of the Columbia's flow—assets in the future—are handicaps now. They add engineering difficulties which must be overcome and conquered before the river can be harnessed. The temporary cofferdams have had to be larger and more durable than many permanent structures; they must withstand five hundred fifty thousand second-feet of water, and already eight shiploads of lumber have gone into their construction. As a government supervisor guides you around the actual work at Grand Coulee, superlatives come as frequently as puffs from his briar pipe. The phrase "the largest in the world" is indispensable to his explanations. In almost every respect the dimensions of the dam establish new records.

The cement-mixing plant is the largest in the world. The spillway will be the largest in the world. The river behind the dam will be backed up into the longest artificial lake in the world, which will extend to the Canadian boundary, one hundred fifty-one miles away, and will bury Kettle Falls, a thirty-six-foot drop fifty miles above Grand Coulee, beneath one hundred feet of water. The powerhouse will be the largest in the world—almost as long as two city blocks. The belt conveyor, which carries dirt from the excavation to a neighboring ravine and dumps it there, is the largest in the world; it is a mile in length and has already dumped a pile of waste as high as a twenty-story skyscraper. The pumps to be installed will be the largest in the world; they must raise five hundred tons of water two hundred eighty feet into the Coulee every second.

Four ocean liners the size of the giant *Queen Mary* could be placed on the crest of the dam, and still they would not stretch from one end to the other. In bulk Grand Coulee will exceed the twenty next largest dams in the country combined. It will contain enough concrete to build a standard automobile highway from Philadelphia to Seattle and back by way of Los Angeles. Sufficient water will flow through the dam each year to provide New York City's drinking supply for a century. In the twin powerhouses, each more than twice as high as the Leaning Tower of Pisa, so much electricity will be generated that all the switches will have to be thrown far away from the plant by remote control; otherwise the men operating the dam would be instantly electrocuted.

Even the quantity of food prepared for the workers reaches a thumping total. Three thousand hot cakes are fried every morning, twenty-four hundred pounds of turkey are roasted each Sunday, and everything from oatmeal to candied sweet potatoes is cooked in similar proportions. At breakfast in the enormous mess hall the workers on each side of me ate six eggs apiece and an equal number of strips of bacon. All these supplies must be transported up the dry floor of the Coulee, and an endless caravan of automobiles and trucks rolls along where only an occasional Indian or sheepherder appeared before.

A few other facts will suggest the sort of problems which the builders have faced. Hauling in sand and gravel by train would have cost several million extra dollars. So a natural deposit was uncovered above the site of the dam, and an immense gravel plant built to handle it. Mud slides continually hampered the work at the east bulwark; but a giant ice machine froze the mud solid and removed that hazard. To prevent the dam from destroying the Columbia River salmon pack—the world's principal supply of Chinook salmon—the greatest spawning-hatchery ever planned will front the downstream side of the completed barrier. (See Chapter 5.)

-4-

What will be the eventual result of this ingenuity and expenditure and effort? Will the vast acreage to be irrigated, and the unequaled bloc of power to be produced, have any salutary effect on the great social and economic problems confronting the nation? Will $404,000,000 be spent to advantage? The answer is locked in the history—past, present, and future—of the approximately million and a half acres lying below the lower end of the Coulee: the Africa-shaped tract of land known as the Columbia basin project. It is there that a network of irrigation canals and subsidiary developments will claim more than half the cost of the Grand Coulee enterprise. The expenditure will be divided as follows:

Dam and power plant	$181,101,000
Interest charges	15,000,000
Irrigation canals	208,532,000
Total	$404,633,000

Forty years ago, when the Northwest was being carved out of the wilderness, the Northern Pacific Railway owned by grant of Congress each alternate section of the Columbia basin project. Lithographs depicting the wonders of this bountiful area were hung in every station, and settlers were encouraged to move West. Gradually the Northern Pacific sections were sold, and the government sections were taken up by homesteaders. For a few seasons the land produced wheat and supported grazing. Improvements were made, good buildings erected, and homes established. There was a brief boom, and money to finance the settlers was loaned by banks, nonresident capitalists, and mortgage companies. No one seemed to realize that the crops could not last, that the eight-inch annual rainfall was not sufficient to maintain even dry farming, and that the only moisture in the ground was the limited supply accumulated beneath a mat of grass and vegetation. The desert had been penetrated too far.

The moisture gave out. The wheat failed; even the bunch grass dried up, and starving cattle roamed the basin seeking fodder. Desperately the farmers searched for water. But they were five hundred feet above the Columbia, and what windmill could raise water one-third that distance? From their arid plateau the settlers looked into the canyon where the second largest stream in the country moved swiftly to the sea. The water to save their farms was within a stone's throw, but it might as well have been in Afghanistan.

The settlers moved on, and the creditors took the abandoned farms. Today, more than a generation later, crumbling barns, rotting farmhouses, and decaying wagon wheels still tell the story of expectations which exceeded the rainfall. And the records of the clerks of Grant, Adams, and Franklin counties tell the dismal story of loans and mortgages which could not be met. Large parcels of the Columbia basin project are listed under such titles as the Washington Trust Company, the Citizens Savings Bank, the Union Central Life Insurance Company, and the Big Bend Land Company. A single bank owns twenty-eight thousand acres. Ninety per cent of the land is in private hands.

This is one of the dilemmas most vexing to Secretary of the Interior Ickes, in whose department the Grand Coulee undertaking has been placed. The average value of the land in the Columbia basin project at present is estimated at fifteen dollars an acre; the average price asked is eighty-six. Refugees from the Dust Bowl of the Dakotas and the slums of Chicago cannot purchase ground at anywhere near the latter sum. It must be available to them at minimum prices. The Bureau of Reclamation has confessed that this is a problem demanding settlement: "Means must be provided for controlling land prices and selling terms to prevent speculation." Many of the owners of the land obviously hope to realize an unearned increment by holding on until the government crisscrosses their arid acres with a web of irrigation canals. Even to obtain the site for the dam proper it was necessary for the government to go into court and whittle down a five-million-dollar demand to a seventeen-thousand-dollar agreement.

President Roosevelt has stated that the great plateau of fertile land to be created by the Grand Coulee enterprise is

largely for the purpose of settlement by people from the East
and the Middle West on whom the burdens of life have
fallen heavily. The policy thus implied makes it imperative
that little or no capital be required for taking up farms. Victims of drought and depression do not have full wallets. A
Bureau of Reclamation report published in 1928 estimated
that "the Columbia Basin project will have to be settled by
people who have from $2500 to $3500." That was before the
crash shook the East, and 100 degrees of heat dried up the
Middle West. Today there are thousands of people who seek
a new start on the Pacific coast, but they are people who are
far from having "$2500 to $3500."

On the roads near Grand Coulee I met scores of dilapidated automobiles from the Dust Bowl. It was pathetic to
hear these drought refugees talk wistfully of a Promised
Land supplied with a steady flow of water from the great
balancing reservoir of the Coulee. The wanderers from the
Middle West seem certain that this most monumental of all
construction enterprises will make the desert uplands bloom.
Even in the presence of the abandoned and rotting failures of
the past, the wayfarers look off hopefully in the distance to
the towering rock bulwarks of the chasm of the Grand Coulee.
Sometimes I think they actually see in their mind's eye the
great river flowing there once more. These people are desperately eager to colonize the vast area the $404,000,000
undertaking will irrigate. But how? Practically all of them
are broke. Where will they get the money?

I asked one of the drought pilgrims whether he would consider taking up a farm in the Columbia basin project. "Sure,"
he replied, "but with what?" From his pocket he took a thin
roll of five-dollar bills wound with a rubber band. "That's all
I have."

A perpetual water right will cost eighty-five dollars an

acre, according to present plans. The toll would be payable to the government over a period of forty years at no interest. Yet there will be other expenses, such as irrigation benefits, and these must be scraped to rock bottom. Nine years ago it was estimated that approximately ten thousand dollars would be necessary to purchase, develop, and equip an eighty-acre farm in the basin. This price range threatens all hopes that Grand Coulee will give a hundred thousand families model homes supplied with cheap power and abundant water.

So the principal question is a human one. Will the victims of natural catastrophes and economic disasters be able to settle on this new territory? The answer depends on whether the government can pare down the financial prerequisites until they are commensurate with the pocketbooks of the people for whom the enterprise has been planned.

An imperative task is the prevention of land speculation. Both the Dust Bowl wanderers and the Alliance Trust Company cannot benefit from the same project. People in Tampa, Florida, and Dayton, Ohio, and Buffalo, New York, are not paying their biggest PWA tax bill for the enrichment of the Northern Pacific Railway and the Union Central Life Insurance Company. Possibly this problem will be solved by the bill recently driven through Congress by Washington's two forward-looking Senators, Lewis Schwellenbach and Homer Bone. The measure permits the Secretary of the Interior to set the price on the nearly two million acres in the Columbia basin tract without basing that price on the increment due to the giant dam.

Of one fact there is little doubt. When the dry bed of the Coulee at last holds water again, the lands of the Columbia basin project will respond to irrigation. Almost identical soil irrigated on a much smaller scale in neighboring Yakima County has produced a wide variety of fruits such as pears, apples, and peaches. Since 1900 the population of Yakima County has increased from 13,000 to 77,000; its assessed valuation has soared from $5,000,000 to seven times that sum. During almost the same period the population of Adams County, which is in the Columbia basin project, has been relatively stationary. The solitary difference between the two counties has been irrigation. If the rate of increase enjoyed in Yakima County applies to the area developed by Grand Coulee Dam, the population of the Columbia basin reclamation land will eventually be 384,000 and the valuation $422,000,000—more than the total cost of the dam and irrigation network.

-5-

The original proposal for this most gigantic of all the nation's irrigation and hydroelectric enterprises goes back more than three decades to 1903, when the Bureau of Reclamation announced that the soil in the Columbia basin was adaptable to irrigation. Another report in 1911 declared the area to be "especially high in the mineral elements to which fertility is often ascribed." But how to get a uniform flow of water onto the land? The Columbia was five hundred feet below the area to be irrigated.

The problem was a sticker for seven years. Then one hot July afternoon in 1918 three men hunched over a cafeteria table in the little town of Ephrata had an idea. "Why not dam the Columbia and pump the water back into the Coulee?" asked Billy Clapp. His crony, Gale Matthews, nodded in agreement. Rufus Woods, the editor of the Wenatchee *Daily World*, brought his fist down on the rickety table with a crash. "Billy has it!" he cried.

Rufus galloped furiously home to Wenatchee, and the next day—July 18, 1918—his paper carried the headline:

FORMULATE BRAND NEW IDEA FOR IRRIGATION
GRANT, ADAMS, FRANKLIN COUNTIES, COV-
ERING MILLION ACRES OR MORE

Last and Newest and Most Ambitious Idea Con-
templates Turning of Columbia River Back into
Its Old Bed in Grand Coulee, the Development
of a Power Plant Equal to Niagara and the
Construction of the Greatest Irrigation
Project in the World—First Conceived
by William Clapp of Ephrata, Wash.

Laughter was the immediate result of Rufus Woods' exuberant outburst. "Baron Munchausen, thou wert a piker!"
editorialized a Spokane paper in discussing the scheme. But
Woods was a fighter. He stumped the State in favor of his
idea. He wrote letters to Washington. Billy Clapp and Gale
Matthews spoke at dozens of political meetings. The "Columbia River Development League" was formed. Mimeographed
descriptions of the greatest dam ever built were mailed to
hundreds of editors, most of whom filed them in the waste-
basket. The proposal was occasionally referred to as "Rufus'
Nightmare."

In 1922 the idea was finally lifted out of the crackpot stage
and given a modicum of respectability. General Goethals said
the plan was sound, and gave it his unequivocal endorsement.
The General had supervised the Panama Canal, and people
in high places listened to what he had to say. Three years
later a special committee of the Department of the Interior
declared that the proposal "should be considered as one of
the great future assets of the nation." In 1926 Secretary of

Commerce Herbert Hoover wrote: "The initiation and construction of the Columbia Basin project is inevitable. It should be undertaken at the earliest possible date. I have familiarized myself with the engineering problems involved, and the time to begin this undertaking is now." A year later Mr. Hoover reiterated his position: "I am decidedly in favor of the Columbia Basin project. It is not only important to the food supply of the nation in the early future, but it is timely to meet the existing economic situation." Even President Coolidge told the Union League Club of Philadelphia, "The Columbia Basin project is not far distant."

However, some of the Union League members, when they contemplated the vast supply of government-controlled electricity incidental to the enterprise, shuddered and decided "not far distant" was too soon. Opposition to "this outrageous proposed extravagance" began to be heard in Congress. During the Hoover Administration a detailed report submitted by army engineers recommended the construction of Grand Coulee and nine other dams on the Columbia River, spanning the stream like the rungs of a giant ladder; but Mr. Hoover had changed his mind since his cabinet service. As President he vetoed the Norris bill providing for the operation of Muscle Shoals, and he had no intention of approving this infinitely larger power plant in the Far West. The army report gathered dust in the drawer of his desk.

In March of 1933 a new President entered the White House. He had promised in his campaign that "the next hydroelectric development to be undertaken by the Federal Government must be that on the Columbia River." Mr. Roosevelt resurrected the army engineers' analysis and authorized the use of $63,000,000 of PWA and other emergency funds, and Grand Coulee was under way. In a number of respects the enterprise was admirably adapted to New

Deal requirements. It offered a constructive method of reliev-
ing unemployment; it coincided with the President's belief
in conservation and reclamation; and it promised the most
important addition to the "yardsticks" with which to control
the rates charged by the private utilities. Mr. Roosevelt also
approved the building of a $75,000,000 hydroelectric project
two hundred ninety miles downstream from Grand Coulee at Bonneville, Oregon, where the Columbia cuts through
the Cascade Mountains. The two dams now under construction are at the extreme upper and lower limits of the ten-
dam proposal advanced by the army engineers. The complete
Columbia River plan—still far in the future—will cost $772,-
000,000 and will ultimately generate almost half as many
kilowatts of electricity as are now produced in the entire
nation.

To date Grand Coulee has been relatively obscured by
other New Deal activities. But this will not be so in the
months ahead. Undoubtedly it will be read about in the headlines as the Republicans and conservative Democrats attempt
to set the brakes on Mr. Roosevelt's spending caravan. Yet
the No. 1 power and irrigation undertaking of American history probably will be completed. It cannot be left stranded
and uncompleted in the mountain wilderness, a hundred-
million-dollar monolith as useless as the Pyramids of Egypt.
The opponents of this costliest of all construction jobs premised most of their hopes on the chance of getting Mr. Roosevelt out of the White House. Congressman Francis Culkin
of the State of New York, who claimed that "in the region of
Grand Coulee, that colossal imposition on the American people, there is no one to sell the power to except coyotes and
jack rabbits," said this foolishness would stop "when we elect
a Republican House and a Republican President." Mr. Roosevelt, now in office at least until the end of 1940, several times

has given his blessing to the titanic enterprise: "We are going ahead with a useful project and we are going to see it through for the benefit of our country."

When the President visited Grand Coulee on his 1937 trip to the Far West, he sat in the tonneau of his automobile above the dam and tried to impress on the newspaper correspondents the fact that the great sums of money appropriated for Coulee supplies and equipment are being spent in no fewer than forty States. The President ate a picnic lunch that day. I remember as I watched him bite into a ham sandwich on whole wheat and lick apple-pie juice from his fingers that I contrasted this mundane performance on the part of Grand Coulee's chief sponsor with the almost fantastic unreality of the massive wall of concrete slowly taking shape in the canyon below.

Grand Coulee, deep in the last American wilderness, is so vast it seems apart from ordinary undertakings. Yet it is gripped by the economic and social and moral dilemmas that beset other projects where men are at work. The A.F. of L. and C.I.O. are locked in a bitter struggle for control of the sixty-eight hundred men building the dam. The M.W.A.K. Company * has given begrudging recognition to the A.F. of L. and ordered the C.I.O. to clear out. A few figures are significant:

Truck drivers: Company, 90 cents an hour; A.F. of L. demand, $1.40; C.I.O. demand, $1.62.

Carpenters: Company, $1.20 an hour; A.F. of L. demand, $1.50; C.I.O. demand, $1.62.

* The M.W.A.K. Company has recently become part of the Consolidated Builders, Inc. This is a larger company, organized to complete the monumental Coulee job. An attorney for the National Labor Relations Board, who looked into labor conditions on the great dam, has told me that both the private contractors and government engineers seem more concerned about cement and steel than about an enlightened attitude toward the workmen.

Steel workers: Company, 90 cents an hour; A.F. of L. demand, $1.30; C.I.O. demand, $1.62.

Labor is not the only point of controversy at Grand Coulee. Various ministers have alleged that deplorable vice conditions are prevalent. Even in an enterprise that seeks to create a Promised Land in the desert fastnesses, there is no escape from the economic and moral questions that rock the world.

-6-

Today, if you alight from the train at Wenatchee and express the slightest interest in Grand Coulee, Rufus Woods will drive you—as he did me—up the floor of the Coulee in his ancient blue Cadillac. On the way he will stop at Ephrata to introduce you to Billy Clapp and Gale Matthews, typical politicians of the American hinterlands. And at the head of the dry river bed, above the site of the structure he was called "Baron Munchausen" for proposing, Rufus, with all the pride of a father displaying a newborn prodigy, will wave his arm and exclaim, "There she is!"

In the canyon below, almost seven thousand men scrape down to granite. Concrete mixing towers rattle twenty-four hours a day. Block on block, the dam rises from the excavation. The Columbia chafes impatiently against the steel bulwarks of the cofferdams. Here the frontier and civilization meet in sharp comparison. Up in Rattlesnake Canyon, where the conveyor continually empties its load of dirt, it was not so long ago that a sheriff's posse ferreted out a horse-thief named "Texas Pete" and hanged him to a convenient ledge. A few miles downstream an Indian spears for salmon. His ancestors were using the same kind of spear when Meriwether Lewis and William Clark reached the scene a century and a quarter ago. The Indian's face is set and hard as he hears the construction noises. He is afraid the dam will spoil the salmon run, which was providing food for his ancestors before Columbus discovered America.

High above the river, the entrance of the Coulee is silently waiting for the Columbia to rush through its rock-bound corridor once more. Until the river flows there again, the head of the prehistoric torrent will hold a town. This new town might be one of the mushroom villages which followed the first railroad west, or studded the trail of the Yukon gold rush. The real-estate agent wears a checkered vest and derby hat. Taxi dancers in gaudy dresses line the walls of twenty beer parlors. Fist fights break up two or three drinking bouts. A dozen brothels with fantastic names cater to several thousand womanless males, and the ladies from the sporting houses swear vehemently as dirt seeps through their sandals and spatters their painted toenails when they walk along the boardwalk to the beauty shops which flank the main street.

The walls of the Coulee, grim and sharp under the stars, frown down on this cluster of rickety buildings and tar-paper shacks. Surely it was not to hold so mean a scene that the forces of uncounted ages carved a great trough through the ramparts of the lava plateau. And the men who at night bury their faces in beer mugs and trudge the steps of the "Swanee Rooms" work by day to achieve for the gaunt Coulee a more useful purpose—that of guiding the river to new farmlands to supply apples and wheat for the people of the earth.

4. Hydroelectric!

The day will come when electricity will be for everyone as the waters of the rivers and the wind of heaven. It should not merely be supplied, but lavished, that men may use it at their will as the air they breathe.   —EMILE ZOLA.

THERE are two hundred seventy-five billion undeveloped kilowatt-hours of hydroelectricity in the United States. This constitutes the latent water-power wealth of the nation. More than 41 per cent of the total amount—one hundred fourteen billion kilowatt-hours—is in the basin of one river, the Columbia.

These figures are amazing *per se*. They are made all the more amazing by the peculiar qualities of electricity. Practically every product except water power can be transported across the earth. Coal taken from a Pennsylvania mine can be burned in a furnace in Manchuria. Trees cut down in Russia can be sawed in an American mill. Wheat grown on the plains of Canada can be baked into bread by a housewife in Sweden. But electricity must be consumed where it is generated. It cannot be transmitted efficiently more than three hundred miles.

That 20 per cent of the country's petroleum is in Oklahoma is of no great significance. Swiftly rolling fast freights and throbbing cargo steamers can carry the product of Oklahoma's wells to any other part of the nation or planet. But suppose the oil would go to waste if it were not used within the State of Oklahoma? This is the dilemma that confronts the country in regard to hydroelectric power. Nearly half the potential electricity of the entire nation is in a region which has less than 3 per cent of the people. And unless the power is consumed in that region, it will be as wasted as it was before man discovered that falling water could light homes and operate factories.

Two statistical charts recently prepared by the National Resources Committee show the problem graphically. The first chart portrays the distribution of the hydroelectricity of the country. Twenty-one little blue generators represent America's undeveloped water-power resources. Approximately eight and three-fourths of these generators are located on the map in the Columbia River basin. The other chart illustrates the population diffusion of the nation by metropolitan districts. Eighty-five dots indicate the citadels of population. Four of the smallest dots are inked on the Columbia River watershed States of Washington, Idaho, Oregon, and Montana.

It is a strange story that the symbols on these charts tell. Outside the Pacific Northwest they show approximately twelve of the little blue generators for eighty-one metropolitan areas; in the Pacific Northwest there are almost nine generators for four metropolitan areas. Reduced to figures the difference is more astounding. For each person living in the Columbia River basin, there are at hand 32,628 kilowatt-hours of potential hydroelectricity. For the rest of the nation the sum is one twenty-fourth that amount, 1,353 kilowatt-hours.

Strangest of all, this disproportion must remain. Electricity is not a resource that can be moved about like apples or timber or zinc. Ordinarily a concentration of a particular product in one locality presents no problem. Half the country's oranges are in California, yet in ninety hours a crate of Sunkist specials can be whisked to New York. But although oranges can be taken across the continent, kilowatt-hours cannot. Transmission methods are still imperfect. Technology is not yet able to convey power long distances. Electricity must be consumed close to its source. Some day, energy produced where the Columbia surges through the granite gorges of the West may drive "L" trains in Chicago and illuminate cabarets in New York. Until then, the river system capable of generating far more hydroelectricity than now is used in the whole nation will either have to be left largely undeveloped or else put to work on a sparsely settled frontier.

So the people of the Columbia River basin are not only the custodians of almost half the nation's latent water power. They also are the people who must consume it—if it is to be consumed at all. Small wonder that for two generations in the Pacific Northwest the issue of hydroelectricity has subordinated all other political and economic questions! What cotton is to the South, what wheat is to the Great Plains, what automobiles are to Detroit, what steel is to Pennsylvania, power is to the Columbia River basin. It is the problem that decides the fate of governors, senators, and presidential electors. The ultimate determining factor in a majority of the political contests in the Pacific Northwest is how forthrightly a candidate approaches, or how expertly he straddles, the question of hydroelectric development.

Let us see why this is so. Comparisons with other parts of the country is the best method of emphasizing the enormous swath which power cuts in the potential destiny of the Northwest. Here are the various areas into which the nation has been divided in the regional planning bills:

Region	Undeveloped Hydroelectricity	Per Cent of U. S. Total
Northeast	21,075,000,000 k.w.h.	7.65
Middle West	13,203,000,000 k.w.h.	4.77
Southeast	41,112,000,000 k.w.h.	14.90
Mountain and plain	15,992,000,000 k.w.h.	5.79
Southwest	6,301,000,000 k.w.h.	2.29
Pacific Southwest	63,800,000,000 k.w.h.	23.20
Pacific Northwest	114,200,000,000 k.w.h.	41.40
Total	275,683,000,000 k.w.h.	100.00

More than half the latent power of the Columbia River watershed is the main river itself. The rest is in the tributary streams. The Columbia alone has sixty-two billion potential kilowatt-hours. This contrasts strikingly with twenty-three billion in the Tennessee River, the key waterway of the TVA. With twenty-one billion kilowatt-hours—one-third the power in the Columbia—the turbulent Colorado is Number Three among America's hydroelectric sources. Fourth is the snarling Snake River, which joins the Columbia after a stormy passage through the sixty-five-hundred-foot crevasse of Hell's Canyon. The Snake is the Columbia's principal tributary. Some conception of the magnitude of the power potentialities of the Columbia may be gained from the fact that the St. Lawrence River, scene of Franklin D. Roosevelt's long-promoted navigation and power scheme, has only five billion kilowatt-hours, or one-twelfth the capacity of the mighty river which drains the Oregon Country.

Not without cause have Presidents of the United States chosen the vast basin of the Columbia as the amphitheater in which to make their most significant pronouncements on the power issue. Both as President and as Secretary of Commerce, Herbert Hoover chose the Northwest as the sounding board for his principal power statements. In this respect, at least, his successor in the White House has emulated him. Almost invariably, Mr. Roosevelt waits until he stands within

sight of the Columbia's foaming reaches to deliver his most
salient power utterances. The dominant power speech of the
stormy 1932 campaign he made at Portland. This was the
famous "yardstick" address. Two years later, at Bonneville
and Grand Coulee, he looked at the swirling rapids where
one hundred fourteen billion kilowatt-hours of electricity
were going to waste and said "More power to you" to the
people who watched that spectacle all the time. In 1937 the
President crossed the continent to dedicate Bonneville Dam,
the first unit of the biggest power plant in the world. There,
in the shadow of the fir-mantled hills that Lewis and Clark
climbed, he set forth the national power policy program. "We
are going to see with our own eyes," Mr. Roosevelt said,
"electricity and power made so cheap that they will become
a standard article of use."

But can power rates in the Northwest be reduced sufficiently for 3 per cent of the people to consume nearly 50 per
cent of the country's supply? The answer is clearly in the
negative. There must be another approach to the problem.
Two solutions have been offered. One is to increase immeas-
urably the population of the Columbia River basin. This
would be done by encouraging Eastern slum dwellers and
Middle Western drought refugees to migrate toward the
sunset in infinitely greater numbers than ever before in American history. The other proposed answer is to make the Pacific
Northwest the manufacturing citadel of the continent, to
create a vast industrial empire out of Oregon, Washington,
Montana, and Idaho.

Either or both of these ideas must be adopted. Otherwise
most of the one hundred fourteen billion sleeping kilowatt-hours in the Columbia River watershed will be as useless
as they were before Benjamin Franklin flew his kite into the
lightning storm. A few statistics tell the story. Two monu-

mental dams are now under construction on the Columbia. Grand Coulee and its irrigation appurtenances will cost $404,633,000. The long, sweeping battlement at Bonneville will cost $75,223,000. This combined expense far exceeds the sum spent on the Panama Canal. It constitutes the most monumental building job of all time and the greatest hydroelectric power system in history. What is the Federal government getting for all this taxpayers' money? It is getting a pair of colossal dams with a combined generating capacity of 14,330,000,000 kilowatt-hours. These *two* gigantic undertakings will produce more power than the 14,082,282,000 kilowatt-hours turned out by the *two hundred sixty* electric plants in the State of New York. Eastern engineers become slightly giddy when they contemplate this contrast. Two dams anchored to the wild, crag-bound canyons of the Northwest can generate more energy than one hundred thirty times that many power projects in the Empire State.

Engineers are not the only individuals dazzled by these statistics. Economists and social scientists also gasp in amazement—and wonder. A few supplementary facts explain their bewilderment. New York has 12,588,000 inhabitants. Its power plants produce approximately fourteen billion kilowatt-hours. The four Columbia River basin States have 3,500,000 people. Right now, the two hundred thirty-two existing electric enterprises in the region generate 6,772,104,000 kilowatt-hours. Who is going to use the more than fourteen billion kilowatt-hours soon to be added by Bonneville and Grand Coulee? Twelve million people in New York, which is an international center of manufacturing and commerce, burn fourteen billion killowatt-hours. How can approximately one-fourth that many people in the frontier States of Oregon, Idaho, Washington, and Montana consume half again as much electricity?

This is the major economic problem confronting the Far West. It also is one of the principal dilemmas facing the whole country. The two staggeringly huge dams on the Columbia River are costing four hundred seventy-nine million dollars. This money comes from taxpayers as far away as Bangor, Maine, and Knoxville, Tennessee. If it is spent in vain, the financial loss will be larger than if an earthquake were to destroy the Panama Canal. One circumstance is apparent: if the enormous blocs of power to be generated at Bonneville and Grand Coulee lie wasted and idle and are not put to economically efficient use, the rest of the energy in the continent's greatest treasure-trove of hydroelectricity probably will not be developed during the lifetime of any man now living.

-2-

The river rumbles and roars. It thrashes against granite walls and gnaws ominously at basalt cliffs. Around jagged rocks it booms like the surf. Miniature geysers of spray are splashed high in the air. Whirlpools form and break, and form again. At the brink of precipitous drops, the river is a chute of hurtling green.

For countless ages the river has surged through the mountains, grinding out a chasm two-thirds of a mile deep. Since the glacial sheets of the distant Pleistocene epoch, no barrier has checked or diverted the river. It has worn down hills and bisected plateaus. Inexorably, it pours to the sea, as relentless and unfettered as the tides. A swollen creek crashes into it from a bluff eight hundred feet above, and the river gathers new force. Where the roaring Snake joins it after a rush through the deepest gorge of the hemisphere, the river snarls like an angry monster. Over falls and cascades it booms the mightiest power anthem in North America. Wild and defiant, the river tumbles unharnessed to the Pacific.

The hours of this freedom are numbered.

Down in the thirty-five-hundred-foot canyon of the Columbia a man waves his arm in signal. Another man in a grotesque traveling crane pulls a lever. The crane reaches out like a heron spearing fish. Trolleys whine and cables jerk. A bucket-shaped steel receptacle moves downward, concrete pours from its maw, and one more timbered frame has been filled. Block by block, level over level, the dam rises from the river. The water foams furiously against massive piers that stretch like kneeling sea horses from shore to shore. The river hurls its force against the dam in white-capped fountains of water and spray, but the great barrier stays anchored to the bedrock far below.

The herculean task is practically completed. The surging stream, the most tumultuous of all the rivers of the nation, is about to be vanquished. Ponderous gates of iron and steel are ready to slide between the spillway piers. The river will be diverted into yawning penstocks. Generators will start to roar. The first kilowatt-hour of the one hundred fourteen billion in the Columbia watershed will be transmitted over steel-towered transmission lines that stretch away across the rugged highlands like a many-legged steed. Public Works Administration Project No. 28 will be in operation at last.

Where Bonneville Dam locks the Columbia River from the crags of the Oregon shore to the timbered slopes of the Washington bank, the fate of the premier power undertaking of all time will be decided. Grand Coulee will not be completed for a number of years. It is at Bonneville that the test will come. The modernistically designed battlement of girders and masonry is virtually finished. Already it has been dedicated by President Roosevelt. Within a few months it will generate hydroelectricity. Will there be a market for its product? The answer to this question concerns more than the comparative handful of people in the Pacific Northwest. It is of consequence to the whole nation.

With the completion of the gigantic fortress at Grand Coulee still considerably in the future, Bonneville Dam is the keystone of the New Deal's power arch. It is the most important—as well as the most expensive—Federal construction project to be started and completed during the Roosevelt administration. Will it be a paying proposition or a losing venture? To meet the interest and retire the debt on $75,-223,000, a lot of hydroelectricity must be sold. Otherwise, the project will fall behind on the interest payments, the principal of the debt will not be amortized, and the adversaries of the New Deal will have a stupendous failure to cite as an example of profligate spending and cockeyed planning.

A great deal is contingent on what will happen where the Pacific's tide makes its last faint ripple in the chasm the Columbia has gouged in the Cascade Mountains. If Bonneville kilowatt-hours hum merrily over a network of transmission lines, and homes are lighted and farms are electrified and factory wheels are turned, the government's power program probably will be extended to encompass the country. More dams will be built on the Columbia and in the Tennessee Valley. The St. Lawrence waterway project will be gotten under way. Passamaquoddy may be started again. The President once more will ride to the tilting grounds to joust with the private utilities.

But should Bonneville fail, all the New Deal power plans would totter perilously close to collapse. If a Federal dam constructed at tidewater on the swiftest river of the continent cannot pay off as a hydroelectric enterprise, what hope is there for other government enterprises in less favorable surroundings? All the claims of the private companies would be substantiated. The great barrier on the Columbia River would become a national monument to extravagance and collectivism, a lonely ridge of concrete as useless as the Pyramids of Egypt. Perhaps its sole function would be to reveal to the generations to come what the monoliths in the Sahara tell us of the people who lived three hundred years before Christ.

Class warfare of a sort has rocked the Northwest over the principal ways proposed for using America's greatest bloc of hydroelectric power. Business men are on one side, farmers on the other. The conflict is sharp and bitter, and threatens to revive the controversy that split the country long ago when the flag had only thirteen stars. It is the break between urbanism and agrarianism all over again. While newspapers in the cities urge the establishment of thriving industrial centers, the country weeklies plead that the Columbia basin be spared the bane of slums and crime and poverty. Sandwiched away between news items in the papers from rural districts are paragraphs such as this:

I view great cities as pestilential to the health, the morals, and the liberties of man.   —THOMAS JEFFERSON, 1800.

The metropolitan newspapers in the region quote great financiers, cite the successes of Ford and Mellon and du Pont, and prophesy the mightiest industrial empire of history on the banks of the Columbia. Away with the ill considered talk of electricity for sheepherders and cowboys deep in the Western hills! Forget the iridescent fantasy of light bulbs in trappers' cabins! Perish the thought of steel transmission towers where now there are not even automobile roads! Industry and commerce are the sinews by which a nation moves.

-3-

Cheap power at tidewater—what more can industry ask? Ocean liners from the distant corners of the world can churn the river to Bonneville. There, in the core of the granite wall of the Cascades, the first unit of the biggest electric system ever conceived spins out an endless supply of kilowatt-hours. These kilowatt-hours drive electric locomotives that bring minerals down from the uplands. They also fire the furnaces in which the raw ore is reduced into the metals of which civilizations are built. Like the portal of some medieval fortress, the gates of the earth's largest locks swing open majestically, and the liners are lifted to the limpid lake behind the dam. Their propellers thrash the placid water far into the wilderness. But it is a wilderness no longer.

Innumerable factories line the river. Through every pass and canyon, railroads twist and wind. Gondola cars are loaded with iron and manganese from the Wyoming hills. The largest phosphate deposits in the world relinquish their Idaho mineral wealth to be made into fertilizer. Fast freights clatter down from Utah, and unload bauxite that high-voltage electricity will convert into sheets of aluminum. Wheels turn and machinery hums. Power bills are negligible compared to anywhere else on the planet. And why not? No costly transmission networks carrying power to remote farmhouses clutter up the scheme. Kilowatt-hours are sold directly from the plant to factories and industries. Massive manufacturing establishments dot the hills. Prosperous cities replace desolate timberlands. Industry converges on America's last frontier.

Steamships with empty hulls come up the swiftly flowing river. They go back downstream, cross the perilous spit at

Astoria—the spit where John Jacob Astor's argonauts perished a century ago—and face the open sea with rich cargoes of metals and chemicals. The headlands of the Oregon coast fade in the haze. The products of Bonneville's power are on the way across the planet to the ports of distant continents. A consignment of aluminum may become a streamlined train that rolls from Berlin to Istanbul at seventy miles an hour. Sacks of chemicals may be shot out of cannons in the European lowlands, where since the days of Attila the Hun peasants have gone to war. Phosphate shipments may give fertility to the soil of Japan or Russia or Norway.

For years every business man and banker and industrialist in the Far West has dreamed this dream. From the time the corps of army engineers first reported that the Columbia River watershed contained almost as much potential power as all the other rivers of the nation combined, storekeepers in Oregon and manufacturers in Washington have visioned an array of Pittsburghs in the Northwest. Are not all the necessary ingredients available—deep harbors, thick stands of timber, untapped pockets of minerals, mild climate, fertile soil, ample rainfall, unlimited hydroelectricity? Surely neither Chicago nor Birmingham nor Cleveland nor even Pittsburgh itself developed into a manufacturing citadel under such favorable conditions as these. Few Chamber of Commerce secretaries between the Rocky Mountains and the Pacific coast fail to learn by heart the recent prophecy of J. Russell Smith, professor of economic geography at Columbia University:

Basing my assertion on past history and economic and industrial conditions of today, it is in the Northwest where I expect American civilization, in many ways, to reach its maximum. Yes; I expect that it will outstrip New York, overcoming the advantage which the metropolis has had of an early start.

This land, which some day may become America's most important industrial principality, now has scarcely any manufacturing at all. The essential prerequisites are at hand, but the factories are not. It is a part of the whole paradox that the region most adaptable to industry because of its enormous power resources has probably less manufacturing than any other area of similar size in the United States. This paucity of factories has given the Columbia River basin a trade balance completely out of kilter, so far as manufacturing is concerned. The situation involves numerous economic complexities.

Annually, the region imports almost five times as much in manufactured goods as it ships out. The value differential in this respect is more than four hundred million dollars. Agricultural, animal, and forest products compose practically all the Northwest's exports. Manufactured articles are virtually 80 per cent of the imports. What happens is obvious. The lumberjack in the Oregon hinterlands cuts down a lofty fir tree. It is sawed into lumber and shipped east to Buffalo or Cleveland, where it is manufactured into a high chair. The lumberjack buys back the high chair for his little girl. He pays the freight both ways. The price of the chair includes the cost of giving the fir tree a round trip overland. This money could have been saved by manufacturing the chair in the locality where the logger felled the tree.

Business men in the Northwest—whether they own a corner grocery or the chain of stores that is driving the corner grocery into bankruptcy—cry out for more factories. Dozens of industrial associations have been formed, and their executive secretaries and public relations experts echo the gospel in every corner of the region. It is evangelism of a sort, with facile orators sketching lavish word-portrayals of a land of prosperity, pay rolls, commerce, and industry. This theme is stressed persistently. At weekly luncheons, Rotary club members in Seattle and Portland and a hundred lesser communities listen in a roseate glow of enthusiasm, as chamber of commerce spokesmen describe the glorious era when every acre of ground within sound of the Columbia's booming hymn of power will be covered by a factory.

Yet fulfillment of the prophecy is far from assured. The dazzling dream of an industrial kingdom in the West depends upon the outcome of a thoroughly mundane controversy. How will the rates be determined for the sale of the fourteen billion kilowatt-hours of hydroelectricity from Bonneville and Grand Coulee? Will there be a special switchboard rate for factories which locate close to the dams, or will the cost of the electricity be identical throughout large areas, regardless of the distance from the projects? Will a farmer at Celilo Falls, fifty-six miles above Bonneville, pay the same base rate as an aluminum plant within sight of the barrier?

The system of low charges to manufacturing establishments is known as the bus-bar rate. This means that a metallurgical reduction plant needing vast blocs of power can build a factory a stone's throw from Bonneville and obtain cheap rates at the switchboard. Transmission costs would be practically nil under such an arrangement. The other method for computing rates is known as the postage-stamp basis. The name explains it. First-class mail requires three cents an ounce, whether from New York to Brooklyn or twenty-eight hundred times that distance, from New York to Tacoma. The postage-stamp power rate is a modified version of this plan. The cost of transmission would be spread over a wide expanse of territory. Each mile from the dam the charge would not increase. For example, under a bus-bar system a kilowatt-hour of Bonneville energy might cost an approximate 2.10 cents at Hood River near the dam, and 3.55 cents at Astoria, one hundred twenty-four miles away. The postage-stamp proposal would charge both towns a hypothetical 2.57 cents.

Advocates of the bus-bar method claim the postage-stamp system would subsidize Astoria at the expense of Hood River. If a manufacturer wants to invest ten million dollars in a steel mill at Bonneville, why should he not get the advantage of proximity to the dam? Is it fair to require his power bill to carry the cost of sending electricity to some cattle rancher several hundred miles away in the mountains? Are not locational benefits to be considered at all? How can the Northwest satisfy its potentialities as a haven for industry, if Eastern investors realize their factories will have to help transmit power to a lot of farmers struggling with marginal land in the Oregon and Washington backwoods?

The rate system put into effect at Bonneville Dam will be the decisive factor in determining whether the Columbia River basin will become the world's greatest manufacturing region or an area of completely electrified farms and small towns. The Chipman Chemical Company of New Jersey told a Congressional committee it would construct an expensive plant on the fir-mantled ridges above Bonneville, provided an assurance of bus-bar rates could be given. In an exuberant moment the Bohn Aluminum & Brass Corporation of Detroit promised to buy every kilowatt-hour available at the dam, with the same proviso, of course, as that demanded by the Chipman corporation. Bus-bar rates would bring the Pennsylvania Salt Manufacturing Company across the continent with the money to build a big sodium chlorate plant. Other industrial concerns have issued similar statements. Dozens of business executives have come West on reconnoitering expeditions, to see for themselves this potential power empire on the

Pacific seaboard. And, no matter how blasé they have been, their eyes have glistened at sight of Bonneville. Everything there has symbolized to them an industrialist's paradise—the great river boiling through its mountain gateway, the downstream sweep to the Pacific and the world beyond, the crenelated wall of the big dam, the vast wilderness with its untapped resources stretching away to countless horizons.

The scouts for big business have gone back over the continental divide with one message: "Give us switchboard rates for manufacturing, and in ten years Bonneville will make Pittsburgh look like Sauk Center." They have promised that humming, modernized manufacturing plants will replace the lean-to villages of the Indian fishermen. Smokestacks and factory roofs will poke through the green tops of the evergreen trees. Industrial cities will blanket the hills and meadows. Bus-bar rates have been held out as the key to unlock the portals to the industrial Garden of Eden.

But there are thousands of farmers in the Oregon, Washington, Idaho, and Montana hinterlands who do not regard a switchboard power policy as the open-sesame to Zion. They are more inclined to look upon it as the key to a Pandora's box. Industries to them mean tenements, strikes, multimillionaires, and crime. "Who wants factories, anyway?" these weather-beaten agriculturalists ask. "We're a damn sight better off than the folks in Pittsburgh, and we intend to stay that way. Let 'em keep their darn factories back East where they belong." I have heard this challenge of the country to the city so many times that when I ask a farmer what he thinks of industrial rates at Bonneville, I know in advance what his answer will be. The farmers are almost unanimously for postage-stamp rates. What do they care about industries? They want the power from America's greatest reservoir of hydroelectricity for themselves.

Only 54 per cent of the farms in the State of Washington are electrified. The figure in Oregon and Idaho is 31 per cent. In Montana it is 8 per cent. These sums aggregate better than the national average of 9 per cent, but they are astonishingly low for a region that has as much potential power as most of the other States combined. Now, the Federal government at last has begun to tap the Columbia's one hundred fourteen billion kilowatt-hours of latent energy. Should the first in line at the power spigot be the corporations from the East or the farmers whose progenitors settled the West? If the hydroelectricity from Bonneville is sold to aluminum and fertilizer manufacturers at switchboard rates, the outcries from the rural areas will reverberate in the Northwest with a thunder like that of the Columbia River itself. On the banks of the swiftest power waterway ever surveyed by man, dwell thousands of farmers who pump by hand, read by kerosene lamps, cook on wood stoves, and watch their wives and daughters stoop for hours over washboards and churns. These people claim the power in the Columbia is their heritage. They contend they have more right to it than industrialists from the other side of the country. A young backwoods farmer in Skamania County in Washington said to me:

"It's easy for them folks in the cities to want to give the power to big business. They got plenty themselves. Wonder what they'd say if they had to live like we do—no lights, no washing machine, no electric icebox, radio run by batteries, no vacuum cleaner, no plumbing, no electric iron, no water taps in the house? We're tired of livin' like hillbillies. We want electricity. To hell with the factories until we get our share! That river belongs to us, not Wall Street."

I looked away over the ridges that stretched to Mount St. Helens' glacier-encrusted cone. It would take lots of money

that the power consumers in the principal hydroelectric territory of the United States were paying exorbitant rates to the
private utilities. At Tennessee Valley Authority rates, he estimated the people of the Pacific Northwest could save $30,-
000,000 annually on their power bills. Representative Walter
M. Pierce of Oregon said the cheapest rates in the Columbia
River basin prevailed in two cities that had municipal plants
—Tacoma in Washington and Eugene in Oregon. The house-
holders of Eugene paid $2.55 for 100 kilowatt-hours. Astoria,
over on the coast, was served by a private company. The cost
there for the same amount of power was $6.50.

This aged pair of public ownership proponents claimed
that bus-bar rates for industry were merely a scheme to protect the overcharges extorted by the utility corporations. Let
the power from Bonneville be transmitted to domestic consumers, and the private companies would reduce their rates
soon enough. How could this be accomplished if all Bonneville's output were sold to factories? Make Bonneville a yardstick! Drive down power rates! At farm conferences and
Grange meetings, resolutions were drafted. The senators and
representatives from the rural regions began to hear from
their constituents. Bonneville for farms and homes! The
chorus swelled, and the politicians listened. The power bill
that went through Congress provided that at least half the
energy should be reserved for public ownership groups.

The onslaught against the power companies was not the
only argument used in Congress. The farm bloc also moved
to the defense of the scenic grandeur of the West. What
would unsightly factories and sprawling industrial centers do
to the beauty of the hinterlands? Who wanted rolling hills
and sylvan lowlands blanketed with manufacturing plants?
Bonneville and Grand Coulee dams alone threatened to destroy the Chinook salmon industry. Factories with their dirt

and pollution would make this threat a certainty. Better no factories at all than to have the resources of the river basin exploited and consumed. Many conservatives who rebelled at the denunciation of the utilities supported these claims of the conservationists. Don't make the West like the East! This became a challenge and a defy throughout the region. Byron G. Carney, a member of the Oregon State senate, put it into terms the farmers could understand:

"This country looks pretty good right now. It isn't going to look that way any longer if a lot of factories are turned loose along the river to use all the power, cut down all the trees, and dig up all the minerals."

In the autumn of 1937 the President traveled overland to Bonneville. He was in excellent humor the crisp, sunny morning his special train clicked onto a siding above the dam. His mood was in sharp contrast to that of the Democratic governor of Oregon and mayor of Portland. They had seen advance copies of Mr. Roosevelt's dedication address, and it did not coincide with their ideas of cheap power for industry. Their faces were glum and dour as the President looked across the river to the steep cliffs of the Washington shore, and then began to speak.

The talk was a repudiation of the people who wanted to establish what the President called "a huge manufacturing center close to the source of power—another Pittsburgh—a vast city of whirling machinery." Mr. Roosevelt promised hydroelectricity to the small rural communities far from Bonneville. He warned against the unhealthy expansion of large cities at the expense of the farm areas. What the Northwest needed, the President said, was not an expansion of industry but an influx of population to settle the hinterlands. It was a speech dedicated to the American countryside, and it was well received. It appealed to everyone to whom kerosene lamps within a stone's throw of one hundred four-teen billion potential kilowatt-hours of electricity were an unpleasant paradox. Even Mark Sullivan and Raymond Moley, two of the President's persistent critics, spoke kindly of it. Mr. Roosevelt had urged that the Pacific Northwest remain a region of sylvan valleys—valleys checkered with farms and dotted with lofty transmission towers. This prospect pleased the nation.

The President went on his way, and still the demand for power for factories would not down. Some Bonneville energy, at least, had to be sold to industry. That was certain. Senator George W. Norris himself, the tireless champion of the farm and home power consumers, said the disposal of compara-tively large blocs of electricity for industrial use was prob-ably essential to a well balanced plan. In some fashion the farm and city factions had to be united. The postage-stamp rate adherents and the bus-bar advocates could not continue to club each other verbally *ad infinitum*. Who could bring them together? The President took Senator Norris's advice and appointed James Delmage Ross as administrator of the greatest power system in the world.

Ross is a remarkable man. He has been a public ownership zealot for more than half his sixty-five years, but he also has a vast respect for projects that pay. A hundred times he has said that there is only one thing as important as making a suc-cess of the humanitarian purpose of Bonneville—and that is amortizing the $75,223,000 debt. The banks have confidence in him, and he has been able to float whopping big bond issues to make Seattle's municipal power plant the largest of its kind ever built. He is a jolly, roly-poly individual with the good nature of a Teddy bear. He exudes honesty and frank-ness. Some one he has never met before, he may keep in his office three or four hours, talking about phosphate deposits, kilowatt-hours, and penstock chutes. No person who has known Ross more than fifteen minutes would think of calling him by another name than "J. D." In 1931, after almost three decades as superintendent of Seattle's public power system, Ross was discharged by a business-man mayor. The community immediately organized for a recall campaign. A few weeks later the mayor had been decisively voted out of office and Ross was reinstated triumphantly. More than sentiment prompted this display of popular feeling. When Ross finished building the Seattle hydroelectric plant in the early days of the century, the private company then serving the city had been selling power at twenty cents a kilowatt-hour. Now, Seattle housewives pay two cents a kilowatt-hour for cooking purposes, and the city has more electric stoves *per capita* than any other place in the nation. Ross has reduced power rates consistently. As soon as he can arrange to buy out the utility concern that still operates in Seattle, he predicts his plant will offer the lowest charges in America.

In the Far West Mr. Ross is referred to as a "one-man TVA." He likes the title. The trouble and strife in the original TVA could have been avoided, he claims, if there had been a one-man administrator instead of a three-man board. Long before the internal bitterness among the directors of the TVA became apparent, Ross said to Mr. Roosevelt:

"Mr. President, a single administrator is better than a board. The sooner you come to a one-man administration, the sooner the government's power program will reach success. Fix responsibility on one man and remove him if he does not keep faith. Help him if he does."

The President has admitted Ross was right. The Bonneville set-up constitutes that admission. "That's fine," Ross said when Mr. Roosevelt showed him Ben Cohen's draft of the Bonneville bill. "All the responsibility is placed on one man. He can't pass the buck to anyone else."

"And *you* are that man," the President said.

Theoretically, Mr. Ross is supposed not to discriminate between the private utilities and the people's power agencies. However, three decades in the public ownership movement are a more urgent stimulus than legal dictum. One wintry night Mr. Ross asked me to drive with him to the country town of Hillsboro, where he was to speak before a mass meeting of farmers. He gave a mild little speech, discussing in matter-of-fact fashion the power problems confronting the Pacific coast.

Then from the rear of the hall a florid, fat man with a taut waistline began an interminable series of questions. He wanted to know about the sanctity of private investment, whether municipal plants paid taxes, what would happen to the widow and orphan stockholders in the utility companies, and how the States could survive if the Federal government took over all the rivers.

The good humor vanished from Mr. Ross's rotund face. He took a sheaf of paper from his pocket. "Let's see what you folks here in Hillsboro pay the Portland General Electric Company for power," he said. "H'mm—$6.46 for 250 kilowatt-hours. I'm sure my friend in the back of the hall will be glad to have me tell you that the publicly owned plant in Tacoma sells the same amount for $3.62."

Mr. Ross looked toward the rear of the room. He pointed to his obese interrogator. "And now, my man," he said, "will you please come forward and tell us just what power company you represent?"

The farmers shouted jubilantly. This was what they had

driven through the blustery Oregon night to hear. Utility companies are not popular in the Pacific Northwest. The region has long been a public ownership stronghold. Power bills are lower in the Columbia River basin than elsewhere in the country, but they are not as low as the farmers think they ought to be. Should sweet potatoes be dear in Georgia? Why not rock-bottom electric rates on the banks of the foaming Columbia? The private utilities have held on successfully in the Northwest largely because of the discredited demagogues using the public ownership movement as a thoroughfare to elective office. The opportunists who prattle for the Townsend Plan and Father Coughlin's money magic also usually hook a ride on the power bandwagon. They abandon their promises the day after election. This has discouraged but not silenced the demand for public ownership.

Farmers and people in small towns cover Mr. Ross's desk with pleas that he eradicate the power companies. Rural folk are much more insistent in this advocacy than are even the extreme left-wingers in the cities. I know many men and women in the country who are conservative on all other issues —they detest "reds," voted for Landon, and believe the child-labor amendment would prevent their sons from doing farm chores—but hate the private utilities. Self-interest is a powerful incentive. These people want cheap electricity. What happens to the rugged individualism they otherwise believe in, they do not much care.

One morning Mr. Ross telephoned me at the *Oregonian*. He had a letter he thought I should see. It was written in a scrawly hand on paper from some grade-school student's tablet. The envelope was postmarked Pendleton—the cattle-country town where the famous Round-up is held each year. Here is what the letter said:

J. D. Ross, Administ. Bonneville Dam.

Dear Sir I write to You, and let you know would like to secure Bonneville Power For to Heat House. also Power to run irigating Pump. Pacific Power & Light Co. Power costs to much money a man cant use there juice to do any good to pay for there Power would soon send a man to the poorhouse. I am using their Juice for Lights only. 15 Kilowatt hours for $1 per Month Which is almost 7 cts per Kilowatt hour. It seems this City Council wont act for to secure Bonneville Power for Us People So I appeal to Direct. Most of the People out here want Bonneville Power But they wont try to get any. Mr. Ross will you please let me know How I can get Bonneville electricity before the chance slips bye. I am a feared I wont get any.

I remain Yours Truly

WM. S ——

From the drawer of his desk Ross pulled a map of Oregon. He traced a line from Bonneville to Pendleton. "You know what I'd like to do?" he asked. "I'd like to send a copy of this letter to everyone in the United States, and then underneath it add one sentence of my own. Here is what that sentence would say:

"This letter was written a few miles from the greatest source of hydroelectricity ever surveyed."

With a push Mr. Ross swung around in his swivel chair. He unloosened another button of his too-tight vest, and looked across the roofs of Portland to the near-by hills. "That sentence would get 'em," he said. "By golly! I wish the President would let me do it."

In addition to his faith in public ownership, his regard for undertakings that pay, and his ability to cut down power rates, Ross's philosophy is made up of a fourth ingredient—showmanship. The Seattle electric plant, high in the Cascade Moun-

tains, is more than a power system. It is a summer resort. Up
the spectacular canyon of the Skagit River, Ross has built a
private railroad and over this scenic route more than 25,000
people travel each year. Near the sheer wall of Diablo Dam,
within sight of glaciers and eternal snows, blooms a flower
garden in which tropical plants grow and flourish. From the
crags above, Ladder Creek Falls tumbles into this mountain
wonderland. At night, colored lights transform the strip of
water into an icy rainbow that twists and shimmers against
the cliffs. Somewhere in a hidden ravine, a loud-speaker plays
Strauss melodies, and *Tales from the Vienna Woods* echoes
between the granite walls of the gorge. No one ever devised
a better way to sell electric power. Housewives who visit
Ross's picturesque resort begin to think of the municipal light
plant in terms of gorgeous flowers and breath-taking waterfalls. From then on, promotion work and advertising are practically superfluous. Puget Sound Power & Light loses a
customer. Its loss is City Light's again.

Ross is sincere about all this. He is an amateur botanist
whose interest in flowers is subordinate only to his zeal in developing new hydroelectric sites. One afternoon, while Ross
was a member of the Securities and Exchange Commission,
he was driving frantically over the twisting roads from Skagit.
In Seattle waited a galaxy of bankers and financiers who
wanted to discuss stock-market problems with him. Bob Beck,
City Light's valuation expert, had the throttle all the way
down to the boards. The car careened around turns at perilous speed.

Suddenly Ross shouted, "Bob! Stop! Stop!"

Brakes whined, and tires smoked. A spray of gravel thrown
up by the wheels hummed like bird shot against the fenders.

Beck looked anxiously at his boss. "What's the matter,
J. D.?" he asked.

Ross pointed to a slope high above the road. "Look, Bob— violets! We'll have to see if we can't transplant them for the gardens at Skagit." He started puffing up the steep hillside.

While the bankers fumed impatiently in Seattle, Ross and his engineer got out their pocketknives and dug up violets on the distant upland ridge.

-5-

The decisions shaping the future of the electric power industry in the United States will be made in the White House and on Capitol Hill—or perhaps in Wall Street, should the New Deal make a definite *rapprochement* with business. The events having the greatest influence on those decisions probably will take place three thousand miles away, in the watershed of the Columbia River. It is in the Columbia's wild and turbulent chasms that the destiny of the electric age in America can best be determined. No other river so closely fulfills Zola's prophecy of electricity as plentiful as the wind of heaven.

Within the next five years, the success or failure of Bonneville Dam will be known. Before that period has elapsed, Grand Coulee's monumental barrier will be in operation. On a scale never before attempted, the people of the Pacific Northwest will be testing the possibilities of an electrified society. Where else so appropriate a place to make the experiment? "In the Columbia River basin," states the Federal Power Commission, "is found the combination of high mountains and heavy precipitation." This is a prosaic way of describing thick sheets of rainfall and swollen mountain rivers locked in their gorges of basalt and granite.

When Waldemar Borquist, Sweden's most celebrated electrical engineer, saw the surging Columbia, he is said to have exclaimed: "If that river were in Europe, its water power might change the course of history!"

J. D. Ross is confident Bonneville Dam will meet the expectations of all the groups that have planned to use its product. He thinks it will provide power for all three important consuming classes—farms, homes, and factories. How? The solution is simple, he contends. There is so much power in the Columbia River it can be sold to everyone at rates fantastically low. "Steinmetz, the great genius," says Mr. Ross, "once predicted the time would come when it would not pay to meter electricity. The first region to see that era will be the Columbia River watershed." Mr. Ross believes low rates are the formula that will answer the problem. Get the electricity cheap enough and the total output of Bonneville and Grand Coulee will be consumed in a few years. Even poverty-stricken refugees from the Dust Bowl will be able to buy the power if the rates are sufficiently low. On the back of a frayed envelope, Mr. Ross shows how it can be done.

In Portland the price per kilowatt-hour is 2.80 cents. The average consumption recorded on each meter is 1110 kilowatt-hours a year. In Fort William in the Canadian province of Ontario, the cost for power is 0.75 cent a kilowatt-hour. Consumption there averages 5240 kilowatt-hours. This ultimately can be accomplished in the Columbia River basin. Thus the consumption of power in the Pacific Northwest can be increased five times, and Bonneville and Grand Coulee will be put to efficient and useful work.

Eventually there will be such demand for hydroelectricity in the States of Oregon, Washington, Idaho, and Montana, Mr. Ross believes, that the other dams proposed by the army engineers will have to be built on the Columbia. If he is right, the taxpayers of America soon may have about a billion dollars in power plants out on the western fringe of the continent. Just make the rates low enough, says Mr. Ross, and steel-latticed transmission towers will stand where now only fir and hemlock trees grow. Electricity will be so abundant in the Northwest that consumers will be charged a nominal flat rate, as though they were paying for water.

Power costs and consumption do not comprise the only national issue which may be settled at Bonneville and Grand Coulee. Still another moot point is at stake. Is hydroelectricity cheaper than steam power? The entire dam-building program of the Roosevelt administration rests on the premise that it is. Yet last year the New Dealers made a slip that still reverberates. The National Resources Committee issued a voluminous analysis of technological trends. At page 259, a report was quoted stating that steam plants could produce power less expensively than dams. Political chaos broke loose. The private utilities chortled—and released the story all over the country the day the President spoke at Bonneville. Mr. Roosevelt was furious. Secretary Ickes hit the ceiling; his subordinates had let him sign the National Resources volume without analyzing its contents. To counteract the devastating effects of the blunder, the Power Authority of the State of New York prepared a report answering the assertion of steam power's advantage. Much of this report was based upon the efficiency with which Bonneville and Grand Coulee will function. After analyzing the probable cost of Bonneville power, Ross blurted, "Anyone who claims steam is cheaper than hydro is either hopelessly ignorant or criminally subsidized."

The situation is vague and indefinite. As these words are written, not a kilowatt-hour of Bonneville's vast supply of power has been sold. It will take at least a year to build transmission lines. If the army engineers have their way, that year may be an epoch. Generals and colonels and majors super-

vised the construction of Bonneville, and they are furiously
indignant that a homespun Republican progressive of the
William Allen White school has superseded them in command. The army has no love for J. D. Ross and his sponsor,
Senator Norris. It frankly believes it is more qualified to
manage Bonneville than any sixty-five-year-old liberal who
talks about conservation and ferns and cheap power for
farmers. What nonsense—trunk lines to homesteaders and an
electric stove in every home! The army politicians have done
their best to impede Ross's activities.* Their original recom-
mendations were said to call only for transmission lines to the
load centers served by private power companies. This would
have left the American taxpayers' $75,000,000 hydroelectric
plant virtually stranded in the wilderness, as silent as the
catacombs. Ross went to Washington wrathfully. "We can't
send electricity through the air," he complained. "We have
to have money for wires—and we don't want those wires to
lead merely to the substations of the private utilities." Without an adequate appropriation for lines and poles, Bonneville
would be an ox team without a yoke. The President listened
sympathetically, and nearly $11,000,000 of PWA funds was
authorized for a transmission network throughout the Northwest. The authorization specifically provided that a humming, 230,000-volt line should connect Bonneville with
Grand Coulee. Thus, by indirection and innuendo as it seems,
a Columbia basin authority to all intent and purposes has
been practically established.

* The public ownership people and the army engineers have long been at polite
but distant odds. Senator Norris once observed that the army corps was composed
of skilled technicians who can build wonderful dams but do not understand the
social usefulness of their own products. The army engineers are said to have been
disdainful of *The River*, the brilliant and dramatic film of the Mississippi which
Pare Lorentz created as a social and economic document. Lorentz now is believed
to be planning a similar cinema record of the Columbia, with Bonneville and
Grand Coulee as the principal points of emphasis.

In this fashion Ross gets things done. Apparently naïve and unsophisticated, he succeeds where such urbane and nimble-witted men as David Lilienthal frequently encounter insurmountable difficulties. The army engineers felt certain they would be placed in supervision of Bonneville Dam. From his desk in the SEC, Ross outmaneuvered them. He also has outfoxed some of the shrewdest and ablest power company strategists in the nation. With such relatively open-minded utilities as the Portland General Electric, the Bonneville administrator gets along reasonably well. Against obdurate and overcapitalized companies, he wars relentlessly. A utility executive once quaintly remarked that the big-waisted, grinning Ross looked as harmless as a third rail and was "just as dangerous." Ross regards the Northwest as the best part of the country—he loves to use Lewis Mumford's phrase of "America's favored spot"—and he thinks of himself as the technological pioneer to develop the region electrically. His engineering assistants are extremely able; ruddy men like Charley Carey and Bob Beck know every hill and ravine that must be spanned by high-tension lines. But susceptibility to adulation is one of Ross's faults, and on his staff are some men who seem to enjoy sinecures because of their adeptness at flattery. The administrator is also frequently vague and indefinite and keeps his own counsel on too many important issues. Until he began to talk before a special Senate hearing on phosphate development in Idaho, none of his subordinates knew what he would say. It was a subject with which Ross was comparatively unfamiliar, and he had permitted no one to help him prepare for the testimony. As a consequence, he had to be extricated from several embarrassing positions by sympathetic committee members. Unwillingness to delegate responsibility is occasionally a virtue, but it becomes a liability when a sixty-five-year-old man attempts almost single-handedly to supervise the world's greatest chunk of electricity on the farthest-flung frontier of the United States. Ross's reluctance to let others perform responsible tasks and his occasional carelessness and lapse of memory have held up important progress in electrifying the hinterlands, when otherwise the course was clear for action. Prompt reports on his part might have resulted in the planning of a huge phosphate plant near Pocatello and the surveying of another great dam at Umatilla, projects now deferred for the future.

Mr. Ross's idea is for towns and rural areas to buy out the power companies in their vicinities. The distributing systems thus acquired could transmit the power produced at Bonneville. For the purpose of determining fair purchase prices, he thinks the utilities should be considered as "going concerns" rather than from the standpoint of "mere physical valuation." This is a somewhat more lenient attitude toward the companies than David Lilienthal has advocated in the TVA. Ross takes the position that haggling over the "last cent" will merely make the companies obdurate and throw the whole proceedings into the courts for years. "The farmers, the Dust Bowl refugees, the home-owners," he says, "need power—now! Let's not beat them out of a decade of cheap electricity by trying to beat the utilities out of a relatively few dollars."

This perspective placed Mr. Ross between Lilienthal and Dr. Arthur Morgan in the bitter strife in the TVA. He viewed the private companies from a less stern viewpoint than Lilienthal, but also emphatically rejected the power network with the utilities sponsored by Dr. Morgan. "My job is to get something done for the people of the West," Ross declared. "I can't do that by laying down to the power companies. Neither can I do it by fighting them for malice or spite or a few final pennies."

How the public power districts near Bonneville should be financed is another bristling question. Ross thinks it is all right for the districts to sell revenue bonds in the open market. His choice of a fiscal agent for the venture is an able, vivacious, and fast-talking broker named Guy Myers. Mr. Myers's address is 35 Wall Street, New York City. The New Deal's bright young economists in the Department of the Interior hold their heads at this. Myers is the most politically vulnerable feature of the Bonneville idea. The utility companies can pound him with visible effect, because the success of the public ownership psychology stems from a suspicion of Wall Street. Ross and his adherents cannot cultivate and fertilize that suspicion, and then shut it off like a water spigot when they propose a man at 35 Wall Street to be the financial supervisor of the new arrangement. Some of Ross's most fervent admirers accuse him of political dullness as dense as a mop in backing Myers. They hope that eventually the districts can be financed with RFC or PWA money or other government funds, rather than by securities tossed into the bond market. The New Deal is primarily responsible for this particular dilemma. It has specified that Bonneville power should go primarily to public districts, but has made no provision for the financing of those districts. And farmers in the Western mountains without electric lights must turn elsewhere for money for power lines! The halfway indefiniteness of the whole set-up has left both the private utilities and the actual and potential power districts bogged down in a morass of confusion.

Myers has a faithful defender in Ross. "Guy shoots absolutely square with everyone," the Bonneville administrator said to me. "He is the best man in the country to handle the

financing for public power setups." Ross's allies contend it is a
new high in hypocrisy for the utilities to assail Myers. They
premise this contention on the latest attempt of the power
companies in Oregon to foil the Bonneville Dam movement.
To their payrolls the companies have added some of the demagogues and quacks who have achieved influence in the Townsend Plan. These charlatans warn their deluded followers not
to be hostile to the electric companies. One rabble-rousing
minister of Townsend prominence solemnly tells the old people they should vote against public utility districts. "The power
companies are willing to pay the 2 per cent transactions tax to
give you your $200 a month," he informs them. "So be sure
to support your good friends." The New Dealers in the State
insist that corporations which capitalize on the hopeless desire
of a lot of bewildered old people for $2400 a year have no
legitimate right to criticize anyone for anything. The Townsend movement is still fairly formidable in Oregon, and I
think nothing is more pathetic. The old people, grasping for
wealth they can never obtain, are exploited by every political
demagogue in the region. They are sold patent medicines,
gland rejuvenators, and seats at seances. They are urged to
vote for all sorts of fakers and mountebanks. The laudations
of the power companies at the Townsend meetings are among
the rawest stunts ever employed to block public ownership.

It is still too early to predict accurately the eventual outcome at Bonneville. Undoubtedly power will be made available to farmers and settlers who now live half a century
behind the times. Probably the rates charged merchants and
residents will be materially reduced. And there likely will be
a lot of new factories and manufacturing plants in the Northwest—only they will not be clustered like pup tents around
the massive dam. They will be spread out in dozens of small
communities. "No one would suggest," said the President at

there is not a transmission line within many miles. Last summer when I was camping and had stopped to get some milk, he told me the Grange in the district was talking about the formation of a people's utility district to distribute Bonneville power. "They'll be gettin' out the petitions pretty soon, I guess," he said. "I'll give 'em a couple o' dozen eggs to pay my share of the printing. It'd sure be somethin' to have electricity here. My oldest son never saw a light switch till I took him to Castle Rock a year or so ago."

The rugged stump rancher still has no electricity. He may have it some day. Perhaps, if he does not, his son will—or maybe his son after him. The Toutle surges past the tumble-down farm like a trough of liquid lightning. A boulder rears out of the center of the stream, and the river snaps at it with angry whitecaps. The boulder was once much bigger than it is now. The farmer has watched it worn down by the river. In another decade the boulder will be gone. The energy the river used on that rock might have been put into a wire. Then it could have operated the stump ranch—only with the electricity it would have been a stump ranch no longer. The power that disintegrated the big boulder could have saved the farmer's strength and his wife's looks, and helped to send their sons to college. Vaguely, the farmer realizes this.

The farmer and his boys get up at five each day. On winter mornings they dress by kerosene lamps, and they labor for fourteen hours in the fields. They have to perform all their tasks by hand. As they trudge home at sundown, the stump rancher pulls out a plug of tobacco and bites off a chunk. He sits down wearily on the ramshackle porch, plants his aching feet on the crumbling rail, and spits across the path into the river. He is getting older, and more and more often he wishes the work on the farm were not so hard. Life would be a lot

5. No More Salmon

Over the knife-edged brink of Celilo Falls the Columbia River poured in a great sheet of green water and frothy, plumed whitecaps. With a roar like massed artillery it crashed on the jagged rocks below. Jets of spray billowed into the air. The clatter of a transcontinental train rolling along the Oregon bank of the river was silenced to a muffled hum by the thunder of the falls. Only a faint treble and wisp of steam against the somber cliffs of the canyon told when the engineer pulled hard on the whistle cord.

Watching the long train as it clicked swiftly on its way to Chicago was a primitive, solitary figure that might have been there more than a century before, eying Lewis and Clark, the first white men to penetrate the frontier. Until the observation car had dwindled to a speck in the distance the tall Indian scanned the railroad right-of-way. Then he looked back at the swirling river. He stood on a frail, ramshackle wooden platform perilously near the brink of the falls. A rope fastened to his waist was tied to a near-by rock: a thin thread of life should he totter from his hazardous perch. Over his shoulder was a long pole that tapered to an arrow point. He held it poised, like a modern collegiate javelin thrower or some spearsman of ancient Rome. And always he watched the river. Each eddy and whitecap and rivulet, he eyed. Minute after minute, while the minutes merged into hours, he stood motionless on the rickety platform. Finally he shrugged his shoulders in a gesture of despair, unfastened the rope around his slender waist, and turned and leaped nonchalantly from rock to rock until he stood on solid ground once more.

Klinquett of the Klikitat tribe pointed at the river that has supplied more salmon than any other waterway in the world. He glanced downstream toward Bonneville and upstream toward Grand Coulee, where the Federal government is building the largest dams in history. He showed his dry salmon spear to the other Indians who clustered anxiously about him. "No salmon like it used to be," Klinquett said stolidly.

George Red Hawk, aged chief of the Cayuse Indians, who was spearing salmon in the Columbia before the line of rail reached the great Northwest, looked grimly at the surging river. "White man's dams," he said, "mean no more Indians' salmon."

And with that masterpiece of understatement in my ears, I thought of the millions of American housewives who every so often buy Columbia River Chinook salmon for their families' dinners, and of the *maîtres d'hôtel* on distant ocean liners who make a specialty of planked salmon *jardinière*, and of the stewards on swiftly rolling dining cars who urge their passengers to eat boiled salmon *hollandaise*, and of temperamental chefs in far-away palaces who prepare salmon soufflé Florentine for their royal trenchermen, and of buxom German *Hausfrauen* stirring vast pots of salmon sweet and sour, and of tobacco-chewing cooks in lumber camps who periodically fry mammoth pans of salmon and hash-browns, and of Foreign Legionnaires in the desert and soldiers on the march and Royal Mounties in the wilderness who smack their lips over canned salmon on brittle chunks of hardtack.

-2-

Prevalent throughout the principal salmon-producing region of the world today is the almost unshakable opinion that within a few years the fighting fish with the flaky pink flesh will be one and the same with the dodo bird: extinct. From the Arctic Ocean on north along the Pacific seaboard to the California border—through Alaska, British Columbia, Washington, and Oregon—thousands of people are convinced that the salmon industry is doomed.

These alarms and fears stem from the fact that the salmon is what the scientists call an anadromous fish. This means that at certain seasons it must ascend rivers from the ocean to breed. If it cannot get upstream to the headwaters of the river, it perishes without spawning, and the species thus ultimately dies out. *The salmon must get up the river!* That is the principal rule with everyone who has ever hauled in a fifty-pound threshing Columbia Chinook—whether with a rod and reel for sport, a gill net for a livelihood, or a spear to feed some Indian squaw and her chubby-faced papoose. And the salmon must get up the Columbia River most of all, because it is there that the world obtains the bulk of its supply of the giant Chinook or king salmon.

The possible destruction of the Chinook salmon runs was a major item on the agenda of the annual convention of the American Indian Federation, held recently in the heart of the Columbia River country at Lewiston, Idaho. A resolution passed overwhelmingly demanded that the Federal government protect the Indians' fishing grounds on the great waterway. One of the chiefs rose solemnly to point out that the red man gave up his lands only when the white man promised that he could fish forever for the giant salmon. "Those rights were given us," the old Indian said, "for as long as the river flows, the sun sets, and the grass grows on near-by hills."

The Indian Federation protested not only that Bonneville may block the passage of the salmon up and down the Columbia, but that the vast lake formed behind the dam will flood choice fishing sites expressly reserved for the Indians by the Treaty of Walla Walla in 1855. This compact was negotiated by bearded Isaac Stevens, first governor of Washington Territory, and proclaimed by President James Buchanan. Ironically, Governor Stevens, who assured the Indians their fishing grounds would be forever protected, was a friend of the army frontiersman, Captain Benjamin Bonneville, for whom is named the dam which may invalidate the promise that has been kept faithfully more than eighty years.

Shall we have a look at the habits of the salmon and see just why PWA dams on the Columbia River threaten to annihilate a large section of the most important fish tribe caught on the Pacific coast? The life cycle of the salmon goes about like this:

The baby salmon emerge four or five months after the parent fish have deposited the eggs high in the mountains, near the headwaters of the river. By September the fingerling salmon are six or seven inches long, and they are carried downstream—millions of them. Those that survive this mad dash eventually reach the sea, and there they remain for three years. They feed on the marine life common to every ocean, and it is possible they do not stray far from the mouth of the river through which they first entered salt water. After three years in the sea, the salmon—a fingerling no longer, but a slim, fighting fish strong enough to conquer rapids and tear a hook from an angler's line—heeds the call of the river, just as once it responded to the urge of the sea. The salmon goes upstream, stemming the spring freshets, and beside it swim

all the other salmon that came down the river three years
before and have withstood the hazards of stream and ocean.
Through rapids, over eighteen- and twenty-foot falls, and
high into the uplands thrash the silver-scaled horde. Finally
the salmon reach the gravel bars and eddies where they themselves were spawned. There they deposit their eggs. This done,
the span of their life has been completed, and they drift
downstream, tail foremost, until they perish naturally a few
days later or are battered to death against some jagged rock.

This is the life pattern of the fish that provides the main
course for so many American family meals. One factor—and
one only—sometimes varies the cycle: inability of the salmon
to gain the headwaters of the river in which they were
spawned.

If either the whims of Nature or the calculated plans of
man keep the salmon from attaining the shallow reaches upstream, then no eggs are deposited and the fish dwindle rapidly in numbers and eventually disappear entirely from that
particular river. The Fraser River in British Columbia used
to produce two million cases of canned salmon each year.
Then a thundering landslide blocked its upper stretches. Now
the river yields about a tenth as many salmon as formerly.
Will this also happen to the turbulent waterway that pro-
duces more salmon than any other river on the planet?
Scientists look at the nearly completed wall of Bonneville
Dam, one hundred eighty feet of steel and concrete from
foundation to parapet, and shake their heads woefully. What
salmon can ascend the Columbia past a barrier the great river
itself cannot budge? How can the fish possibly get by Bonneville? And what about Grand Coulee Dam, three hundred
miles farther upstream, which will make Bonneville look like
something constructed with children's building blocks? If the
fish by some modern miracle pass Bonneville, what will

occur when they come to the monstrous wall of Grand Coulee, a wall nearly a mile long and five hundred feet high?

These questions are answered in extremely gloomy fashion
—both by distinguished, morning-coated scientists in Washington and New York, and by picturesque, buckskin-clad Indians in the fastnesses of the Far West.

Arthur Newton Pack, president of the American Nature
Association, declares that the dams being constructed on the
Columbia River are likely to spell the doom of a fishing industry that annually gives employment to more than 25,000
people. A similar opinion is held by E. D. Clark, secretary of
the Association of Pacific Fisheries, who claims that the absolutely most disastrous occurrence that can happen to a salmon
stream is to be blocked by a dam—or by several dams. The
encroachment of civilization and industry, says Mr. Clark,
has almost invariably meant the end of salmon runs. He
points out that the situation is infinitely more serious where
the Columbia River is concerned, because it is the main source
of the giant Chinook, which is the choice eating salmon. It is
Chinook salmon that mother buys at the corner butcher shop
when she wants a thick, flaky chunk of pink fish to bake with
lemon and tomato sauce for the family's dinner.

The alarming predicament of the Chinook salmon is one
of the few topics on which the proponents and the adversaries
of Bonneville and Grand Coulee are partially agreed. "The
development of the Columbia River for power and agriculture imperils an ancient industry, the salmon fisheries," admits Frank T. Bell, United States Commissioner of Fisheries
and one of the original advocates of the Columbia River
dams.

But, most of all, the Indians in the Northwest are convinced they have seen the last great spring salmon migration
up the Columbia. The red men are highly indignant about it,

because one of the main considerations they received for the land that once was theirs was the promise of perpetual fishing rights on the world's greatest salmon stream. Now, they claim, the white man is making those rights as worthless as the ashes of last moon's campfires. Gloom and foreboding gripped the annual Feast of the Salmon at Celilo Falls this year. One by one, the Indians arose and said the white engineers from Washington were taking away the red man's fish. No more will the giant salmon ascend the Columbia, and the Indian fishermen must become farmers or starve, old Oscar Charley warned his tribespeople. A dismal nodding of heads followed.

After the temporary cofferdams at Bonneville had jammed the salmon in the lower river last spring, the Indians descended menacingly on the army engineers in charge of construction, and for a few minutes another Custer's massacre threatened. The engineers finally solved the crisis by blasting a hole in the barrier blocking the stream. The Indians went away muttering imprecations and wondering what will happen when the Columbia is blocked from shore to shore with a towering, fortresslike wall.

-3-

Whatever gap there is at Bonneville will have to be provided for in advance, and to this end the government is spending $7,077, 200 for the most unique stairways and elevators of all time.

Imagine a hundred or so swimming pools, each a little higher than the next and the whole series strung through the hills like a monstrous, many-linked dragon, and you will have some idea of the most costly stairways ever planned—the salmon "ladders" at Bonneville Dam. The pools will be the steps of the stairways, and each step will be a miniature swimming tank, forty feet wide, fifteen feet long and six feet deep. Water will tumble in undersized falls from pool to pool, starting with the pools at the top of the dam and ending with those at the base. There will be one of these mammoth stairways along each bank of the river and one twisting up the tree-covered island that divides the spillway dam and powerhouse. The steps will connect with canals, and the entire system will be fifty-nine hundred feet long, or five times the height of the Empire State Building.

Up these enormous stairs, that might have been used by the giant who chased Jack of the Beanstalk across the sky, the Chinook salmon of the Columbia River will jump merrily from pool to pool until they reach the water above the dam. At least, the thousands of people engaged in the fishing industry along the Pacific coast fervently hope that they will. On whether the fish in the Columbia leap up the watery levels of the vast stairs being built through the hills around Bonneville Dam depends the fate of the Chinook salmon.

It will be entirely up to the salmon, say the naturalists. The dam will be there, and so will the stairways. The fish can fight the impregnable barrier of steel and concrete until they die without spawning. Or they can gain the upper river and their breeding grounds by flipping blithely up the gentle, one-foot levels of the $7,077,200 steps. It is just that simple—the difference between survival and destruction for one of the major industries of the Far West. The total value of the Columbia River fishery to our economic structure exceeds $15,-000,000, with an annual income of at least $10,000,000.

The noted scientists who have studied the situation claim it is extremely important that the salmon find the big stairways with an absolute minimum of delay. Salmon on their way to spawn have only a limited amount of energy. They never eat from the time they enter fresh water from the sea until they die high in the mountains after breeding. If the female salmon, each carrying from twenty-five hundred to five thousand eggs, spend their strength fighting the dam, they will not be able to ascend the long series of pools when they finally discover them. The men building the dam are aware of this.

Frank Buck never tried any harder to get a Bengal tiger into a cage than the army engineers are trying to lure the 100,000 Chinook salmon that pass Bonneville each day at spawning time into the entrance of the mammoth stairways. Fronting the downstream face of the powerhouse will be elaborate collecting troughs, with water running at right angles to the flow of the river. Once a salmon flips into these troughs, it will be carried almost automatically to the giant steps. There also will be four fish lifts, which will be in a class by themselves so far as elevators are concerned.

The fish elevators are probably best described as a hybrid between an old-fashioned lift and a ship lock. They will be huge chambers six hundred feet square, and they will be lifted from the lower river to the upper river as fast as they are filled with water and salmon. Once above the dam, the floor of the elevator will be tilted so that no salmon, however reluctant it is to leave the impromptu joy ride, will be able to remain for the round trip. The elevators will operate in pairs, like the cable cars on a mountain scenic railway. When one lift is emptying its load of salmon above the dam, the other will be receiving fish at the base of the barrier. The water filling the chamber will provide the ship-lock part of this complex arrangement, and the rising floor of the lift will furnish the elevator touch. Each of the four fish lifts will be able to accommodate thirty thousand salmon passengers a day. It will require twenty or twenty-five trained men to operate them.

In addition to the elevators and stairways, there will be a whole series of fingerling passes to get the baby salmon back down the river without being smashed in the turbines and generators. The power equipment at Bonneville has been especially constructed to leave large openings for the fingerling salmon. Chief George Red Hawk thinks this is even more important than the ladders and lifts to get the fish above the dam. He is afraid the little salmon, seaward bound, will encounter more difficulties at the dam than the parent fish, headed for their spawning grounds in the upper river.

One thing is certain: no salmon will be able to get past Grand Coulee, which will be three times as high as Bonneville and more than four times as long. Instead of elevators and seven-million-dollar stairways, it would take dirigibles and airplanes to scoot the salmon past Grand Coulee. So the government will not even attempt that impossible feat, but will try to catch the parent salmon and strip them of the precious eggs by artificial means. For this purpose, the largest fish hatchery in the world is planned to be built on the Columbia River just below Grand Coulee. But first the salmon must get by Bonneville, because a large proportion of the fish spawn in shallow tributaries and eddies along the three-hundred-mile stretch between the two dams.

William L. Finley, vice president of the Izaak Walton League of America, is willing to admit the Chinooks may have some chance at Bonneville, but contends that Grand Coulee will kill as dead as a coffin nail the runs of salmon that now spawn in the extreme headwaters of the Columbia River.

All the gadgets and equipment at both dams are as much of an experiment as the first steamboat, and many of the men in the salmon industry are either reading the want ads these days or else planning to sue the government for enough in damages to retire comfortably. Congress has been deluged with resolutions, complaints, and protests, and the Senate has requested an investigation of the entire Chinook salmon situation on the Columbia.

The Secretary of Commerce has just announced that his department will begin a survey of the fifteen thousand miles of rivers, creeks, and streams open to the millions of the salmon that swim up the Columbia each year.

The peril that Bonneville and Grand Coulee constitute to the salmon industry has given the opponents of industrial power rates their most effective argument. What will happen to the grandeur and majesty of the West if its rivers are lined with factories? Now, the Columbia is crystal-clear and ice-cold. Sewage and waste material do not contaminate its rush of white water. Indian fishermen and forest rangers can scoop up its drops and drink them without fear of typhoid or other water-borne diseases. The river is full of oxygen, and the fish coming upstream have a maximum of energy to thrash their way to their mountain spawning grounds. Sometimes so many of the silvery shapes jam the Columbia that a man might almost venture across the broad river on a pontoon bridge of salmon.

This would not be so if the waterway became a lane of factories. Waste material would be dumped into the river constantly. Sewage would clog its reaches. The stream that now flows as clear as spring water to the Pacific would become a torrent of garbage and pollution. The wild life of the whole region would be imperiled. Not long ago in the *Survey Graphic* Stuart Chase told how relatively minor developments on the Klamath and Salmon rivers in the high Siskiyous threatened the natural wonders of that area. Salmon died in the streams and deer fled from the forests. Even the comparatively few manufacturing plants near Portland have turned the Willamette River into a sluice of filth and dirt. The industrial empire that business men vision on the Columbia would destroy the game birds and animals that now inhabit the mighty river basin. Eagles do not soar above smokestacks, salmon do not swim into pollution, and panthers and bears do not roam within sound of whirring machinery.

The world's greatest runs of Chinook salmon may use the seven-million-dollar ladders to pass Bonneville. Conceivably, they may even survive the frowning battlements of Grand Coulee. But they will never come up the Columbia again if there are new Pittsburghs where the river penetrates the ramparts of the mountains.

-4-

The dilemma caused by the construction of the Bonneville and Grand Coulee dams would be far less alarming were it not for the crisis confronting the world's other great source of salmon—Alaska. What Brazil is to the planet's coffee cups, Alaska and the Columbia River are to the globe's supply of salmon. Practically every tin of canned salmon comes from one of these places. And the salmon runs in Alaska have fallen off from 20 to 80 per cent in the past year because of an invasion of fishing fleets from Japan. The situation is so ominous that Senator Schwellenbach of Washington claims it menaces the peace of the United States.

All Japan's imperialism has not been confined to China. Occidental waters are as fertile raiding territory as Oriental lands. The choppy waves of Bristol Bay, the principal swimming ground of the famous Alaskan red salmon, have been churned lately by the propellers of Japanese cannery ships. Just as the Nipponese military juggernaut rolls across China without regard for the amenities of civilization, so do these fishing vessels from Tokyo completely overlook conservation rules and principles in their quest for the finny wealth of the ocean.

Heavily weighted nets scoop crabs off the bottom of the bay—and with them the marine life on which the salmon feeds. Other nets and fish traps cork up the mouths of rivers, and salmon runs are cut off before they even can enter the stream which leads to their distant spawning beds. Bonneville is one hundred fifty miles from the mouth of the Columbia, and the American government is spending seven million dollars to prevent it from being an impassable barrier. But Japanese fish nets guard the very mouths of the Alaskan rivers, and their main purpose is to snare the salmon on their last weary hegira into the highlands.

The salmon supply in the continent's northern waters cannot survive this reckless and indiscriminate plundering. Already the annual pack has been reduced 1,690,413 cases. The Japanese invasion is responsible. The circumstances are not only alarming to salmon packers and fishermen. They threaten the welfare of Alaska. Salmon is the Territory's greatest source of wealth. Since Seward bought Alaska from Russia for precisely the same amount as the Bonneville fish ladders is costing, the territory has produced $467,732,633 worth of gold. But the salmon catch has been worth more than twice that much—$956,502,270. Alaska's economy cannot stand the destruction of this income by Japanese imperialism. The salmon industry pays 75 per cent of the taxes of the territory.

The fishermen have a powerful union and they are ready to act. Unless Tokyo withdraws its cannery vessels from

Alaskan bays and inlets, the fishermen will picket all Japanese ships docked along the Pacific coast. Through that picket line the longshoremen will not pass. This would throw trade between the United States and Japan into confusion. The fishermen are prepared to make good their threat. They have nothing to do most of the year. The Alaskan salmon-fishing season lasts only about a month. Trudging a picket line, particularly when it is in defense of their livelihood, is as good a way as any for the fishermen to pass the long months in the "States" between their expeditions into the North.

Men who follow the sea in British Columbia have insisted that Ottawa make official diplomatic representations to Tokyo. American fishermen are demanding similar procedure of Washington. Whether the Japanese will really respond to these complaints is dubious. World opinion has not meant much in previous situations. Japan has promised to get out of Alaska, but so far has taken no positive action to do so. Its boats continue to scoop the fish off the bottom of the sea. The fate of the red salmon in Alaska remains as doubtful and uncertain as the fate of the Chinook salmon in the Pacific Northwest.

The precise shade of black—or whether it is not black at all—will be determined some time late in 1938 or in 1939. By that time the Japanese government will be forced to adopt some sort of policy on its invasion of Alaskan waters. And long before that the waterway at Bonneville will be entirely blocked. The open water between the piers will be cut off. The fish runs of the next year or so will show whether the people of the earth will ever again eat the great Chinook salmon from the Columbia River.

When the ponderous steel gates are fixed in place and the river completely barricaded, final judgment will be written on the fate of the Chinook salmon. Then, the only way the salmon can pass will be by the seven-million-dollar stairways and lifts. In the spring and autumn, more than ten million fish will head upstream from the blue Pacific. Leaping waterfalls and thrashing through rapids, they will come to the great crenelated battlement of Bonneville. Will they stop there and die without spawning, or will they use the steps and elevators and canals to reach their breeding grounds in the upper river? And if the salmon pass the dam, will they find their way through the forty-five mile tranquil lake which will form behind the barrier? Salmon invariably follow a river's current when they are swimming upstream to spawn. Will there be enough flow above the dam to guide them into the distant highlands, or will they thrash about aimlessly in limpid Bonneville Lake until they perish from starvation and exhaustion?

This spring brought no answer to these questions, because the salmon run mysteriously was a fragment of its customary proportions. Some naturalists attributed this to the biological changes the dam has caused in the stream. Most of the people who have opposed the construction of Bonneville for other reasons—private ownership advocates, for example—are certain the barrier means ruin to the salmon industry. However, these individuals are in an anomalous position. They are the group which wants more industry along the rushing river. And it is the encroachment of civilization and industry that has done as much to reduce the salmon runs as almost any other single factor. In 1884 more than 620,000 cases of rich Chinook salmon were taken from the Columbia. Last year the haul was less than half that. Frank M. Warren, a pioneer packer, gives this reason: "Civilization and wild life don't mix." Yet the civilization now on the banks of the Columbia

is only a very fragmentary sort. Suppose the river really de-
velops into the industrial wonderland which the business men
visualize. What will become of the salmon then?

Morton Tompkins, the overseer of the Oregon State
Grange, has questioned the sincerity of many of the groups
that now fervently protest the damage to the salmon industry.
"These groups," he said to me, as we ate lunch in the immacu-
late kitchen of his farmhouse in the Willamette Valley, "never
were conservationists when the lumber companies were ruining tracts of forest land." Selective logging is a new development. Secretary Ickes insists it is too new. There was a time
when timber operators went into the woodlands and tore out
the whole countryside. Vast forests were gutted. Green hills
were left bare and ugly. The owners of the logging camps did
not even want the government to build roads and trails to be
used in fighting forest fires; they were afraid the presence of
Uncle Sam meant an end to their depredations. For interests
akin to these to condemn Bonneville Dam from a conservation
viewpoint does not, in Tompkins' opinion, ring entirely true.
Is it the welfare of the salmon for which they fear? Or, possibly, are they thinking of the electricity which will be sold to
farms and homes and stores at cheap rates? There is no doubt
in Tompkins' mind that the concern of big commercial interests for natural resources is a recent occurrence. He admits
there is a grave danger the salmon runs may be destroyed;
but he thinks big business, except that engaged in the canning
industry, is worried about fish less and hydroelectric power
more. "The salmon ladders are costing $7,000,000," the
leader of the farmers said. "That's one of the most conscientious efforts at conservation in the history of the country."

Countless fishermen, naturalists, Indians, and sportsmen
will line the river to watch the salmon finally face the wall
at Bonneville. Men who fish for sport are also deeply con-

cerned. There are few thrills comparable to having a fifty-pound Chinook on the end of a line. Columbia River salmon fishing has regularly attracted anglers like Herbert Hoover and Zane Grey, and many years ago a mustached little Englishman visited the Pacific Northwest. Asked what he wanted to do most of all, he replied, "Go salmon fishing." So Rudyard Kipling waded out into the Clackamas, one of the Columbia's woodland tributaries, and pulled in a giant Chinook below the trestle where the interurban line from Oregon City to Portland spanned the foaming river.

The food of the Indians, the future of an industry, the sport of thousands of anglers, and the usefulness of the most elaborate and costly fish equipment ever built will be at stake when the salmon runs of the near future reach the massive barrier at Bonneville.

United States Commissioner of Fisheries Bell admits he is not certain what will happen, but states he is hopeful the giant stairways and lifts will meet the crisis.

And Chief George Red Hawk, whose father was spearing fish at Celilo Falls when young Lieutenant Ulysses Simpson Grant was stationed at an army post just down the Columbia, looks at the principal salmon river of the world and says, "Soon we know—for sure."

6. Government by the People

The day will come when every State in this Union will have the initiative and referendum. When that day comes the people will rule; the people will rule.   —ABRAHAM LINCOLN.

THE Pacific Northwest has a greater abundance of the necessary goods of life than any other proportionate area in the world. It has half the timber of the United States. It also has 42 per cent of the hydroelectricity, one-fourth of the wool, one-fifth of the wheat, and practically all the Chinook salmon. Individuals as far apart in time and perspective as Thomas Jefferson and Viscount Bryce and Theodore Roosevelt have proclaimed it one of the richest and most beautiful regions on earth.

Two-fifths of a century ago the people of the sovereign State of Oregon thought they knew how this Promised Land could be made as prosperous as it was bountiful. They were certain they had found the formula for a social and economic well-being commensurate with Nature's prodigality. All that was needed was to give the power to make laws directly to the electorate. Let the voters rule themselves without recourse to the slow-moving machinery of representative government. Then—no more procrastination, no more obeisance to corporate wealth, no more thwarting of the wishes of the majority, no more poverty in the midst of plenty, no more restrictions on liberty and freedom, no more legislative runarounds. The will of the people would prevail in its purest and most unadulterated form. The populace would be as happy as their fair land was lush. The Saturnian age would be reached.

With these hopes the initiative and referendum were introduced to the Western hemisphere in 1902. That year the citizens of Oregon were placed in complete and direct custody of their fate. Laws could be enacted without looking to any branch of the State government; laws adopted by the legislature could be killed if the people did not want them. The same applied to constitutional amendments. The power to govern was taken from the State capitol and put in the marketplace and on the hillside. Men with sheaves of petition strode through city streets and trudged along country roads. They became the lawmakers of Oregon. The signatures of 8 per cent of the voters of the State placed any proposal on the ballot for the people to decide on it. The signatures of 5 per cent of the voters could force a referendum on any proposition enacted by the legislature.

Here was democracy pure and simple. What the people wanted they could have. No longer would the demands of the voters have to be conditioned to the delays of the legislative process. "Oregon has evolved the best system of government that exists in the world today," said Senator Jonathan Bourne, Jr. "It is an absolute government by the people." His speech on the initiative and referendum was the most widely circulated address ever delivered in Congress. Nine million copies were printed. People in every part of America read about the State that was run almost as democratically as a New England town meeting. Oregon became a political laboratory of tremendous significance. Writers traveled across the globe to see a commonwealth twice as large as England governed on the same basis as one of the *Landesgemeinden* of tiny Switzerland. A new era in history was foreseen. "The Oregon System" was hailed as a logical sequence in the development of democracy. At last, the people themselves could confront directly the great problems facing civilization.

"Popular government is superseding delegated government," said Senator Bourne and his allies. They predicted— grim prophecy!—the ultimate subordination of legislatures and Congresses and Reichstags and Parliaments and Diets. With initiative and referendum petitions, the people could become masters of their destinies. Into limbo would pass the shocking incongruities and ugly paradoxes that existed under representative government. The aphorism "The People Rule" would be given true literal meaning. "In Oregon," wrote Burton J. Hendrick in *McClure's*, "it is on the farms that the laws are really made and not at the State capitol."

Thirty-six years have gone by since then. During that almost two-fifths of a century the initiative and referendum have been in effect in Oregon. The voters have had direct and sweeping control over the laws and constitution of the State. Their dominion has been the broadest grant of power ever held by an American electorate. For nearly four decades each Oregon citizen able to qualify for voting and to write his name on a petition has been a potential and actual member of the State legislature—a legislature of nearly half a million souls.

How has it worked out? What has been the result of one of the most daring innovations in the political history of the United States? Can the people govern themselves? Has direct government proved superior to representative government? Have the initiative and referendum been successful? Has the lodging of legislative sovereignty in the people made the bounteous Columbia River basin the Elysian field of freedom and contentment that the sponsors of this bold undertaking thought it would? Is Oregon any better off than the rest of the country? Has it become America's Promised Land? How has the Pacific Northwest reacted to the startling experiment that has taken place within its far-flung borders?

This is a propitious time to search for the answers to these inquiries. All over the world "How much democracy?" is a question of unrivaled importance. In many nations democracy is dead. Even in the countries in which it is most alive, it does not survive without travail. The attempt of President Roosevelt to increase the membership of the Supreme Court was predicated upon an attitude toward democracy. The President and his followers contended the Court was setting aside the mandates of the electorate. Chief Justice Hughes and other defenders of the tribunal pleaded that the nation should not be left at the mercy of temporary majorities. One group demanded more power for the people; the other asked that the decisions of the voters be cushioned by the slow process of constitutional government. Some of the President's adherents revived the old Bull Moose idea of a national referendum on important Supreme Court opinions. Their adversaries scoffed at the notion of the entire country's being qualified to pass upon grave and complex constitutional disputes.

"With how much power can the people be safely entrusted?" has been asked many times in Congress and White House and courtroom in recent years. Should there be brakes on the omnibus of popular authority, or should it roll unimpeded over the American countryside? Not alone the Supreme Court struggle has brought these inquiries into the political amphitheater. President Roosevelt, who sought more power for the electorate in the Court controversy, clamped the White House vise onto Congress with unprecedented pressure to force the rejection of the Ludlow amendment which would have given the people control over the war-making power. He said a popular referendum on war was not consistent with the principles of representative government.

The people or their representatives? Whose verdict is more to be trusted—the electorate, or the individuals to whom the electorate has delegated authority? These have been questions of varying significance for the past two generations. Just now they are more significant than ever, made so by the temper and problems of the times. Fortunately, they may be answered with a degree of verisimilitude. One State, at least, has provided an indication of what happens when the people vote directly on constitutional and legislative issues. Oregon's citizens have had for thirty-six years the right to enact laws and constitutional amendments entirely on their own volition. Petitions circulated among the people, rather than legislators' *ayes* and governors' signatures, have been the instruments of democracy. The initiative and referendum have become so much a part of the political economy of the State that they are known everywhere as "the Oregon System."

Direct legislation exists in twenty-one other States, but not to the extent that it does in Oregon. Practically all these States have been content with modified copies of the original product. Maryland and New Mexico, for example, have the referendum but not the initiative. The voters of Utah, Montana, Idaho, Maine, Washington, and South Dakota can initiate laws but not constitutional amendments. A number of other States use what is called the *indirect* initiative; this means that proposals sponsored by a specified number of signatures are sent to the legislature instead of to a popular vote. But in Oregon, according to Dr. Charles A. Beard, the system of lawmaking by petition has been "complete and thoroughgoing . . . and extensively tried."

It is in the tumultuous, sparsely settled State nestling in

the heart of the wild and magnificent Columbia River country that the most authoritative test of direct popular sovereignty in America has taken place. It is a test that began in
1902. It is still going on today.

-2-

When Oregon became the first commonwealth in this hemisphere to adopt a full-fledged version of the initiative and
referendum, Lincoln Steffens and other veteran combatants
on the battlefield of political reform argued that the innovation would enable the people to decide their salient and crucial problems more democratically. It would open the passes
to the Promised Land, they said.

Not long ago Oregon commemorated that event. On the
thirty-fifth anniversary of the introduction of direct legislation to the New World, one referendum campaign was under
way: the pool-hall operators and cigar-store proprietors of the
State were circulating petitions to legalize slot machines and
pin-ball games.

This particular type of commemoration may have been co-
incidence. Unfortunately, it was not unfitting. The initiative
and referendum were brought forth to accomplish bold reforms. Instead, they have been used to authorize new county
jails and regulate the sale of oleomargarine. No objective has
been too trivial or piddling to command the operation of the
great governmental institution that was to have made Oregon
a Canaan in the Far West.

The voters of the State will not be surprised when they
eventually go to the polls to decide whether beer halls and
honky-tonks can augment their take with money machines.
Oregon's electorate has voted on far less significant proposals

than that. The initiative and referendum had been in effect only a few years when the zealous circulation of petitions and several feverish election campaigns accomplished the specifying of the duties of the State printer and forbade the contemplated purchase of a stretch of toll road. One early campaign centered around whether hotel sheets should be 81 inches wide and 103 inches long; the voters decided they should.

Here are a few of the other attempted uses to which direct legislation has been put: abolishing the Wallowa County high school, increasing the bounty on sage rats and jack rabbits, eliminating the desert land board, regulating the size of cattle herds in Umatilla County, giving naturopaths and chiropractors the right to prescribe medicine, forbidding the smoking of cigarettes, closing Nestucca Bay to commercial fishing, specifying the salaries of the officials of Clackamas County, moving the State University forty-one miles farther north, providing for the maintenance of the Klamath Falls commercial club, requiring the railroads to give free passes to public officials, reducing the charge for automobile licenses, allowing dentists to advertise rates and remedies, prohibiting compulsory vaccination for smallpox, establishing a normal school at Pendleton.

This fribble trumpery was not the aim of the reformers who long ago persuaded a pioneer commonwealth to try a great experiment. The founders of the initiative and referendum thought so basic a governmental change would be used in major causes only. Their main objective was the adoption of the single tax. They believed the writing into the State constitution of the philosophy of Henry George's *Progress and Poverty* would make the Promised Land dream come true. It was obvious the legislature would not accept such a theory. Perhaps the people might. That was how the seed of the initiative and referendum first came to be planted in the political soil of the United States—a fallow ground that never before, through more than a century of history, had felt the roots of any but representative government.

Why not penalize the vast land resources of the Northwest that lay idle rather than the few scattered acres that were productive? Three unusual men asked frontier Oregon this question. One of them was Joseph Fels, the multimillionaire soap manufacturer. Henry George's doctrines were his shibboleth. He thought them infallible, and selected the bountiful outpost States of the Columbia River country as the place to vindicate this belief. To Fels, from the bustle and hum and overcrowding of the industrial East, the Pacific Northwest seemed a rich, primeval wilderness. He wanted its economic destiny to be guided by the single tax. So did an idealistic young lawyer from Colorado named William S. U'Ren. He had been a blacksmith who read Jefferson and George and Bentham between turns at the forge. The third member of the triumvirate was the scion of a New Bedford family grown wealthy in the textile mills. Jonathan Bourne, Jr., had left Harvard to go to sea. He was shipwrecked off the Formosa coast and had landed weary and tattered in Oregon. There he caught the vision of the country and decided to stay.

Fels was interested only in *Progress and Poverty*. The single tax encompassed his perspective. But U'Ren and Bourne were political as well as economic reformers. They had another thunderbolt in their quiver—the initiative and referendum. For years they had been fascinated by the prospect of wresting control of Oregon's limitless resources from the corrupt and demagogic politicians who ruled the State legislature. The best weapon to accomplish this feat seemed to be the government by petition that little Switzerland had established a generation earlier in 1874. Why not try it in Oregon? Surely the single tax could be passed in no other way. It had not as much chance in the legislature as a swimmer in the rapids of the Columbia.

U'Ren and Bourne convinced the twinkling little Jewish philanthropist they were right. Fels's money went to support the People's Power League, that had been formed to change the government from one of delegated authority to direct power vested in the people. It was the solitary hope for the single tax. The legislature would have to be reduced to a nullity before Oregon could become the Promised Land that the manufacturer of Fels-Naptha visioned.

In 1902 there occurred the most sweeping American political alteration since the founding of the Republic. The initiative and referendum were added to the Oregon constitution. The Fels Fund had done its work. Direct popular sovereignty superseded representative government in the Pacific Northwest. The nation quivered to the shock of the deed. There seemed to be no limit to the potential results of what had taken place. Out of this strange, uncushioned democracy might emerge a series of weird reforms that would ultimately bring about the downfall of democracy itself.

That was nearly four decades ago. The results—either direful or auspicious—of the initiative and referendum are still largely potential. Scarcely anything has happened. The people have used these extraordinary powers to gain practically no advances that other States have not attained in the customary legislative fashion. With lofty hopes Oregon's people went to the polls on that historic election day in 1902. Those hopes are still to be realized. The State is not yet the new Canaan of plenty that the original sponsors of direct legislation planned. Its citizens enjoy no more political freedom or economic security than those of the States in which the initiative and referendum have never even been proposed.

Lush though Oregon is in natural wealth, the annual *per capita* income of its people is only $394. This contrasts with $607 in Connecticut. Direct legislation has meant little improvement in the general welfare. Joseph Fels died a disillusioned man. He saw that "the Oregon System" had been an end in itself rather than the means to the single tax. The pioneers who struggled overland or sailed the tempestuous passage around the Horn had earned their farms too hard to risk putting *Progress and Poverty* into the statute books. Five times Fels's adherents got enough signatures to place the single tax on the ballot. On each occasion the voters turned thumbs down.

It was at the goading of radicals and progressives and reformers that Oregon braved the untried governmental adventure of the initiative and referendum. U'Ren and Bourne and their followers were political insurgents. Liberals all over the country thrilled to what they had done. Lincoln Steffens wrote enthusiastically about the momentous event. Charles Erskine Scott Wood, the bearded freethinker, boasted that Oregon was his home State. The agitation for "the Oregon System" was the first political rebellion observed by a little boy in the Portland Academy named John Reed. The political science classes at Princeton heard Woodrow Wilson apologize for claiming the initiative and referendum were a lot of theoretical bosh. "Fighting Bob" La Follette wanted Wisconsin to be the next State to adopt the idea. Across the continent in the White House the new President, Theodore Roosevelt, watched approvingly. If legislatures would not bust the trusts, initiative petitions might. The Populist movements in the Middle West stirred restlessly. Here was a new cudgel that could flatten the farmers' enemies forever!

"The Oregon System" was swept in on a wave of reform.

Almost ever since it has lain stranded on the beach of reaction. It has been a step backward as often as it has been a stride toward the Promised Land.

-3-

In 1922 the State was gripped by Ku Klux Klan hysteria. Fiery crosses burned on the hills, and initiative petitions to close all religious and private schools were circulated in the streets and marketplaces. Sufficient signatures were obtained in a few days. The measure was adopted at the polls, 115,506 votes to 103,685. What no legislature had ever dared to do, the people had done with the weapon of "the Oregon System." Religious freedom had been abridged, and the law later was declared unconstitutional by the United States Supreme Court.*

Although it was easy to get enough signatures to violate the Bill of Rights in 1922, it was impossible to accumulate enough to protect it in 1928. That year an attempt was made to initiate a bill repealing the Oregon criminal syndicalism law, an anachronism surviving from the days of wartime fervor. The petition never came to a vote; it failed for want of signers. The same year more than sufficient names were obtained to a measure to promote commercial fishing on the Umpqua River.

Oregon's public officials interpreted the indifference to the criminal syndicalism repeal petition as a popular mandate to bear down on minority groups. Left-wing heads were cracked, and men were thrown into jail for making speeches. Then the Supreme Court outlawed the statute in a case that Mr. Chief Justice Hughes described as one of the most drastic

* *Pierce* v. *Society of Sisters,* 268 U.S. 510.

curtailments of free speech and assembly ever to occur in the United States.*

Thus has the country twice been treated to the spectacle of the supposed citadel of American conservatism, the Supreme Court, undoing the damage to civil liberties inflicted by the nation's most thoroughgoing experiment in absolute democracy.

Practically nothing has resulted from Oregon's thirty-six years of experience with direct legislation. What meager outcome there has been has not offered much encouragement. Confusion in the economic sphere has paralleled oppression in the field of freedom. The initiative and referendum have helped to make the power laws of the State a hopeless botch. This is serious business in a region that has 42 per cent of the hydroelectricity of the whole country.

In 1930 the voters overwhelmingly elected a Jewish department store proprietor governor on a public ownership platform. They also adopted several initiative petitions creating the legal framework for people's utility districts. A year or so later the electorate voted on a bond issue that would have given some substance and financing to the power program. Approval was thought to be only a formality, but the people wiped out the proposition. Governor Meier shook his head perplexedly—and spent the rest of his term dallying with a State police force he organized under the expert supervision of General Smedley Butler.

Not long after the Federal government began construction of the giant dam at Bonneville on the Columbia River, Secretary of the Interior Ickes sent to Oregon a bill providing for transmission lines. It was initiated by the State Grange, and the necessary signatures were readily put to the petitions.

---

* *De Jonge* v. *Oregon*, 299 U.S. 353. This was the first unanimous free-speech decision in the history of the Supreme Court.

On election day the voters buried the measure beneath an avalanche of adverse ballots. The legislature accepted this as an irrefutable verdict against building a power distribution system. So Bonneville Dam is nearly completed now, and not a wire taps the energy put on the Federal "backbone" lines. It is as isolated as the clock stroke of one. Yet the $75,000,000 battlement is wildly cherished by the same voters who annihilated the transmission-line proposal. Republicans and Democrats alike must hail its wonders effusively. The candidate who directs a skeptical word toward it commits political hara-kiri.

One hundred and fifty miles down the Columbia from Bonneville, the gill-net fishermen at the mouth of the river used to claim that the fish wheelers upstream destroyed the Chinook salmon just as they were about to spawn. The fish wheelers, in turn, charged that the gill netters scooped up the salmon before they could enter the river from the sea. One summer each faction got out petitions to prevent the other type of fishing. At the polls the voters did not choose between the propositions. They adopted both of them! This practically meant no more commercial salmon fishing in the Columbia River. The salmon canneries were threatened with ruin. The neglected legislature had to intervene hastily to save one of the West's principal industries from immediate extinction.

Such occurrences as these have led to continual reiteration of the question: "Do the people realize how they are voting?" But the workings of the initiative and referendum at the ballot box cannot be understood until there has been some analysis of the happenings on the street corners and in the tall timber. The obtaining of the required quota of signatures is a necessary prelude to election day. What occurs when the petitions are circulated?

-4-

"The business of getting names" is what Burton J. Hendrick long ago called the preliminary operation of "the Oregon System." And it *is* a business—a business of consequence to the State. Sixteen thousand signatures can place before the voters a scheme to increase the bounty on coyotes or a plan to abolish the capitalistic system. Some people can get signers to either of these ideas with equal facility. Whether a certain petition reaches the ballot, and another fails ignominiously, frequently depends far more upon the glibness and zeal of the signature seekers than upon the merits of the cause. Many petition pushers earn ten or fifteen cents a name. Some receive as high as twenty-five cents in important campaigns. Legislative efforts have been made to eliminate the paid name getter, but it is a practice that can be carried on *sub rosa* with ease. Occasionally a fast-talking young man will make fifty dollars a day seeking signatures on a busy street.

A prepossessing appearance and an unwillingness to take "No!" for an answer are more essential to triumphant initiative and referendum sponsorship than a knowledge of the problem at issue. A few years ago a group of college students achieved remarkable success with a petition levying new taxes for education when they had pretty coeds canvass signatures from men on the Portland thoroughfares. Almost two generations of experience with direct legislation have shown that dimples and slender ankles win signers quicker than political and economic logic. Professor Waldo Schumacher of the University of Oregon recently made a study of the people pushing initiative petitions. He found most of them colossally ignorant of the proposals they were sponsoring. I have been urged to sign a tax limitation measure by a man who could

not tell me the first thing about the scheme. He had a thick
sheaf of signed petitions, and I was the only person, he said,
who had asked him any questions.

A large proportion of initiative and referendum signatures
are gotten in the marketplaces of Portland and a few other
cities. Women walk through these streets laden with bundles.
They have no time to stop and argue. They cannot move on
when some one stands in front of them and pokes an expos-
tulative finger in their faces. It is much simpler to sign the
petition than to refuse and be harassed. The same applies to
signature seekers who enter busy offices or ring residential
doorbells. Sign and be done with it! Many people adopt that
philosophy. A member of the desert land board even put his
signature to an initiative petition abolishing his own job.

Subterfuge and sophistry are as much a part of direct legislation as are professional name getters. In a legislative body
a law must mean approximately what it is alleged to say.
This is not always the case when statutes are adopted out in
the streets and countryside. If the gamblers have an initiative
to permit slot machines, they call it a proposal to stimulate
business. If an infinitesimal portion of the gambling take is to
be diverted to relief, the bill is given an eleemosynary slant
and described as an aid to the needy. A law is designed to
throw a mountain river wide open to commercial fishing, but
the people who sign it and vote on it are told it is a conservation measure. A sales-tax measure carries a clause throwing a
few pennies to rural schools; the bill is no longer a sales tax
but an educational proposal. Allocate a handful of silver to
the farm fairs in all thirty-six counties, and a scheme to
legalize dog racing becomes a bill to promote agriculture. A
plan to let advertising dentists list the price of their bridge-
work and allow lady chiropractors to describe the revivifying
effects of their treatments is presented to the electorate as a

twentieth century Valley Forge in defense of the freedom of the press.

Much of the responsibility for the bogging down of "the Oregon System" must rest upon the factions that have exploited it for selfish purposes. The men who introduced an outpost commonwealth to a new form of democracy were mainly altruists. They visioned a Promised Land in the American wilderness. Those who followed them have not been so idealistic. They have looked upon the initiative and referendum as a means to personal aggrandizement rather than as a way to better the general welfare. A distressingly large number of the proposals sponsored by petition have been started by groups that want to put money in their own wallets.

An example tells the story.

A Willamette Valley community felt it was losing business to the near-by seat of the State University. Why not move the University to town No. 1? Accordingly, the local Chamber of Commerce got out initiative petitions providing for such a change. This is a typical instance of the petty jealousies and antagonisms that direct legislation has served. Property owners continually initiate sales-tax bills to put the burden of taxation on the consumers. Back the consumers inevitably come with plans to get more revenue from real estate. The truck companies try to sock the railroads, and the railroads try to sock the truck companies. The naturopaths attempt to encroach on the field of medicine, and the doctors grimly stand them off. Every year new petitions seek to lift the conservation restrictions from nearly all the rich watersheds of the Columbia River basin. Where timbered mountains dip into fish-clogged streams, "the Oregon System" ironically has been used not to attain the Promised Land but to strip it bare.

Direct legislation has become a welter of self-seeking. The

scramble for economic advantages predominates all other types of proposals. There are twenty petitions to legalize gambling or exempt some group from taxation to one to improve the State school system or promote civil liberties. Fifteen or twenty thousand dollars have gone into petitions to let advertising dentists promote their wares. Only $901 could be raised to finance an initiative to abolish compulsory military training in the colleges.

The indiscriminate use of direct legislation has made the people increasingly suspicious. They have come to regard as phony many of the propositions that face them at the polls. They are always looking for a joker. "Vote 'No' on everything," is a common warning. It is becoming ever harder to win a favorable decision on any initiative proposal. Out of 243 measures submitted, 159 have been defeated on election day. Some of the wariness on the part of the people stems from the fact that so many proposals are initiated as amendments to the State constitution. This has developed into a racket. Suppose loan sharks want to fix a high rate of interest. Their petitions call for a constitutional amendment instead of a law. Then the legislature cannot touch the proposal if it passes. It can be undone only by another popular referendum. Constitutional amendments require no more signatures and no more affirmative ballots than ordinary bills. As a result the State constitution is a conglomeration of special privilege grants to minority groups. One article has 38 sections. In the *Oregon Blue Book* the full text of the United States Constitution covers nine pages; that of the State, twenty-three.

For a long time conservatives reveled in the tendency to vote "No." Now they are not so sure it is a good thing. No longer do they merely want to preserve the *status quo*. They are alarmed by the labor situation. The grim warfare between the Far West's labor titans, Dave Beck and Harry

Bridges, has made business men shiver apprehensively. They want a series of laws incorporating and controlling trade unions. These measures failed in the Oregon legislature, where the labor vote is a constant threat to aspiring politicians. Conservatives fear they will fail, too, on the initiative ballot unless the impulse to vote "No" is overcome.

The principal reason for the preponderant number of "No" votes is that the people are skeptical of anything they do not understand. They do not understand most of the schemes presented to them by direct legislation. Oregon's citizens, for example, are largely tolerant and fair. They were induced to close religious schools by a bill that was ambiguous and masqueraded. It was presented as a measure to promote education rather than stifle it. Most of the direct legislative proposals reach the voting booth in similar confusing form. The founders of the initiative and referendum forgot to see to it that the measures would appear on the ballot in words intelligible to the average man. Legalisms are not made for the general run of people. Simple language is the key to most men's reasoning. Yet direct legislation invariably confronts the voters with such verbal complexities as this:

For amendment of Section 32, Article I, Oregon Constitution, for the purpose of permitting taxes to be levied upon different classes of property at different rates, but providing that taxation must be uniform upon each separate class within the territorial limits of the authority levying the tax. . . .

What happens when the masses of the people face riddles of this sort? Oregon's experience indicates that they do the natural thing. They vote "No." People will not pluck in the dark when they are adding some scheme to their constitution or statute books. Before they vote "Yes" they want to know on what they are voting.

The initiative and referendum procedure allows the Oregon attorney general to prepare the material that is printed on the ballot. This gives a relatively minor States official vast power over the laws of the commonwealth. The language in which a proposition is presented often becomes the determining factor in the proposition's fate at the polls. Many times this has been true.

Several years ago the churches and other peace groups sponsored an initiative to forbid compulsory military training in the Oregon schools. After the bill had been defeated, two reporters for the Portland *Oregonian* interviewed scores of people who had voted exactly opposite to their inclinations, because the proposal had been so ambiguously worded on the ballot.

In 1935 the State legislature diverted $1,000,000 from the old-age pension fund to general relief. Referendum petitions put the act before the people. Had it been expressed in simple terms, the social security enthusiasts would have gone against it unhesitatingly. But the attorney general nebulously called the measure "BILL AMENDING OLD-AGE ASSISTANCE ACT OF 1935." Way down at the tail end of a paragraph of complicated language was the only mention of the diverted $1,000,000. Most of the old people and Townsend Plan devotees never saw it. They apparently voted for the bill.

Oregon will decide within the next year on an initiative measure calling for the incorporation of labor unions. The petitions are already in circulation. It will be the first time in American history that a general electorate will have a chance to vote on this bristling issue. Yet it may be determined not on its merits but on the prejudices of a State attorney general. If organized labor can get onto the ballot the hint that the bill is aimed against working people, the measure will lose. If employers' organizations succeed in having it described merely as a means of ending labor warfare and violence, the measure will pass. Direct legislation gives a single official that much obscure power.

Frequently the electorate is so bewildered by the involved wording of initiative propositions that from 20 to 40 per cent of the people appearing at the polls do not vote on them at all. A publication known as *The Voters' Pamphlet* has been distributed in an attempt to eliminate this bewilderment. The pamphlet consists of the arguments for and against all proposals referred to the people. Pages in the pamphlet cost $100 apiece and are paid for from the treasuries of the organizations sponsoring or opposing measures. The space is generally bought by such groups as the Grange, the power companies, the labor unions, the churches, the banks, the temperance societies, the gambling interests, the real-estate agencies, and the pension clubs. The pamphlet is published by the State and mailed to every registered voter.

The Voters' Pamphlet represents an effort to make direct legislation work, but Dr. James Duff Barnett, head of the University of Oregon political science department, is doubtful if one person in a hundred gives it even a cursory examination.

-5-

The initiative and referendum comprise the only important governmental reform ever to start in the Far West. To date the reform has not been a success. Yet the people are still hopeful. I have a Republican friend who looks ahead to the time when direct legislation will be a bulwark against the intimidation of the State legislature by radical minorities. And I know a curly-haired young Socialist who assures me "the Oregon System" will eventually end capitalism in the State and establish a system of production-for-use.

Neither conservative nor left-wing factions in Oregon would consent to the abandonment of the initiative and referendum. Possibly conservatives feel this way because, as Dr. Beard has pointed out, the drastic changes prophesied as a result of direct legislation have not taken place. Business groups also think that some day the initiative and referendum may set aside crackpot schemes adopted by a labor-dominated legislature.

Radicals want legislation by petition to stay for a different reason. They claim they have not really started to use it. They expect to do so soon. Public ownership of all utilities is the first item on their initiative agenda.

But all the faith in direct legislation is not premised on materialistic considerations. Pride is a factor. No other great governmental innovation ever came out of the West. Oregon cannot admit defeat after only thirty-six years. The initiative and referendum are entitled to additional time. The Republic itself traveled a rough course the first four decades.

The humorous, the ironic, and the tragic results of direct legislation are all part of Oregon's heritage. The best political tales on the sundown side of the Mississippi concern the bold experiment of government by signatures.

A bill to prohibit free railroad passes was once adopted by Oregon's people when they were in an anti-corporation mood. The vote was 57,281 to 16,799, yet the measure never became a law. The zealous but clumsy petitioners not only had neglected to attach an enacting clause, but also had worded the bill so that it gave the railroads greater latitude in the issuance of free passes than they had enjoyed before!

The outcome of direct legislation has not always been as comical as this. The recall of public officials was a part of "the

Oregon System." One of the men who urged its inclusion most vigorously was a homespun Portland physician named Harry Lane. In 1912 he was elected to the United States Senate. Five years later he was one of the "little group of willful men" who until the end opposed American participation in the War. Federal government officials are not legally subject to the recall, but petitions were circulated by a silk-stocking brigade against Dr. Lane for his alleged treason. The avowed purpose was to humiliate him. Thousands of signatures were collected. In six weeks the pacifist Senator was dead, the victim of a nervous breakdown.

Oregon is not proud of that episode. Nor does it boast of the time in 1922 when initiative petitions imperiled religious liberty. In extenuation the State can cite only one major accomplishment that has resulted from direct legislation. It occurred thirty years ago.

In 1908 United States Senators were still chosen by State legislatures. The Federal Constitution specified this method. The Populists agitated against it militantly, but U'Ren and his adherents were the first to find a way around it. They drafted a brief pledge for State legislators:

I further state to the people of Oregon, as well as to the people of my legislative district, that during my term of office I shall always vote for that candidate for United States Senator in Congress who has received the highest number of the people's votes for that position.

This promise was called Statement No. 1. It was practically impossible to get elected to the legislature without subscribing to it. On election day, 1908, the people adopted an initiative measure instructing the State legislature to vote for the popular choice for United States Senator. The country was astonished to read that for the first time a member of the upper hall of Congress had been elected by direct vote of the people. Jonathan Bourne, Jr., was the people's choice.

Five years later the nation followed Oregon's leadership. The seventeenth amendment to the Constitution, providing for the popular election of Senators, was decisively ratified.

Statement No. 1 made history. But it has been the only significant outcome of thirty-six years of absolute democracy. Practically all the other results have proved either trivial or undesirable. "The initiative and referendum," wrote the late Dr. Charles H. Chapman, president of the University of Oregon, "were the State's chance to move in one leap from foul politics to the golden prime of democracy, but the chance was not taken. The system was adopted formally and that was the end of it."

The debacle of direct legislation has shown both conservatives and radicals that the Promised Land cannot be achieved as if by magic. Mere tinkering with the forms of democracy will not hasten its fulfillment. "The Oregon System" has not protected business men from the grimmest labor hostilities in the country. Neither has it kept poor people from practically starving to death in the most bountiful section of the United States.

The situation has proved conclusively that voters who elect unsatisfactory legislatures are not likely to do any better themselves. It also has indicated that when the people are able to master the intricacies of direct government, they will probably elect legislatures that will make these other controls unnecessary.

Yet the initiative and referendum will probably always be a "stick behind the door"—a defense bludgeon for either conservatives or left-wingers to wield in periods of stress. Its presence at least will have a certain psychological effect. Ruthless pressure groups, high-handed corporations, and tyrannical public officials may not dare acts they would perpetrate if the initiative and referendum were not there.

The Oregon experiment has made clear that before the initiative and referendum can succeed in America, there must be a wholesale discarding of the linguistic mumbo-jumbo which surrounds the legislative process. Proposals on the ballot must not be smothered in legalistic rigmarole. A bill to raise school teachers' salaries to a certain amount should say just that, instead of hemming and hawing about mandatory levies and twenty-mill limitations. The simplification talents of Thurman W. Arnold and others who have urged straight-forward economic and political language might help make "the Oregon System" work.

Of course, it must not be forgotten that hand in hand with this necessity is the duty to educate the people to these unique responsibilities and obligations. A half-million souls in a hinterland fastness twice as big as Czechoslovakia cannot become a giant legislature without some preparation. U'Ren and Bourne thought they could take the cowboy off his range and the woodsman off his trap line and interest them in complex questions of political theory and taxation. The procedure was wrong. The voters had to be educated first. Now, that job must be done if direct legislation is ever to be anything greatly more than abstract scribblings in Oregon's State constitution.

The chance for the initiative and referendum of which Dr. Chapman wrote is not gone forever. It remains. For nearly forty years it has been passed by, but there is still the possibility that America's most thoroughgoing test of democracy will help to bring about a Promised Land where the Columbia surges to the sea.

7. The Thunderer from the Idaho Hills

No PERSON in American public life so typifies the magnificent promise and scant fulfillment of the Pacific Northwest as the seventy-three-year-old Idaho lawyer whom Walter Lippmann once called the region's greatest citizen.

William Edgar Borah has served in the United States Senate since 1907—longer than any other living man. During most of that time he has been one of the country's significant figures. On occasion his importance and prestige have eclipsed that of Presidents. All over the world his words are listened to attentively. People in far-away places who have no conception of where Idaho is know about Senator Borah. He is the great orator of Congress. His speeches fill the Senate galleries and burst into the newspaper headlines. Few men have so captured the imagination of the American people. Impressive in appearance and dramatic in action, he has long symbolized to the nation at large the independence and freedom of the Western ranges. He is almost regarded as the prototype of the hinterland statesman. His career has been singularly free of the offal of politics. No scandal or hint of intrigue has ever blurred his name. Seldom are his motives suspect; Woodrow Wilson believed Borah was sincere in his opposition to the League of Nations. The Idaho Senator is respected by reactionary and radical alike. Humanitarianism is widely recognized as one of his dominant qualities. Each Presidential election finds him one of the more honorable and desirable White House potentialities. He is an old man now, but in a recent *Fortune* poll to determine possible favorites to succeed Roosevelt the name of Borah led all the rest. His ability to fill the Presidency has never been questioned. His speeches are clear and lucid and crammed with facts. He can be logical or emotional, as situations require. In debate he is an alert and competent foe. His knowledge is a storehouse he has not begun to exhaust. He combines the polish and dignity of Eastern urbanism with the democracy and simplicity of the Western backwoods. Never has pomp or stuffiness diminished Borah's usefulness or importance. He frankly confesses when he thinks he has made a mistake; he is sorry now that he voted for the World War and against the confirmation of Brandeis as a member of the Supreme Court. Borah detests ceremony and the pretense of Olympian wisdom. He rides streetcars to his office in Washington and walks downtown in Boise. To a question he is not afraid to reply, "I don't know."

For nearly two generations this long-maned lawyer from a wilderness State—a State with sixty-two times as much land as New York City and one-eighteenth as many people—has been one of the strong and enduring public figures of the American scene.

Like the bountiful section of the country whose most notable citizen he assuredly is, Borah has all the attributes of greatness. He has been benevolently endowed with talents, as the Northwest has been richly supplied with resources. Both have failed to fulfill the hope they invariably inspire. The Columbia River basin, for all its fertility and abundance, has given its people no extra quota of happiness and freedom and security. And the river basin's most illustrious citizen, the Senator of the thundering oratory and leonine head, has scarcely any tangible and affirmative accomplishments to his credit.

Borah has been in the Senate three decades. Yet his name is associated with no major legislative acts. The history books mention him for the things he has fought rather than for what he has sponsored. His forte is not advocacy: it is opposition. The League of Nations, the military expeditions sent to Nicaragua by Coolidge, the NRA, the New Deal scheme to enlarge the Supreme Court, and innumerable other ideas launched with high hopes have floundered on the reefs of Borah's hostile speeches. Practically every organized political group in the nation has winced under his criticism. He attacks with the fury of the winds that sweep down on Idaho from the twelve-thousand-foot ramparts of Borah Peak. In an hour he did more to kill the anti-lynching bill than all the Southern Senators had been able to do during two weeks of interminable jabber.

Since 1907 Borah has assailed the remedies and plans proposed by others. No one else in Congress has been so effective in exposing unsoundness and inadequacy. He condemned the NRA, for example, because it buttressed monopoly and raised prices. Now, the Roosevelt administration admits that these charges have proved lamentably true. The vulnerable point of Borah's brilliant strictures against the NRA was his failure to suggest a substitute program to correct the abuses the NRA was expected to mitigate. Seldom has he advanced an alternative for the measures and policies he arraigns. That has been his weakness.

The Senator tore into Hoover's Food Administration in 1918, but offered no stopgap ideas on the subject. In 1932 he was thoroughly disgusted with Hoover as a President, yet supported none of the other candidates. He recently urged that the South be left free to work out the Negro problem: how the South should do the job, Borah did not say. By far the most eloquent protests against every League of Nations and World Court proposal have been delivered by Borah: never has he put forth any realistic specific alternatives for the country's foreign relations. No one, not even Roosevelt, has matched Borah's picturesque and poignant description of the drought victims seeking refuge in Idaho and the rest of the Northwest; and although the $404,000,000 Grand Coulee project may be the most colossal debacle in American history, it at least is a scheme to take care of these wandering farmers: the distinguished Senator has had no definite plan at all.

Borah has been poked at more inquisitively than any other man in public life. For years commentators and historians have tried to figure out what makes him tick. The shrewdest chroniclers are puzzled by him. How can a Senator be classified who delights the Southern reactionaries with a masterly indictment of the anti-lynching bill, and then makes them shiver apprehensively for their starvation-wage textile factories when he pleads for tolerance of the sit-down strikes? Who dares even attempt to catalogue a man who is against the Child Labor amendment and for recognition of Soviet Russia, who has been against Brandeis and for Cardozo for the Supreme Court, who is denounced in both *The Red Network* and the *New Masses*, and who can stump the country for Herbert Hoover in 1928 and the State of Nebraska for George W. Norris in 1930?

Borah is the great American enigma. Washington correspondents with a dull afternoon can always psychoanalyze him in the columns of their papers. Against the background of the national capital he has been dissected and examined by a thousand typewriters. Scarcely ever have these investigations extended across the continent to the frontier commonwealth where Borah does not even own a house yet where the State's highest mountain is named for him. Idaho is the setting against which both the strengths and the frailties of the dean of the United States Senate stand out most clearly. His story is the story of the State almost from the day it was admitted to the Union.

-2-

In the autumn of 1891 a young lawyer from Kansas rode westward on one of the swaying trains that puffed over the continental divide and down into the vast basin of the Columbia River. Three months earlier Idaho had become the forty-third star in the American flag.

On the train a gambler advised twenty-five-year-old William Edgar Borah to get off at Boise. A business man warned him he had better go on to Portland. Borah got off at Boise —but before he went down the steps of the day coach he heeded the business man's admonishment to look in his pockets and see how much money he had. He found $15.77 and decided that was enough to live on until he could earn more.

In this fashion the round-faced attorney from the plains adjusted his habits to the frontier on which he had arrived. He accepted the gambler's counsel and tempered it with the business man's caution.

His first legal client, the gambler obtained for him. The man had shot a Chinese cook in cold blood. He was arrested for first-degree murder, and Borah stood by in open-mouthed amazement when the judge reduced the charge to manslaughter because only a Chinaman had been killed! The defendant was promptly acquitted. Borah pocketed the thirty-five-dollar fee and advised the slayer to keep on moving and get out of the State. He wanted no more clients like that.

Borah descended from a pious Baptist father of German ancestry. At home he and his six sisters and three brothers had been taught to fear God, work hard, and live righteously. The Idaho of 1891 shocked him. Indians still rode on occasional raids, and the frontier was looted by the riffraff of the Union and Confederate armies who had wandered westward after the War. Vigilantes patrolled the hinterlands, and grim-jawed sheriffs wore sagging cartridge belts in town. Six-shooters frequently subordinated courts as a method of arbitration. Joaquin Miller even was said to have held up a man over on the Oregon border. The State was wild and tumultuous. Organized society was only a few years removed from the blockhouse era.

Early Idaho was uncontrolled and free. The railroads were comparatively new. Not all the transcontinental lines had yet spanned the mountains. The lumber industry was in its embryo stage. Rich deposits of minerals were still to be converted into mines. Homestead acreage was easily available. Pastures lush with grass waited the farmer with herds to graze. Sagebrush flats needed only water to make them fertile, and the rancher who could dig a ditch from the Columbia or the Snake might harvest potatoes and apples as big as horses' hoofs.

This wilderness commonwealth made a lasting impression on the prairie-bred lawyer who had settled in Boise. As Borah built his career he was counsel for many of the rough-and-ready individuals who survived on the frontier by their wits. His Baptist training inhibited him from gambling and drinking and smoking with these people, but it did not prevent him from being their lawyer. The cases of the derelicts and toughs who came to his office, he pleaded with eloquence and understanding. He achieved local fame. Whole villages turned out to hear his jury addresses in behalf of the State's fly-by-night characters. Substantial clients began to bring him their troubles. He was sought out by miners and stockmen and orchardists and timber operators who had turned the bounty of the open spaces into bank accounts with six digits.

Most of these men of wealth had once been poor. The affluent rancher had ridden the range as a cowboy in chaps and sombrero. The prosperous Jewish merchant had peddled trinkets from camp to camp and been the butt of the lumberjacks' jokes. Their success had a profound effect on their legal counselor. Here were little fellows who had broken the bank. They had done so in a State in which there was neither great concentration of capital nor rigid governmental control. Borah's new clients were personifications of the fairness and equality of free enterprise. In the untrammeled hurly-burly of the frontier they had made good. What they had done, others could do. This was the American system at its best. Everyone had a chance to be a millionaire. Idaho offered opportunities unlimited, and there was no private monopoly or government bureau to intervene.

Borah has not forgotten his original glimpse of the State he has represented in the Senate for thirty-one years. His faith is in that sort of an area. He wants the country to be free of both governmental restrictions and capitalistic encroachment. In that objective he thinks the hope of America lies. The present remoteness of such a system has never diminished the intensity of Borah's attacks on bureaucracy and monopoly. He assails them incessantly; that is why he is often in the anomalous position of being an ally of Carter Glass one day and of Bob La Follette the next.

The Idaho of today is not the Idaho that a young man from Kansas saw half a century ago. The Union Pacific cuts a swath through the lower end of the State—and a sphere of influence in the legislature. Lumber mills fix prices and fight the labor unions. Rival leaders struggle for the allegiance of the men who work in the zinc mines. Electric Bond & Share squats across the rivers, and the people pay light bills half again as high as the rates in the Tennessee Valley Authority. Government bureaus dictate crop quotas and irrigation allotments, and a labor board orders what men shall work and what men shall not. A hedge of rights and deeds and easements and privileges surrounds the frontier that once was free for the taking. Much of Idaho's income and wealth goes back across the country to absentee landlords and inventors. The average earnings of the inhabitants of the State are only $345 annually. The simple commercial relationships of long ago have given way to interference from the left and the right. There are labor unions and price pegging, and chain stores and holding companies. The Promised Land rolls to the Idaho horizons, but developing this last American wilderness is not the simple act of settlement that it was in 1891.

When William E. Borah rises majestically in the Senate and challenges both the conservatives who believe in rampant capitalism and the progressives who want government ownership and management, he looks back to the Idaho that preceded Electric Bond & Share at the waterfall and the C.I.O. in the sawmill. On this glance in retrospect are premised the thundering speeches which once impelled George Bernard Shaw to say, "Borah is the only American whose brains seem properly baked; the others are either crumbs or gruel."

At the age of seventy-three, Borah seeks again for the day of the little fellow. He remembers the Idaho when the logger in the lumber camp could become a timber operator, the clerk in the country store could be a successful merchant—

and a lawyer with $15.77 in his pocket could become the most illustrious United States Senator.

-3-

"I have looked him up and find that he is safe and sane," approvingly reported Nelson W. Aldrich when Idaho sent a new Senator to Washington in 1907.

The Republican boss had investigated superficially. He knew that Borah had prosecuted Big Bill Haywood and several other radicals for the murder of a former governor of Idaho. What he did not know was that the State's case had been conducted so impartially that Haywood himself said: "Borah was fair. He did not try to convict me by arousing prejudice against my cause."

Agitators were rare in outpost Idaho. Bitterness and hatred against the defendants ran high. Borah never pandered to this animosity. During the trial he came across a Socialist newspaper in which Haywood had scornfully connected Theodore Roosevelt with the slain governor. Borah turned to Clarence Darrow, the defense counsel. He pointed to the passage about Roosevelt, then gestured toward the jury. "I shall not use that," he volunteered. "All those men are Republicans."

The Senator's biographer, Claudius O. Johnson, has observed how needless it is to contrast this tolerance toward a radical in a frontier State with the trials of Sacco and Vanzetti in cultured Massachusetts and Mooney in civilized California. Haywood was acquitted.

The politicians in Washington who expected Borah to be a regular Republican judged him by the prosperity of his important clients. Of the clients who came from little farms and dingy pool halls they were unaware. Nor could they know about the allegiance to democracy that life in an outpost commonwealth on the Western frontier might instill in a man of strong character and stubborn convictions. They learned that Borah was the confidant of Calvin Cobb, aristocratic editor of the unyieldingly conservative *Idaho Statesman*—but not that he had risked his life to save a Negro bootblack from a lynch mob.

Borah was twenty-two miles away when he heard that a cowering colored man was threatened by rioters in the town of Nampa. He telephoned for the details and was told that the mob suspected Jim, a bootblack from Boise, of shooting a policeman. Borah hurried to the Union Pacific yards and persuaded one of his engineer friends to start at once for Nampa with a locomotive and coach. Railroading in the West was not as formal then as it is now! As the abbreviated train lurched along the bumpy roadbed, Borah walked through the coach pulling down all the shades. The train ground to a halt near the Nampa jail, where several hundred attackers were battering at the doors. Inside quavered the terrified Negro.

Borah pushed his way to the front of the mob. Ascending the steps he shouted, "Do you want the fair name of Nampa to be stained by a lynching?" Some one in the crowd hooted, and again the mob pushed forward. Borah stood off the rioters with one hand and pointed dramatically to the train with the other.

"No lynch law shall hold sway here!" he cried. "We have men on hand to prevent it. We have brought the militia from Boise!"

The mob looked apprehensively at the dark and silent car. It eyed the firm jaw and defiant glance of the young attorney. Then it broke. Borah strode into the jail and grabbed the trembling bootblack. They walked unmolested back through the crowd and boarded the ominously shuttered coach. The train began the twenty-two-mile return run to Boise.

A thoroughgoing faith in the Bill of Rights is part of Borah's background. This emanates from his lonely faith that if everyone starts from scratch, the race is fair. He does not want freedom jeopardized by holding companies, Federal bureaus, or mass antagonisms. This philosophy he first put into practice long ago.

The Mormons have always been Idaho's dominant minority. They are more numerous there than in any State except neighboring Utah. In 1891, when Borah was a newcomer to the Columbia River country, the Mormons were the target for every opportunist in politics. A speech on polygamy was the surest way to draw a crowd. Salacious descriptions of Mormon elders surrounded by bevies of nightgowned women —their wives—were inevitable preludes to bristling defenses of "one wife and the purity of the American home."

This demagogy disgusted Borah. He demanded that the defamers of the Mormons prove their charges. More than any other person, he drove religious intolerance out of Idaho politics. The men who talked of sin and debauchery in the Mormon Church could not support their accusations. Borah dryly remarked that the Latter-day Saints seemed just as decorous as the men persecuting them. Mormonism faded as a political issue. Years later Borah wrote:

"I am a believer in the fundamental principles of religious liberty. If the time ever comes when I have to sacrifice my office for those principles, I shall unhesitatingly do so."

-4-

Swank skiers and "socialite" dude ranchers from the East come down out of the Sun Valley highlands to observe the

great statesman who had been Idaho's Senator since Theodore
Roosevelt was in the White House. The glimpse they get of
William E. Borah does not conform to the Beacon Street
notion of a distinguished public figure.

Borah and his slender, white-haired wife live in an unpretentious suite of rooms at the Hotel Owyhee in Boise. The
Owyhee is not Boise's newest hotel. The Senator goes out
seldom. Most of the time he and Mrs. Borah eat alone in the
hotel dining room. She is continually looking for new recipes
for onion soup, which the Senator loves. He dislikes foreign
food and fancy dishes, and sticks to such American staples as
fried chicken and mashed potatoes with country gravy. Borah
hates to be disturbed by autograph hunters and lion collec-
tors. Inquisitive tourists and snooty travelers annoy him. He
regards artificiality as a curse. Real people monopolize his
interest. He will spend a whole afternoon talking with a griz-
zled farmer from the hills who drives to Boise to peddle a
load of potatoes or a side of beef.

In Washington, Borah is the thundering orator whose
words are heard beyond the seas. In Idaho, he is as plain as
when he rented a room over a brewery and practiced law and
slept in that one room. Borah's office now is almost equally
modest. It is a few blocks from the Owyhee, and he walks to
it whenever the streets are not drenched by rain. As he am-
bles along leisurely, he usually stops to chat with two or
three people on the way. Generally they are not notables.
More than likely they will be farmers or truck drivers or
the fruit vender from whom Mrs. Borah buys the pears and
peaches and apples that invariably top the table in the suite
at the Owyhee.

Idaho is large in area but not in population. It is still part
of the frontier. Snobbishness breeds hard in the wilderness.
The only believers in social distinctions are a few of the

ephemeral visitors at Sun Valley and a handful of their imitators in Boise. The most illustrious citizen in Idaho's history is in neither category. Borah would rather attend a Grange meeting than a lavish social function. He declines offers to go on remunerative lecture tours, yet seldom turns down an invitation to speak at an Idaho farm gathering.

Borah is a plain man who has achieved greatness in politics. The frontier clings to him more closely than do the accouterments of fame. He wears drab suits and shoestring ties. Generally his Stetson hat is too small for him. His long mane of hair reaches to the collar of his overcoat. His appearance as well as his philosophy goes back to the outpost era. As he strolls down one of Boise's tree-shaded avenues, he might be a lone survivor of the old Idaho when Indian war whoops and the hoofs of paint ponies still echoed in the dry river beds.

It is because of these things that William E. Borah has been returned to the United States Senate more than any other living man. His personal democracy, his heroic appearance and demeanor, his hatred of sham and sycophancy—these are the attributes which appeal to the wilderness State that has given him six consecutive Senatorial terms. Morton R. Stone, an engineer who helped lay the Milwaukee line through the Idaho mountains, once sagely observed that the State was doubtful of Borah's ideas but downright in sympathy with his personality. The pioneer and the argonaut like a man whom renown cannot spoil. They detest stiffness and formality. They admire determination and action. Borah fulfills all these demands. What matter, then, his opinions? It is how a mans stands rather than what he stands for that counts.

What do trappers in the Sawtooth Range and boatmen on the Snake River know about the World Court and States' rights and the sending of an ambassador to the Soviet Union?

But they do recognize a forthright Senator when they see him in action. The voters of Idaho are so devoted to Borah personally that they will accept utterances from him that might incite them to violence against some one else. In 1918 he condemned the espionage laws as drumhead government; he carried the State decisively that November. The same year Kate Richards O'Hare was forcibly thrown out of Twin Falls for saying almost the same thing.

When the senior Senator delivers an eloquent address on foreign affairs at the New Meadows Grange, his listeners are far from convinced that the League of Nations should be shunned like a rumbling volcano. What they are convinced of is that a man of such powerful oratory, firm convictions, and democratic behavior should represent Idaho in the United States Senate as long as he lives.

Despite his stern appearance and militant speeches, Borah is not a vindictive or angry man. He and his political foes get along fairly amicably. Borah seldom carries political grudges into personal and private life. He is essentially gentle and kind. There is nothing he likes better than to tell about the tenderness and humility of his good friend, the late Justice Holmes. Little children instantly claim his attention. Never a father himself, he is a sort of patron saint to many of the youngsters in Boise. He used to ride horseback along the town's byways. The children would time his coming and wait for him to jog past. Frequently he would dismount to sit with them, talking over Betty's broken dolly and Dickie's lost baseball bat. Some of Borah's friends say the fact he has no children is the great sorrow of his life.

This gentleness dominates much of the Senator's behavior. He has the oratorical equipment to blast unmercifully Senator James P. Pope, an outspoken New Dealer from Idaho, who has differed with Borah on numerous questions. Yet only once has he ever taken his perverse colleague to task—and then with a quip rather than a denunciation. Borah returned to Idaho in the summer of 1935, when Pope was issuing a series of indiscreet statements on the European situation. Most of the statements concerned Italian designs on Ethiopia. As Borah descended from his Pullman, a reporter sought his opinion on Pope's remarks.

Borah paused on the steps of the car. "If Senator Pope can avert war between Italy and Ethiopia," he observed wryly, "he is certainly entitled to a great deal of credit."

Personal bitterness is repugnant to Borah. He believes political animosities should stop at the forum edge. He had an opportunity to put this belief into practice when the President visited Idaho in the autumn of 1937. The trip came not long after the defeat of the savagely debated Court plan. Borah had helped prepare the report which condemned the President's scheme as violating "every sacred tradition of American democracy." On the bright September morning that Mr. Roosevelt drove into Capitol Square at Boise, the senior Senator stood on the platform with him. The galaxy of correspondents that had accompanied the President gasped and got out their pencils. Borah had assailed the Court bill ferociously. His speeches had played an important part in the failure of the proposal. Would he continue the battle now, nearly a continent removed from Capitol Hill? Was the President about to be rebuked in the hinterlands? The newspapermen waited intently.

Senator Borah stepped to the front of the platform. He looked about him. The greatest crowd in Idaho's history jammed the square. It would not even have been a big football audience in the East. But it was a magnificent effort for Idaho. Out of the valleys to the south and down from the mountains to the east had come the people who dwelt in the wilderness. Borah looked out over the faces of the men and women who six times had entrusted him with a Senator's commission. He glanced at the near-by trees filled with small boys who would read about him in future years. He turned toward Mr. Roosevelt. Then he looked at the crowd again.

"My friends and neighbors," the Senator said, "this is a wonderful day for our little town. Our great President has come."

-5-

Deo volente, William E. Borah can serve another two terms in the Senate. Then he will have been in the upper chamber longer than any man in the nation's history. What will he leave behind him if he does?

Borah is more widely known than any other American who has not occupied the White House. To the rest of the world he epitomizes statesmanship in the United States. Yet his record is largely one of dissent. Constructive achievement is almost totally absent. True, he assisted in such reforms as the direct election of Senators and the passage of the income-tax amendment; but he was not a leader, and the innovations would have taken place without him. La Follette drove through the Seamen's Act, and Norris sponsored the TVA. Borah, just as able as these illustrious Americans, can point to no such deeds.

Why? The main reason is Borah's contradictory philosophy—the philosophy that goes back to the Idaho of the frontier period. His suspicion of monopolies and business combines keeps him out of the banquet halls of the conservatives. His mistrust of bureaucracy and governmental tyranny impels him to loiter only on the extreme periphery of the camp of the progressives. With no set formula, with no specific remedy, he wanders a lonely course between the two battle lines. Amidst the complexities of modern civilization, he searches for a day that is long past.

Idaho has influenced Borah far more than Borah has influenced Idaho. The State has left on his mind the imprint of an outpost commonwealth in which neither corporations nor government restricted opportunity. That picture the Senator has never forgotten. He has had no such tangible effect on Idaho. For more than three decades the Gem State has been represented in Washington by a great man. Yet it is much the same as the commonwealths that have been represented by mediocrities. Borah has been one of the few truly notable Americans of the last half-century. But Idaho's political and social economy bears small evidence of his greatness. The State is like the rest of the Columbia River basin—a Promised Land that has yet to fulfill the hope and promise that it inspires.

Despite this lack of visible accomplishment, Borah has been a force for good. He has refused to take part in political manipulations. Scandal and dishonor have never touched him. There are many petty schemes the State's politicians might undertake were it not for his presence. He has been a constant threat to chicanery and falsehood. Even though he has not put his vast capacities to the work they might do, there is something magnificent and heroic about him. It is this magnificence and heroism that a frontier State has followed, when it did not know along what trail he led.

"The next few years belong to me," Borah once said at an Idaho political meeting. "Nobody but God Almighty can take them away from me; and during that period I am going to say precisely what I think, and advocate the policies in which I believe, regardless of the political consequences to the Republican party."

Against the range of distant hills, his maned head was resolute and powerful—like the head of a lion.

8. Beck—An American Phenomenon

ONLY the Far West could produce a labor leader like Dave Beck. None but an outpost region could give him the latitude and elbowroom for the activities that have made him the most unusual union boss in the country's history. There never has been a duplicate of this squat-shouldered, beefy-jowled teamster organizer who believes a primary function of labor is to show capital how to make a return on its investment.

"I run this place just like a business—just like the Standard Oil Company or the Northern Pacific Railway," said Beck to me, as he expansively waved a fat hand around his carefully appointed, dark-paneled office. "Our business is selling labor. We use businesslike methods. Business people have confidence in us."

Beck is obese and pudgy, a condition against which he is now directing an intensive course in physical training. He wears well tailored tweeds and Oxford grays, with shirts and ties carefully selected to match. His office is done in harmonious brown tones, and the fittings are rich and elegant. There is a heavy carpet on the floor. Beck keeps appointments meticulously and has subordinates who are crisp and efficient.

His enemies call him, among other names, a "labor racketeer." They claim he makes nearly five thousand dollars a week. His supporters contend not only that he is one of the most militant foes of Communism in the country, but also that he understands the problems of business and industry more thoroughly than many leading financiers.

"Some of the finest people I know are employers," says Beck frequently. "I realize that labor cannot prosper unless business men and invested capital are given reasonable and adequate protection."

Beck is an international organizer for the Teamsters' Union. He is also the chief strategist of the American Federation of Labor forces on the sunset side of the Mississippi River. On his domelike head and soft shoulders rest the hopes for A.F. of L. dominance in a region twenty times as large as England. William Green has given Beck *carte blanche* in the labor warfare being waged between the height of land and the Pacific coast. As Beck fares, so fares the A.F. of L. in the West. Green could have chosen no aide more formidable. Beck is resourceful, shrewd, and able. He combines tenacity with ruthlessness. He is never licked. He has been down many times, and always he has come struggling back. Leadership in his union he won through aggressiveness and determination. The same qualities enable him to maintain labor leadership along the fifteen-hundred-mile sweep of seaboard between Vancouver Island and the seas that break off San Pedro.

Some labor bosses coöperate with business and capital. Beck forms an alliance with them. His viewpoint is that of the business man. Not for many years has he looked at industrial questions from the perspective of the worker. He pooh-poohs the idea of referendums among the rank and file of the unions. What do laboring stiffs know about complex questions of union policy? How can truck drivers and eighteen-dollar-a-week grocery clerks decide jurisdictional problems and strike calls? What are a union's officers for, anyway? Billion-dollar corporations entrust decisions to their boards of directors. The stockholders delegate authority. Should not labor unions do the same thing?

Beck thinks in terms of business. He is versed in business folklore. He observes business mores. Labor, he believes, should assist business in making a profit. Capital investment, price stabilization, fair competition, reasonable returns—these are the terms in which Beck speaks. His forums are the American Legion, the Elks, the Chambers of Commerce, the Rotary clubs, and the realty boards. He advocates a policy of labor supervision of business management unique in the United States. Although only forty-two years old, he has extended this policy southward into the valleys of Oregon and eastward into the cattle country and sagebrush hills. Beck contends that labor should insure existing business a legitimate profit, even to the extent of forcing new competitors out of the community. Here is a typical statement by him on business in his city:

"There are too many filling stations in Seattle. More are threatened. We're going to close some of them. First, I advise promoters against starting new stations. If that doesn't work, the Teamsters' Union simply will refuse to serve them. They won't last very long."

Beck wants to rule benevolently like a Kublai Khan, but his benevolence prevails mainly when there is fresh in people's memories the fact that he can behave equally like Kublai's grandfather, the fierce and savage Genghis. The hard-slugging, swift-attacking "goon squad" of the Teamsters' Union is a legend as well as an accomplished fact throughout the Far West. Not many of Beck's foes escape knowledge of its merciless fury.

The members of the Newsboys' Union in Seattle rebelled against the despotism imposed upon them by the old-line leadership of the A.F. of L. The "goon squad" moved into the situation and went to work. The newsboys applied for a temporary injunction. Hearings lasted for twenty days before Judge James T. Ronald of the Superior Court of the State of Washington. Judge Ronald, in his opinion, while denying the application, gave an account of many of the facts. He said that newsboys actually had been dragged out of a meeting of the Central Labor Council and thrown down a steep flight of stairs. Crippled news vendors on street corners were beaten up by bruisers and plug-uglies armed with brass knuckles. Jaws were broken and faces smashed. A small, weak man was disfigured with marks the judge said "he will carry to his grave." Several of the thugs and bullies perpetrating these deeds made their getaway in a car bearing license plate A-95046, which Judge Ronald stated was registered in the name of the president of the Labor Council. No arrest or investigation was ever made. The judge said the treatment of the insurgent newsboys was "so shameless and disgraceful as to parallel the lawlessness witnessed at times in certain saloons in pioneer days.

"If such is unionism, which I am unwilling to believe," Judge Ronald warned, "then the world is witnessing the beginning of the end."

Not long ago Beck said, "We have passed the peak of misunderstanding between labor and capital." He prophesied that the way would soon be open for permanent and lasting peace. As he uttered these soothing words, his subordinates in Portland sent a new business agent out on the picket line. This recruit to teamster ranks was Leo Lomski, known in the prize ring as the "Aberdeen Assassin."

There have been labor bosses before who enjoyed brief reigns as political czars. Beck has not built his empire on so flimsy a foundation. He also is an economic overlord. Fickle changes at the ballot box do not shake his temple to the ground; it is supported by more than one pillar. Restricting competition, keeping up prices, and regulating business practices are essential features of Beck's technique. He knows more about many businesses in the Northwest than do the owners and managers themselves. Political reversals may deprive Beck of his influence with the police force and the sheriff's office, but they fail to break his economic grip. Beck has just sustained a crushing political defeat; yet his conquerors in the political sphere face a long, weary struggle to curtail, let alone eliminate, his economic dominance.

Most unions are concerned exclusively with wages, hours, and conditions of labor. Those along the Pacific slope controlled by Dave Beck have a wider variety of interests. Prices form a major worry. Here is a clause from a contract between the bakery truck drivers and their employers in Portland:

It is mutually understood by all parties of this agreement and agreed that in order to maintain the ability to pay the schedule of wages and hours specified in this agreement and otherwise perform the provisions of this agreement, *the employer must be able to obtain and maintain adequate prices for the bakery products sold, and the failure of the employer to obtain such prices will jeopardize the interests of the members of the union employed in the bakery industry* . . . and the members of Local 499 *agree to co-operate to the fullest extent with the employers to create and maintain the conditions herein specified, in order to maintain a stabilized condition at all times.**

The last phrase is a favorite with Beck. He continually insists that industry must be stabilized. This labor policy had its inevitable outcome when a joint committee of bakery owners and union officials agreed upon an increase in bread prices. A large, modernized establishment refused to comply with the order. New equipment and efficient methods enabled it to pay

* Italics mine.

the union scale and at the same time give the consumers lower prices. A picket line was flung around the place. The bakery could not move its products. Bread and pies mildewed on its shelves. There was no dispute as to wages or hours or union recognition. The charge for bread composed the whole issue. The concern could not make deliveries again until it acquiesced in the boost in prices. The real sufferers, of course, were the thousands of Oregon families who need bread and struggle along on inadequate finances.

-2-

The taxicab driver knew exactly where to go when I said I had an appointment with Dave Beck. The driver was a member of the Teamsters' Union and paid his dues in the modernistic new headquarters Dave has built out in the Seattle suburbs. He told me he had been employed on a bakery truck when Dave Beck came along and started organizing. The bakeries had pleaded they could not afford to raise wages to the union scale. So Dave investigated. He computed the number of bakeries in the city per potential customers. He surveyed the prices of raw materials and looked over books and bank accounts.

Pretty soon, the cab driver said, Dave knew more about coffee cake and hard rolls and Boston cream pie than the bakers themselves. Then he made a report. The bakeries, he announced, were not getting enough money for their goods. He also said there were sufficient bakeries in Seattle to supply the present consumer demand. If the bakeries would sign contracts with the unions Dave Beck would see to it that neither price cutters nor immediate new competition obtained men to drive their trucks. Without truck drivers, he pointed out, no shop could move its products. The bakeries, my cabby informant explained proudly, signed.

I thought over what the driver had told me, as I waited in a comfortable reception room to see the man whose claim it is that he has organized "everything on wheels," including automobile salesmen. Promptly at ten o'clock a statuesque, blonde secretary in a black dress and sheer stockings swung open the double doors leading to Dave Beck's office.

After we had shaken hands and the pleasantries were over, I related to the round-faced man behind the massive, ornate desk the story the cabby had told. "Is that the policy of labor in the Pacific Northwest?" I asked.

Dave Beck glanced impatiently at an electric clock. "Let me explain something to you, briefly," he said. "If you travel from here to Spokane by train, you pay the same fare, no matter which line you take. Is that right?"

I agreed it was.

Beck went on: "Now, let's see why that's so. The government regulates railroad rates. It doesn't permit each line to run berserk underbidding competitors for your business. If that were allowed, for how long do you think American trainmen would get the highest wages in the world? If fares between here and Spokane can be stabilized, why can't we apply the same principle to the prices charged for rye bread and chocolate pies?" Beck pounded the desk for emphasis as he said, "We recognize that labor cannot receive a fair wage from business unless business receives a just profit on its investment."

Across the desk from me, Beck started dictating a telegram to his secretary over an interoffice communication system. He snapped off the instrument and resumed our conversation. He told me that he ran the Teamsters' Union just like a big business.

And with that brief statement, uttered so vauntingly, I felt that I understood Dave Beck. I knew what made him tick. The most powerful A.F. of L. leader west of the Mississippi would like to be a business man.

Seattle accepts pretty much for granted the fact that Dave Beck is the quasi-economic dictator of the city, and generally its actual or potential political dictator. Many times the late Mayor John F. Dore admitted, "Union labor runs this town." The congressman from the Seattle district is a member of the Teamsters' Union. Washington's United States senator from Seattle was formerly the teamsters' attorney.

What do the business men of the Pacific Northwest think of this union leader?

The head of one of Seattle's important industries said: "I have dealt with labor union officials all over the country. Dave Beck is the only such official who ever showed any sympathy with the difficulties faced by the business man. He has never asked more than the traffic will bear. Most union leaders make all sorts of exorbitant demands, regardless of whether business can meet them. If Dave Beck makes a demand for higher wages for his men, he sits down with you and figures out how you can meet the increased pay roll. And let me tell you—he's a shrewd and canny business man. I'd make him my superintendent in a minute."

The proprietor of a big restaurant said Beck submitted a complete report showing the city's eating establishments what prices they had to charge to pay union wages. "That fellow knew everything about my place," the restaurant man declared. "He knew how much it cost to prepare each meat order. He knew how I could cut corners and reduce expenses. He knew as much about cooking as my chef."

The Seattle *Post-Intelligencer* is the newspaper which a stockade of Beck's teamster pickets helped to keep closed for more than one hundred days because it discharged two union sympathizers. Now, in the publisher's office at the *Post-Intelligencer* sits John Boettiger, son-in-law of the President of the United States. Boettiger is one of Dave Beck's most zealous boosters. "Seattle has better labor conditions than most other cities," Boettiger said. "Strikes are few and far between compared to other places, and Dave Beck sees to it that union contracts are inviolate. When he signs a contract, he keeps it. Employers know that, and they have confidence in him."

Arrayed actively against this shrewd and competent labor despot is a combination of conservatives and radicals. One of the conservatives is a woman who told me business in the Northwest was compromising all its principles by signing closed-shop agreements with Dave Beck. She and some of her society friends once had marched to the State capitol, carrying signs that blared, "Down With Beck-ism." The radicals declare that Beck's price-fixing agreements are a sock at the consumers. They also charge that Beck is only half-hearted in his support of the New Deal, despite the elegantly framed picture of the President on the wall of his office. Incidentally, the teamster boss is against a third term for Roosevelt.

Both segments of Beck's opposition felt the bitter wrath of Mayor Dore, who until his death was the closest ally of this extraordinary labor strategist. The women who carried their banners of protest down the Sound to the capitol at Olympia, the Mayor denounced as "perfumed, fur-clad hussies." Beck's C.I.O. adversaries, he threatened to send to "jail, a hospital, or the morgue."

The ever available assistance of Mayor Dore was a tribute to Dave Beck's persuasive powers and political wisdom. Dore was once a militant foe of labor. He promised the voters the Labor Temple would have nothing to say at the City Hall. Part of his legal practice was bringing injunction suits against

the Teamsters' Union. In 1932 Dore won office as a reactionary. He denounced the mildly liberal incumbent for permitting Communist demonstrations, and he promised that no
appointments would be dictated by organized labor. He reduced taxes and sliced the budget in half. When he was up
for reelection in 1934, the Seattle *Business Chronicle* called
on the "substantial elements of citizenship" to back him to
the limit. But Dore was beaten by a young man named Smith
who had been a star halfback at the State University. Smith's
administration was hilarious, if nothing else. His chief contribution was a series of weird contests to "put Seattle on the
map." He persuaded newsreel cameramen to photograph his
diaper-changing derby, in which a galaxy of prominent business men dashed fifty yards to a sawboard-trestle holding a
row of naked babies. The entrant who pinned on the diaper
first was the winner. There also was a "Put-Out-the-Cat" contest, the "Iceman's-Dash-for-a-Housewife's-Kiss" contest, and
similar occurrences. After two years Seattle had enough of
this type of statesmanship. It was ready for a change—and so
was John F. Dore. He had produced for the business men,
and they had failed him on election day. So he sought other
political clients. "I'm all through with business men," he said.
"I've had my fill of them." On the eve of the municipal election in the late winter of 1936, he turned to the Teamsters'
Hall, which once he had inferred was a den of racketeers and
terrorists. There he was received joyfully by Dave Beck. The
latter was just as eager to arrange terms with Dore's leading
opponent, a young attorney named Arthur B. Langlie. But
Langlie was the candidate of the New Order of Cincinnatus,
a group of young men advocating integrity and impartiality
in politics, and he refused Beck's invitation to a parley.

Beck recognized Dore as a man of his word. He had performed faithfully and ably for business. Now he would go

demeanor, that "You will be sorry if you take this beer," "You want to keep your place whole, don't you?"

John F. Dore is buried on one of Seattle's green hills, and Dave Beck was among the pallbearers who carried him on his last journey. The Mayor's tempestuous career has come to an end. Yet his complaint against Beck's union still officially pends in court—and his unprecedented praise and defense of Beck will long be remembered by the Northwest's people. No paradox so well epitomizes the fantastic political and economic sovereignty that Dave Beck fights for in the Columbia River basin.

-3-

The year before America entered the war was notable in Dave Beck's career, for two reasons. In 1916 he came into his majority and was able to vote; he also got a job driving a teetery old laundry truck over Seattle's steep streets. The next year he went to war, and was stationed with a navy air corps bombing squadron in the North Sea. He came back and drove the laundry truck again. But he did more than that. He looked into the laundry business. He decided there was more to labor unionism than merely demanding higher wages. The employer had to make enough profit to meet the pay increases.

Even while he was driving the laundry truck Dave Beck tried to study Pacific Northwest business and industry. He read the financial pages. In 1924 he was elected secretary of his union. A year later the teamsters held their national convention in Seattle, and Daniel Tobin, the drivers' elderly president, was impressed with the burly young man. He hired Beck as an international organizer.

Today Dave Beck is one of the Pacific coast's substantial citizens. He has been Seattle's boxing commissioner, a Civil Service commissioner, Exalted Ruler of the Elks, and a member of the State Parole Board. He and his wife and seventeen-year-old Dave, Jr., live in a comfortable home in the quiet Ravenna district and have a modest summer cottage on Bainbridge Island in Puget Sound.

Beck drives a large Lincoln automobile. His salary is $12,000 annually. The most traditional party of the year in the Northwest is "Dave Beck's Round-Up," held just before each Christmas at the exclusive Washington Athletic Club. It is attended by bankers, senators, state supreme court justices, congressmen, industrialists, and newspaper editors. Beck's liberal adversaries jestingly say, "Oh! Everyone is at Dave's 'Round-Up'—that is, everyone except working people." Beck is continually invited to speak to dignified luncheon clubs and staid commercial groups. Invariably he amazes his listeners with his genuine understanding of business and finance.

Thoroughness and efficiency are Beck's standards, whether in the conference room or on the picket line. Not long ago he felt the teamsters' jurisdictional sovereignty was threatened by the raids of other unions. He announced that three thousand of the West's sturdiest truck drivers would start at once taking lessons in boxing, wrestling, and jujitsu. Some new teamsters' business agents were hired; many of them boasted formidable records as prize fighters.

The distinguishing feature of this unusual labor leader is his admiration and knowledge of business—and business's confidence in him. "That fellow may have been only a laundry truck driver," said one of the newspaper correspondents on President Roosevelt's train last autumn who interviewed

Beck, "but he sounded to me like the dean of the Harvard School of Business Administration!"

"We aren't looking for a fight," said Beck when he revealed that his most muscular teamsters were about to receive instructions in pugilism. "The idea isn't to make our young men handy with their 'dukes.' We simply want to build a big, strong union."

And Beck has a big, strong union—one of the biggest and strongest in the United States. In the Northwest it wields what occasionally amounts to absolute power. On each such occasion it demonstrates that the A.F. of L. has chosen its most tenacious, resourceful, and ruthless leader to hold the Pacific seaboard against the sallies of the C.I.O.

For many years a bitter internecine labor struggle has been waged between the teamsters and the brewery workers. Each has claimed jurisdiction over the men who drive beer trucks. A stalemate had lasted for a decade, until Dave Beck finally broke it. He announced that if the teamsters could not deliver beer throughout the rest of the country, then the brewery workers could not brew it in the Columbia River basin. Henceforth, he said, teamsters would perform that function. So the truck drivers' union took over the brewery workers in the Northwest. The "white label" of the teamsters became a necessary passport before any beer could slide down thirsty throats in the vast Columbia River country. An impenetrable boycott was slapped on the "red-label beer" produced elsewhere in the nation by bona fide brewery workers.

Beer from the East came into the Northwest on freight trains and was unloaded in warehouses. There it fermented and gathered dust and age. Beck's truck drivers would not move it. Federal courts in Tacoma and Portland ordered them to lift the embargo, but the injunctions were ignored.

The "goon squad" appeared to exercise greater sovereignty than the government of the United States. All the beer consumed in the Columbia basin was produced by the breweries in that region—breweries where both the brewery workers and the beer deliverers came under the jurisdiction of Dave Beck. A few taverns and honky-tonks with more temerity than judgment insisted on selling red-label beer still on hand. The "goon squad" grimly arrived and dumped the boycotted brew in the gutter. "Terrorism stalks," deplored the *Oregonian;* but the embargo accomplished its purpose. After years of battling the teamsters on even terms, the brewery workers had been conquered on one sector by the pudgy labor boss of the cities and hinterlands of the Northwest.

The belligerent longshoremen and timber workers, traditional enemies of Beck's capitalistically inclined unionism, met defiantly and proclaimed they would not drink teamster-union beer. Only red-label brew, made by the brewery workers, could quench their thirsts. The ultimatum was delivered to Beck in his lavish citadel. He laughed softly. "They'll either drink Beck's beer or they'll go a hell of a long way for a drink," his office announced.

The longshoremen and timber workers drank Dave Beck's beer.

Transportation is the key to industry, particularly in a region of deep harbors and vast distances like the Far West. This has given Beck a measure of power and control far beyond that possessed by the ordinary union boss. In the great and spacious Promised Land of the Columbia basin, he has unlimited scope for the strategic boycotts and shrewd maneuvers that have made him a figure of almost legendary omnipotence. It required sit-down strikes and a sympathetic governor at Lansing to compel General Motors to bargain with the C.I.O. In much simpler fashion were the automobile manufacturers quelled by Dave Beck. He did not like the way automobiles were being caravaned west to save railroad tariffs. He said men got only one dollar a day for driving the new cars across the country, and then were dumped onto the labor market in Seattle and other Northwest cities. Those men should be unionized, he said. He also claimed that the licenses of the drivers did not correspond with the engine numbers. Teamster pickets closed down automobile agencies selling cars wheeled westward by nonunion drivers, and the Seattle city administration ordered the moot automobiles impounded. "That ends the caravans coming into Seattle," announced Beck. The announcement was final.

In keeping with the eccentricity of Northwest politics, it is the business men who look most kindly upon this czar who rules from the truck drivers' modernistic headquarters. Beck is a dictator, but to the business men he is an understanding one. He helps them maintain high prices, and little sympathy is wasted on the consumers chewed up in the jaws of this situation. Beck can tell a caterer why he should get fifteen cents more for an order of pigs' knuckles and sauerkraut, and he can explain to a barber why haircuts should be sixty cents instead of half a dollar. "Organize the Boss" is Beck's maxim. It is the employers, rather than the employees, whom he impresses with the wisdom and advantage of "signing up." The business men have implicit confidence in him, and he reciprocates this trust. Although closed-shop Seattle pays higher wages than open-shop Los Angeles, the business men along Puget Sound are not disturbed. Many of them approve enthusiastically. Price increases have more than taken care of the wage rise, and the teamsters—by violence and threats and refusals to truck—keep out price-cutting competition. The *Business Chronicle* reported that in 1936, Seattle's index number for living costs was 144.4 as compared with 138.4 and

135.5, respectively, in the considerably larger cities of Los Angeles and San Francisco.

With this condition business in Seattle has been fairly content. The real victims have been the middle-class consumers whose incomes remain nearly static. In most American communities capital and labor are at each other's throats; in Seattle, the most thoroughly unionized community of all, they are stanch allies. The late Mayor Dore was not far from the truth when he said: "Seattle is 95 per cent unionized. Big business in the city is satisfied, and it wants it to remain that way." Listen to the analysis made by the editor of a conservative weekly periodical, Harold D. Chadwick of the reliable *Argus*:

There is considerable merit to Beck's argument that employers are just as much responsible as he is for the conditions which put trucking, laundry, brewing, cleaning and dyeing, dairy and baking industries completely under his dictatorship. The same is true of auto repairing. Beck's pluguglies will not permit chiseling in any of these industries. They will not permit new competition to enter the field. They maintain prices at levels that are satisfactory to the bosses. And the bosses, no matter what they say in indignation meetings, are very happy about the situation. Therefore, they, more than Beck, are the racketeers.

So far as business relationships and problems are concerned, the average labor leader is a total loss. Business is a field far from his domain; in business dealings he is about as drab and listless as a suit of long underwear. Beck is the reverse of this rule. He is more competent and alert than the business men themselves. For efficiency, his research department obscures the Better Business outfits. Some oil companies told him they could not afford to pay their drivers the union scale. The Teamsters' Union ordered its statisticians and accountants to investigate. They reported back to Beck that the oil companies were paying unjustifiably high rents for their filling stations. The pudgy labor boss helped straighten out the situation.

The trade associations and union-employer organizations formed in the Northwest are sardonically referred to as "Dave Beck's voluntary NRA." The ironic title is not entirely inappropriate. Beck believes that indiscriminate price cutting and chiseling are sure routes to business chaos. His methods may be a combination of those of Genghis and Kublai Khan, but his philosophy is that of Hugh S. Johnson. He believes that any price war ultimately is fought with the wages of the workers in that particular industry. His technique is to warn the plants and establishments hacking away at the price structure that they cannot get any more trucking. Not long ago, in discussing breweries undercutting the price of beer, he said: "We are going to those breweries that are lowering prices and forcing everybody else to do the same and tell them we won't let our men work for them. We say to them that if they want to go on like that, it is all right but we won't work for them."

"Dave Beck's voluntary NRA" operates in unique fashion. The cleaning and dyeing industry in Seattle has been corralled into an association headed by William Short, one of Beck's allies who formerly was president of the Washington State Federation of Labor. "Dues" are 1 per cent of the retail volume of each establishment, or 3 per cent of the wholesale volume. "Make checks payable to W. M. Short, administrator," admonish the payment blanks. The "dues" are pungled up every week and are based upon the gross volume of business. The *News* published by the left-wing Washington Commonwealth Federation contends that although the wages of the workers in the cleaning and dyeing industry have been reduced as much as 30 per cent in past years, the association has geared up Seattle cleaning prices until they are the highest in the nation.

Various food concerns in this region which the President of the United States regards as America's Promised Land cannot put a Bakers' Union label on their products unless they join the Washington State Bakers' Association. Without a Bakers' Union label, the teamsters will not make deliveries, and merchandise will rot and spoil. The wife of the owner of a macaroni factory alleged to the *News* that her husband paid more than $400 a month for good standing in the association.

"What does the association do for you in return for your dues?" the owner himself was later asked.

"We are protected from price cutting on the part of other companies."

"What would happen to you if you failed to pay your association dues and dropped from membership?"

The macaroni manufacturer's reply came swiftly. "Well, we have never tried that."

The Bakers' Association makes no bones about collecting a percentage of the industry's receipts and issuing labels to the various firms. It insists that these practices are perfectly legal.

Housewives scrimping to make thin wallets nourish plump children know nothing about legality. But they do know about exorbitant prices.

-*4*-

I have a letter from one of the organizers of a law and order league ostensibly formed to combat labor violence in the Northwest. He writes: "While Dave Beck's leadership has been responsible for the growth of the closed shop in Seattle, he should not be confused with such Communist leadership as that of Bridges.* There is nothing Communistic or radical about him. His success with employers is due to the fact that he makes the best agreement that he can and then sees that it is kept."

From the perspective a large segment of the region's employers looks at the beefy boss of the truck drivers. Beck speaks continually against Communism. He is always willing to appear at an American Legion meeting or Junior Chamber of Commerce luncheon and wave the flag. Sitdown strikes are his *bête noire;* he also is wary of even ordinary strikes, and brags that the forty thousand teamsters in the Northwest have seldom had a strike lasting more than five days. He boasts about the time in 1932 that he persuaded the laundry truck drivers to meet the depression by reducing their contract wage from forty dollars to thirty dollars a week. An able, earnest, and convincing speaker, Beck's frequent public appearances win him friends and ameliorate differences. The trade associations become minor evils, indeed, when contrasted in the business mind with the ominous specter of Communism. To many business men "Dave Beck's voluntary NRA" has meant welcome stability. It also has meant bargaining with labor spokesmen who keep agreements and understand business problems. This seems an industrial Elysium compared to the mutterings about working-class solidarity and production-for-use that come in on the breezes that blow from the woods and waterfront.

Beck is widely regarded in the Northwest as the principal barrier separating industry from the C.I.O. Many business men believe that his elimination from the labor amphitheater would leave the arena as wide open as a moat to the radicals in the trade-union movement. They pray that his defenses are

* Harry Bridges, head of the Longshoremen's Union and C.I.O. chairman in the West. (See Chapters 9 and 10.)

sturdy, and that his bastions will hold. Beck has approved the labor relations program of the Chamber of Commerce, and he has said, "Labor is working in very close harmony with the industrial organizations in Seattle." Why teeter this delicately balanced arrangement? Why take a chance that the devil-may-care timber and maritime workers may replace the substantial labor forces led by Beck? In the recent city elections the *Argus*, the most dependable interpreter of the attitude of business and industry, supported not young Mr. Langlie, the conservative candidate promising impartiality to both labor organizations but subservience to neither, but Mayor Dore, the unequivocal adherent of Beck and the A.F. of L. "Langlie has openly declared that he will make Seattle an open labor town and allow the Lewis and Bridges elements to enter unhampered," the *Argus* warned. "That would promptly result in a new period of labor turmoil and in the undoing of all the progress that has been accomplished by civic bodies, the employers, and the Labor Temple in creating harmony and economic coöperation in Seattle."

Langlie had a different conception of harmony. "One of the principal reasons for the increase in living costs in the past two years," he said, "has been the combinations effected between certain businesses and certain labor czars. They have through such combinations prevented competition and have succeeded in increasing prices of household necessities to the extent that the average housekeeper was made to suffer." Langlie was elected overwhelmingly, a success assured by the schism in the labor forces. However, it is far from certain the new mayor will be able to break up the combinations he thus denounced. The mayor of near-by Portland bombastically berates labor extremism, but lolled complacently at the City Hall while a teamster picket line "stabilized" the price of bread. Langlie will try to make performance dovetail with his promises; that is certain. He is honest and reliable, with a strain of Swedish perseverance. The New Order of Cincinnatus, which was his original political sponsor, places its principal emphasis on political decency, morality, and integrity.

As these words are written, three A.F. of L. teamsters are on trial in Seattle for allegedly beating up the owner-drivers of a C.I.O. coal yard. The arrests were part of Langlie's law-and-order policy. Since they occurred, Dave Beck has been gingerly hinting that perhaps the two labor factions should unite at least for political action. The burly teamster boss still detests the labor radicals and their leader, Harry Bridges. His psychology is that of the business man and not that of the proletarian. But he is realistic and shrewd, and he seems to realize that the national A.F. of L. program of preferring even law-and-order zealots to pro-C.I.O. laborites may mean, ultimately, the hamstringing of both labor groups. The methods by which the A.F. of L. seeks to destroy the C.I.O. are methods by which the A.F. of L. itself some day may be destroyed. Does Beck think this? Perhaps he does. One of his partisans said to me, "Dave doesn't believe in compromise, but neither does he believe in suicide."

The election of Arthur Langlie as mayor of Seattle was a blow to the prestige of the handsome, broad-shouldered man who is Dave Beck's most celebrated ally: John Boettiger, the husband of Anna Roosevelt Dall.

When Boettiger arrived in Seattle to become resident publisher of the Hearst *Post-Intelligencer*, he found Beck and Mayor Dore zooming along triumphantly. He cagily put in with them. Outright backing for the "voluntary NRA" he avoided, but the *Post-Intelligencer's* financial editor wrote a series of articles attempting to prove that labor conditions were more satisfactory in Seattle than in many other American cities. "Myth Refuted," one of the articles was empirically headlined, in discussing the city's reputation as a place of labor strife. Boettiger also published a full-page essay by an advertising agency, the general theme of which was that Seattle is really a "model industrial community." In all these episodes Boettiger refrained from crossing the Rubicon. He did not endorse Beck and Dore in so many words, but gave the implication that Seattle had a splendid and healthy industrial climate—all the while that Beck sat in Teamsters' Hall, and Dore sat in the City Hall and said, "Union labor runs this town." When Beck gave unqualified sanction to the labor relations plan of the Chamber of Commerce, the *Business Chronicle* scathingly referred to the "strange alliance between the Seattle Chamber of Commerce and Dave Beck, highly approved in editorials and public speeches by John Boettiger." And Franklyn Waltman wrote in the Washington *Post*, "Dave Beck and John Boettiger have become great friends and consultants." *Time*'s new picture magazine, *Life*, published a photograph of Beck and Boettiger warmly shaking hands, and contended, "Beck can and does instantly shut down any balking businessman or unwelcome competitor, by picketing or by stopping truck deliveries."

"Conditions are as near perfect as they could be anywhere," Boettiger wrote lyrically about Seattle not long after reaching the Northwest's Promised Land. Even as he published these words under his own name, country newspapers back in the hinterlands were discussing Seattle editorially under such titles as "A Leper Among Cities," "Seattle Wrecked," and "The Shame of Seattle." Boettiger's formula for putting Seattle over the top was for its citizens to become boosters. Here is what the President's son-in-law counseled:

"Can we become a city of boosters, imbued with the sort of spirit that would make all of us say, 'Seattle is MY town and I'm going to FIGHT for it!' "

The election of Langlie was an indication that the voters did not regard this ebullient advice as Seattle's password to the new Canaan. Langlie in his campaign attacked the partiality of the city administration for the A.F. of L. over the C.I.O. and insisted on neutrality as between the rival factions. He assailed racketeering, intimidation, coercion, and violence in the ranks of labor, and said the unions had to clean house. The people accepted this thirty-eight-year-old conservative's version of labor conditions in Seattle, rather than the *Post-Intelligencer's* fantasy of a "model industrial community."

Boettiger has been in frequent skirmishes with the National Labor Relations Board because of his refusals to bargain with the American Newspaper Guild. Each time he appears before the board, some of Seattle's citizens muse on the curious fact that he is the son-in-law of the most important advocate of collective bargaining in the nation's history. The *Post-Intelligencer's* financial editor admitted that he had discussed with Dave Beck the possibility of chartering a rival union to the Guild. Boettiger has been charged with discriminatory firings, and an organizer for the C.I.O. lumberjacks said he had encountered some hardboiled employers in the woods, but wrote in the *Timber Worker* that a new kind to him was the son-in-law of the great New Deal President of the United States. Drew Pearson and Robert S. Allen declared in their "Washington Merry-Go-Round" column: "One of the first things which John Boettiger did when he became publisher of the *Post-Intelligencer* was to form a friendship with Dave Beck. Some say it was the other way around, and that Dave Beck decided to take the President's son-in-law into camp. In either case, the two are now boon companions and apparently it pays." The *Guild Reporter* recently claimed that dispatches by Westbrook Pegler on Beck and the labor movement in the West were omitted and distorted in Boettiger's paper. The

Seattle newspapers were strangely silent on the hearing of the *Post-Intelligencer* before the Labor board. The silence also extended to the *Post-Intelligencer*.

Boettiger praises his illustrious relative with glittering phrases. Yet he is scarcely even perfunctory in support of the New Deal's reforms. He calls the President "the most idolized living American," but did not back up "the most idolized living American" and Secretary Ickes in a controversy with the State of Washington administration over the size of the new Olympic National Park. Instead, he attacked Ickes for the pugnacity of his methods. This episode emphasized that the Boettigers' affinity with the New Deal is a matter of kinship rather than conviction. Ickes was demanding that protection of the forests be the primary consideration in establishing the new park. The State administration was thinking in terms of timber revenue. Boettiger counseled Ickes to have an open mind on the question. He said the Secretary's outbursts were not settling the issue. Then Ickes decided to see the Olympic peninsula for himself. Who else for him and his bride to stop with in Seattle except the relatives of the President? "Secretary Ickes—Welcome Visitor," the *Post-Intelligencer* now editorialized. Apparently entertaining Ickes was one thing; supporting his application of New Deal conservation ideas to the Washington woodlands was another. The Boettigers have shown a parallel attitude in regard to the Newspaper Guild. No one is more welcome in their home than the President's wife. But members of the Guild contend that when Mrs. Roosevelt joined the organization, the Associated Press story of the event was not published in the *Post-Intelligencer*. Upon being invited to emulate her mother's act, Mrs. Boettiger said she knew nothing about the Guild, and as the wife of the publisher was reluctant to take any action that might be hostile to the policy of the paper. The Guild also was involved in a controversy between Boettiger and the political editor of the *Post-Intelligencer*, Lester Hunt. The President's son-in-law pulled Hunt off a story in which he seemed to be sympathetic to plans for a special session of the legislature to consider New Deal legislation. Hunt, hitherto a strong neutral in the editorial office, immediately joined the Guild.

The people who take exception to these occurrences also criticize members of Mr. Roosevelt's family for working for the newspaper publisher who smeared the President so unscrupulously in the 1936 campaign. Tousle-haired Howard Costigan, able young secretary of the Washington Commonwealth Federation, one of the most effective New Deal political organizations in the Northwest, told me he wished the President's son-in-law could definitely be classified among the President's adherents.

It is scarcely surprising that Boettiger is not as enthusiastic as he might be in his attitude toward the New Deal. Prior to his marriage to Anna Roosevelt Dall, he was on the Washington staff of the Chicago *Tribune*. For that newspaper he fashioned some bitter criticism of the Roosevelt administration. As early as 1934 he wrote that the New Deal "has shown slim results." He also noted that the *Literary Digest* poll *(sic)* showed the President's policies slipping in popular favor. Mrs. Charles H. Sabin of the Liberty League was described by Boettiger as "one of the few genuinely feminine women to achieve public and political prominence." Is it significant that Boettiger's future mother-in-law was not included in this euphemistic laudation? When a prominent Republican savagely condemned a speech by the President, Boettiger called the act "a show of courage." He said the New Deal's recognition of Russia was a grotesque failure, and contended the New Dealers wanted Congress composed of "members pledged slavishly to support the President."

Now, as the son-in-law of Mr. Roosevelt, Boettiger is not moved to ecstasy by the New Deal. He seems to be less emotionally susceptible than when he was attacking the administration for the *Tribune*. In the summer of 1934 a Republican meeting in Michigan brought from him this effort:

Eighty years ago today staunch sons of America rallied stubbornly beneath a cluster of oaks in this city and calling themselves for the first time Republicans, launched a struggle against slavery. Now these oaks are greater and stronger and higher, and today under their protective branches another group of Republicans, far outnumbering those pioneers of 1854, and coming from all over the country, called for a rebirth of their party and for a revival of the historic struggle against slavery.

But today it is not the enslavery of blacks that brought the fiery words of challenge from the lips of the Republicans. They battled what they called an effort to enslave the people under a New Deal, which they said gave promise only of regimentation and slavery, in fields, in shops, and in homes all over the land. They saw Americans spitted on the experimental irons of the brain trust of Washington. . . . The great oaks seeming to symbolize the strength of the country which the Republican Party has helped often to nourish, in all their strong majesty echoed the speakers' cries for a return to government under the Constitution of the United States.

A year after he wrote this Republican Party odyssey, Boettiger married the President's daughter.* The *Tribune* proudly confided, "The approaching marriage was known to the *Tribune* which preserved the secret at Boettiger's request."

Both Boettiger and his wife are in the employ of Hearst, and are occasionally entertained by the publisher who inferred the President was a Communist ally in the 1936 cam-

---

* Boettiger as well as Mrs. Dall had been married before. His divorced wife, Mrs. Alice Boettiger, lives in Winnetka, Illinois.

paign. Mrs. Boettiger edits the "Homemaker" section of the *Post-Intelligencer*. She and her husband are not particularly popular in Seattle, and have made little effort to crash the precincts of local society. They live in an unpretentious frame house, and overlook few opportunities to travel off to see the President. Whenever Mr. Roosevelt is in the Far West, they are conspicuously at his side. They were the subject of a loud guffaw throughout the State when Congressmen John Coffee childishly boasted that the presence of the President's daughter was undoubtedly somewhat responsible for the great chunks of Federal money allotted for such Washington projects as Grand Coulee Dam and the Bonneville transmission system.

Boettiger and his wife are extremely conscious of the kinship that makes them not as ordinary people. Under his own name the publisher of the *Post-Intelligencer* writes pontifically about matters that concern the Northwest. He gives his readers scant chance to forget he is related to the President. In appraising the State's chances, for example, of having a National Park established on the timbered Olympic Peninsula, he did not neglect to mention what was said on the subject by "President Roosevelt, during his visit here." Of course, during that visit the President was sequestered at the tree-shaded home of Mr. John Boettiger. Under the gay title of "Happy Days Are Here Again," Boettiger recently surveyed business conditions. He could not deny that he was in close contact with the President:

"We aver that our opinions are based upon broad observations. . . . But we can't dney that we are also influenced by the calm confidence of the President. He isn't selling the country short, and neither are we."

Nor does Mrs. Boettiger hesitate to allude to her distinguished family connections. "Imagine my happiness," she wrote not long ago in the women's department of the *Post-Intelligencer*, "when my mother told me that she would be delighted to be the guest of honor at the meeting being held this afternoon in the Civic Auditorium!" And after the President's wife had departed for the East, her daughter sighed for the benefit of Mr. Hearst's Seattle readers: "Somehow or other this week seems a bit dullish after the excitement of my mother's visit. . . . And, on the way to the airport to catch her plane for Moscow, Idaho, we were already making plans for her next trip. May it be soon!" Mrs. Boettiger also wrote in detail about her trip eastward with her husband to be a bridesmaid at the wedding of her brother John. Her by-line in the *Post-Intelligencer* is Anna Roosevelt Boettiger, and so no one forgets that she is not merely the wife of a resident Hearst publisher who once wrote anti-New-Deal dispatches for the Chicago *Tribune*. Her husband's salary from Hearst is credibly put at about $37,000 annually.

President Roosevelt himself takes an interest in the *Post-Intelligencer*. It is probably the only enterprise in the country at outs with the Labor Board on which the President looks favorably. On the paper's seventy-fifth anniversary, he sent a letter beginning "Dear John" to the son-in-law who had been with the publication about eighteen months of those seventy-five years. "The seventy-fifth anniversary of the *Post-Intelligencer*," wrote Mr. Roosevelt of the newspaper that had assailed him so bitterly in the 1936 campaign, "is an event of interest not only in the life of the community of Seattle but in American newspaperdom." Another newspaper in the Northwest wanting a similar letter was informed that "any communications and statements which he [the President] makes to the press, he makes to all—treating the press collectively and on a basis of strict impartiality or parity." The condemnation that has followed such happenings as this is perhaps why, in recent weeks, the *Post-Intelligencer* has shown a slightly increasing sympathy with the policies of the President.

The Boettigers had an opportunity, when they first arrived from the East and settled down in the Northwest's Promised Land, to become the foremost family of the region. They were on a frontier where Mr. Roosevelt is more genuinely popular than anywhere else in the country. Boettiger himself makes an impressive appearance, and his wife has some of the charm that has made her mother universally admired. Yet that opportunity they muffed. They began to bungle it the night Boettiger was photographed at a banquet with great *joie de vivre* in the company of Dave Beck and Mayor Dore, and when the *Post-Intelligencer* heralded as a "model industrial community" a city in which a pudgy labor boss could unsmilingly proclaim:

"There are too many filling stations in Seattle. More are threatened. We're going to close some of them. First, I advise promoters against starting new stations. If that doesn't work, the Teamsters' Union simply will refuse to serve them. They won't last very long."

-5-

The city and region where Dave Beck has become America's most extraordinary labor leader are a new part of the country. On a journey to the United States in the eighties, a round-faced, young Englishman named Rudyard Kipling was impressed in the East by a highly developed civilization but in the Northwest by an expansive wilderness. Arthur Langlie, Seattle's new mayor, believes that this time-lag between the regions is largely responsible for the events that have created

an unprecedented labor situation. As the Northwest matures
and comes of age, he thinks its industrial pattern will conform
more closely to the national weave.

Only the passage of at least a generation can test the truth
of this analysis. At present the former laundry driver who
now is squishy-muscled from long years of comparative inactivity is the No. 1 labor phenomenon of the nation. Beck takes
almost for granted the sovereignty that his union exercises
over the economic functions of the vast Columbia River basin.
"It has been charged," he said a few months ago, "that labor
is operating a racket in the milk industry."

And then, self-righteously, "Why, if we let milk come into
the Seattle market without restriction every dairy in Seattle
would be bankrupt in two weeks."

Some of the police power of the State is exercised and the
business supervisory work of the commercial associations is
performed along the continent's sundown rim by the Teamsters' Union. Beck and his aides halted automobile shipments
of citrus fruit being hauled northward along the coast. The
drivers of the caravans worked only for eating money. "Railroads and responsible trucking companies couldn't meet such
competition, so we put a stop to it," said Beck. "Was that
racketeering? Why, we were doing work that properly belongs to the Chamber of Commerce."

This kingly attitude of self-conferred omnipotence has led
to some strange conclusions. A galaxy of teamster business
agents, secretaries, muscle men, stooges, and "goons" are in
county jails and rural lockups in the State of Oregon. Scattered all through the picturesque Willamette Valley, from
Portland south into the orchard area, dozens of truck drivers
and their allies have been arrested. The revelations from this
wholesale round-up have been interesting. Al Rosser, the
boss of the teamsters in Oregon and the *ex officio* overlord of

the labor movement in that State, was never elected by his subjects. Beck merely appointed him, like a hinterland Mussolini sending one of his marshals to rule a subjugated territory. Ben Osborne, the liberal head of the State Federation of Labor, could do nothing to restrain Rosser's activities. The elective officers of Oregon's teamsters proved to be the flimsiest sort of figureheads. The president of a big truck drivers' local testified, "I did Rosser's bidding at all times, without question and without explanation." Many of the so-called "goons" * have received prison sentences, and today Rosser himself sits in jail in the tiny backwoods town of Dallas, where he was jolted with a conviction for arson in connection with the burning of a lumberyard.

There were other corollary exposures. A peek at teamster records showed payments to the Federal Laboratories for tear-gas equipment. Among the "goons" arrested was a select assortment of prize fighters; these men did not belong to the Teamsters' Union, but were given ten dollars a day and a button showing "dues paid" when there was picket duty to be done. Several alleged "goons" turned out to be leaders in a lofty-sounding organization known as "Americans, Incorporated." The main objective of this outfit has been the red-baiting of anyone slightly liberal. Each week it issues a sort of frontier *index expurgatorius* of alleged subversive influences. Included in the forces thus ferreted out have been the *Oregonian*, the traditionally Republican newspaper of the Far West, and Mrs. Nan Wood Honeyman, a gray-haired, aristo-

---

* The origin of the term "goon" is obscure, although from Puget Sound to Mexico it is the common designation for teamster picket patrols. The Oregon City *Enterprise* thinks the term is really "goop." Another newspaper contends it is a corruption of "gooney." The word first was used in Seattle by Beck's left-wing and Communist adversaries. They took it from the *Popeye the Sailor* comic strip, in which the "goon" is a weird and terrible monster from another planet. Jim Marshall of *Collier's* thinks the term belongs in the next dictionary of the American language.

cratic member of a wealthy and socially élite Portland family
who represents her district with distinction in Congress! Of
course, any alleged "goons" active in Americans, Incorporated,
affirm their solemn devotion to law and order.

Such facts as these have damaged the whole labor movement in the Northwest. They have given public officials in-
discriminately opposed to all unions a whip to crack at will.
The great majority of labor organizations watched disapprov-
ingly as the teamsters committed their depredations. The
rank and file of the truck drivers resented what was taking
place. There were no protests because no one dared venture
them. In the Portland *News-Telegram* a reporter wrote, "It
is no secret in labor circles that Dave Beck of Seattle and Al
Rosser have held a 'goondoggling' dictatorship over the local
labor movement for a number of years. It also is no secret
that legitimate unionists have been actually afraid to challenge that dominance for fear of retaliation on themselves."
The groups and individuals hostile to any form of labor activity are using the "goon squad" revelations to impel the
adoption of laws that would reduce the unions to a virtual
nullity. There is a chance the effort may succeed. If it does,
a little coterie of tyrannical union bosses will have been responsible for setting back the labor movement in the Northwest a quarter of a century.

Beck was never connected with the beat-ups, bombings, and
other outrages in Oregon; but they were largely perpetrated
by men responsible to him, and they apparently induced Dan
Tobin to proclaim in warning at a Western conference of the
truck drivers: "If you associate with characters that are not
law-abiding and that commit crime and are shady or near-
racketeers, we advise you now to look out, watch your step,
because one of these days you are going to get caught and

when you do, we warn you now it is no use coming to us to help you."

The opponents of Beck, especially those who direct their fusillade from the left, lose no opportunity to claim he is through. This prophecy is premised more on wish than on observation. Political and economic influence of great dimensions, the blue-eyed, raspy-voiced teamster leader still wields. The late Mayor Dore ran close behind the C.I.O. candidate in the recent Seattle elections, and all his votes were personally delivered by Beck. The mayor lay wanly in a hospital throughout the campaign, and to most people he was a man on whom the mark of the grave had already been stamped. The strength that Beck was able to place behind an invalid will not soon be forgotten by politicians with their eye on the main chance.

All the attacks against Beck have not been effective. His foes contend that he makes fabulous sums of money. This charge generally proves a dud. Is it not directed at all labor leaders, whether they be a Beck extolling big business or a Bridges fraternizing with the Communists? Always, Beck answers: "What does anyone think I possess in influence with the Federal government that it can't check on me? You can see the records of the Internal Revenue Department any time you want." This reply has seemed logical, and there has been no refutation of it. Beck's left-wing foes have not been conspicuously consistent. His capitalistic tendencies that now make them shiver for the fate of democracy, they overlooked when he collaborated in their schemes. In the autumn of 1936 he helped them shut down the *Post-Intelligencer*. His teamsters were part of the living battlement that closed the newspaper and subsequently brought about the cross-country hegira of the Boettigers. Then, the Communists were Beck's eager allies. A short time later the big schism occurred between the A.F. of L. and the C.I.O. The Communists suddenly discovered that Dave Beck was really a sinister Fascist. They revealed that the totalitarian state was brought closer by his concept of "Organizing the Boss," his economic supervision of competition and prices, his indifference to rank-and-file stirrings and to union referendums. Yet all these manifestations were clearly evident when Beck and the left-wingers worked together to barricade Mr. Hearst out of Seattle, and when Beck's obedient servant, Mayor Dore, was saying, "I don't care now if the *Post-Intelligencer* ever publishes, and I think it would be a good thing for the town if it didn't."

Erwin D. Canham of the *Christian Science Monitor* thinks Dave Beck is a tremendously significant portent, "a cloud already a whole lot bigger than a man's hand." The other newspaper correspondents who traveled westward with the President were practically unanimous in agreeing that the most remarkable phenomena observed on the six-thousand-mile transcontinental journey were not the geysers of Yellowstone Park nor the giant dams at Grand Coulee and Bonneville but the burly teamster in Seattle and his lithe adversary from the waterfront, Harry Bridges.

Do Dave Beck and his economic edicts about milk, filling stations, Boston cream pies, citrus fruits, beer, and automobile caravans really represent the portent of which Canham spoke? Does he indicate a national trend? Will he continue as the most extraordinary and influential individual in the Promised Land of the American West? These questions cannot be answered until there has been some analysis of the jaunty little Australian who strolls cockily along the docks of the Pacific coast, and who in practically all particulars is the diametric opposite of Dave Beck.

9. Bridges—Thunder on the Waterfront

ONE bleak afternoon a generation ago a storm with the wrath of the Furies caught the ketch *Val Marie* off Australia's barren Ninety-Mile beach. The little ship struggled and twisted like a swimmer with the prescience of doom. Then it slowly sank. A young seaman named Alfred Renton Bridges would have sunk with it except for his father's mandolin. He clutched the musical instrument as he went overboard and its buoyancy kept him afloat until help arrived.

There are some sharp and emphatic opinions along the Pacific seaboard today as to whether that mandolin performed a good service for the United States in general and the Far West in particular. The sailor whom it saved from death in an angry sea has become the most radical labor leader ever to assume major proportions in this country.

"We take the stand that we as workers have nothing in common with the employers," Alfred Renton (Harry) Bridges observed not long ago before a luncheon club on the University of Washington campus. "We are in a class struggle, and we subscribe to the belief that if the employer is not in business his products will still be necessary and we still will be providing them when there is no employing class. We frankly believe that day is coming."

A gasp shook America's Promised Land. This statement
had not been made by some lone Communist haranguing
from a soapbox in downtown San Francisco or Seattle. It had
been uttered by the chief strategist of all the Committee for
Industrial Organization workers between the Big Muddy and
the Pacific Ocean. So if Dave Beck is the most phenomenal
individual on the sundown side of the Rocky Mountains,
Harry Bridges is certainly the most controversial one. Bridges
is president of the Pacific Coast Longshoremen's Association.
He also has been appointed by John L. Lewis to be chairman
of the Western battalions of the C.I.O.

Beck and Bridges are enemies. In appearance, philosophy,
and tactics they are exact opposites. Only one thing have they
in common: the fact that they are the most vehemently debated and widely discussed men ever to play a part in the
destiny of the great area that stretches westward from the
plains. For five years they have been the dominant perform-
ers in the huge amphitheater of the Far West. A nod from
Bridges has meant silence along the San Francisco waterfront.
A blunt command from Beck has raised the price of bread in
Portland.

Once the two men were allies. Then it was that their cohorts closed down the *Post-Intelligencer* for more than a
hundred days. In dozens of hotel lobbies, on scores of railroad cars, in hundreds of living rooms, at thousands of farm
gatherings, the people of the Pacific seaboard argue about
these powerful labor bosses whose activities so affect their day-
to-day lives. The heavy jowls of Dave Beck and the thin face
of Harry Bridges are familiar to people in Washington and
Oregon who are not certain what their senators or governors
look like.

Bridges is lean and angular. His clothes are drab and inex-
pensive, and he frequently goes on trips without taking along

an extra shirt. His office is unpretentiously furnished with plain chairs and a battered desk. The floor is bare. He is careless about his appointments, and the people under him are often neglectful of important correspondence.

Bridges' antagonists charge that he is an "alleged alien Communist who seeks by strikes and revolution to overthrow the American system of government." His adherents claim he is scrupulously honest and has brought greedy industrialists to their knees by refusing many chances to sell out his followers. "What a union representative should never forget," Bridges advises, "is the power of the men behind him. If you know how to say 'No!' and say it often enough and in enough different ways, you can really get somewhere."

Where else are there two such complete contrasts as the sloppily garbed Bridges in his cell-bare headquarters and the sartorially correct Beck in the sumptuous office at Teamsters' Hall? Beck believes labor and capital should be intertwined in the weaving of the fabric of the profit system. Bridges thinks labor should operate business on a nonprofit basis. He talks about working-class solidarity, rank-and-file control, and economic democracy. He speaks before production-for-use societies, public ownership groups, the League for Peace and Democracy, the International Labor Defense, and the American Newspaper Guild.

Until four years ago Dave Beck ruled labor supreme in the expansive area of the Far West. He was the most powerful labor spokesman in America outside William Green and John L. Lewis. Then, in 1934, the country at large first heard about the slender longshoreman who was as opposite in every respect from Dave Beck as a man could be.

On July 16, 1934, the city of San Francisco was ominously silent. Business ceased to function. Factory wheels stopped. Streetcars never left the barns. Only nineteen restaurants were permitted to open. People stood in line for hours waiting for food. It was the most sweeping general strike in American history—a strike called to protest the slaying by police of two members of a stevedore picket line. The national leaders of labor tried desperately to avert the mass walkout. They condemned it publicly as illegal and unauthorized. The governor of California called it an alien plot. "Rats!" was the epithet General Johnson of the NRA hurled at the strike fomenters.

Across the continent flew newspaper reporters and other observers to see who had persuaded the workers of the Pacific coast's biggest seaport to disregard the warnings of their political and economic spokesmen. The trail led to a shabby office near the docks that extended like long fingers out into the bay. There the correspondents found the man they sought. He surprised them. They had expected to see a burly, hard-boiled individual. Instead, the man behind the general strike turned out to be a soft-spoken little fellow with a Cockney accent—Harry Bridges, president of the Longshoremen's Union.

That was in 1934. The intervening four years have been filled with demands that Bridges be deported to his native Australia. But he is still very much in the United States, and now threatens to supersede Dave Beck as the principal labor leader of the Pacific coast. For months he and Beck have been battling each other to control warehouses and the timber industry, and most observers regard their fight as a showdown. Even though labor patches up its differences nationally, Beck and Bridges will probably continue to wage guerrilla warfare in the Far West. Their philosophies and aims differ *toto caelo*.

-2-

I met Bridges as he sat in his dingy room in a hotel near the Portland waterfront. He tilted his feet on the wheezing radiator, and said, "Well, what can I do for you?"

He did not look like a dangerous radical. Had I seen him behind the tie counter in a department store I should not have given him a second glance. With his sharp face and high forehead, he might have been a bookkeeper or accountant or clerk. He was dressed plainly. His vest was unbuttoned, his tightly knotted tie was askew, and cigarette ashes flecked his trousers. He acted suspicious and defiant and soon blurted out belligerently, "You belong to the Guild?" My affirmative reply made him a little more friendly. He said he had not much respect for newspapermen who would not join a union. I remember thinking at the time that perhaps an employer had just as much right to insist that a newspaperman interviewing him not belong to the Guild.

I had dinner with Bridges and a brilliant young labor attorney named Harry Gross. Bridges monopolized the conversation. He ordered chicken à la king and left most of it in the casserole. He talked with the eagerness and intensity of a zealot and waved aside impatiently any dissident questions. Gross, who since has died from tuberculosis, supplemented and amplified Bridges' remarks. The slender and pale leader of the longshoremen listened intently, but seemed eager to begin talking again himself. He gabbed cockily and said he was undisturbed by the incessantly bitter attacks against him by both employers and the A.F. of L.

Bridges' answer to every question was exactly the opposite of Beck's. The beefy teamster had pooh-poohed the suggestion of referendums among the members on all questions of union strategy.

Bridges said: "No union is a good union unless the rank and file controls it. Labor leaders cannot sell out their followers when all decisions are subject to referendums."

Teamster meetings and conferences are brief and snappy. Sometimes longshoremen and maritime conventions stretch out like sessions of Congress, lasting for weeks and weeks.

Bridges is as unwilling to give sovereignty to a union leader as he is to give it to a bank president. He trusts only the workers themselves. One day, in a meeting with other union officials, a question of policy arose. Bridges had not yet made his stand in the matter. He excused himself and strode out into the union hall, where he motioned to a group of stevedores. "Here's the situation, fellows," he said when they assembled around him. "What's your opinion?" He listened as each man spoke up, then returned to the union conference and argued along the lines advanced by the majority of the workers in the outer hall.

Bridges mistrusts business and industry. He looks upon the relationship between capital and labor as a struggle. He is intensely suspicious of anything associated with wealth. Generally he stops at third-class hotels. Once he took a room at the leading hotel in a large Pacific coast city. A day later he left angrily, claiming his room had been tapped with dictograph machines.

At home he lives as unpretentiously as when he is traveling. He and his wife and twelve-year-old daughter Betty live in a house that costs thirty-five dollars a month rent. They drive a 1935 Ford on which all the payments had not been made last summer. Bridges' salary is seventy-five dollars a week. During the 1934 strike he turned this back into the union treasury to be used for strike benefits, and went on Federal relief.

"Harry Bridges is scrupulously honest," said one of the steamship line officials whom Bridges denounces so furiously. "He wouldn't betray the longshoremen for a first mortgage on every vessel afloat. But that doesn't prevent him from being a very dangerous man. All zealots and fanatics are honest. Bridges can see no good in business and whips up the workers to hate and mistrust their employers. This makes for suspicions and antagonisms that simply don't fit into the American scheme of doing things."

I knew Harry Bridges had been the son of a prosperous real-estate salesman in Kensington, Australia. This could not account for the most extreme left-wing beliefs yet advocated from the seats of labor power in the United States. What could? I talked to Bridges' friends and enemies to find out.

As a boy in Australia, Alfred Renton Bridges had liked best of all to do two things—play his mandolin and listen to the men who followed the sea. When he was seventeen he went to sea himself. Two shipwrecks, including his fortuitous rescue in the *Val Marie* disaster, did not discourage him. He kept on. His parents at home, one of them a devout Irish-Catholic, called him "Alf." His sailor mates nicknamed him "Harry."

Bridges shipped on other vessels. He loved the sea, but rebelled against the strict discipline imposed on shipboard. In 1920 he was on the barkentine *Ysabel*. The captain ordered the crew to work on Easter Monday. Bridges led the men in objecting to the command, and his career of protest and insurgency was under way. As a further indication of his anger, Bridges left the *Ysabel* when it docked at San Francisco.

For the next few years Bridges shipped out of San Francisco. On one occasion his boat tied up at New Orleans during a seamen's strike. The demands of the workers seemed reasonable to "Limo" Bridges, as some of his shipmates called him. So he marched in the picket line. A policeman threw him into jail.

"Why am I here?" Bridges shrieked from behind his cell door.

"For bein' a striker, buddy," one of his jailers said.

Bridges was a confirmed enemy of the shipowners by the time he got back to the Golden Gate. He married Agnes Brown, who had been born in the Black Craig Hills of Scotland, and settled down in San Francisco as a longshoremen. Twice he was injured in dock accidents. He became convinced that the companies did not provide proper safeguards for the men at work. He tried to organize the stevedores, but the embryo union ran into financial difficulties. The steamship lines formed the notorious Blue Book company union, and Bridges' further organization efforts were sharply blocked.

As these events occurred, he adopted increasingly radical positions. At night he would drink beer with the longshoremen and sailors and urge them to unite in a solid front against their employers. He never joined the Communist party; but the Communists supported his views, and he followed their strategy. He contended that the steamship companies were getting rich on government mail subsidies, and demanded that this money be passed on to the workers in bonuses and wage increases.

Bridges was blacklisted, and in 1932 he and his family had to subsist for a time on local relief handouts. He was one of the best winch drivers on the Embarcadero, the great half-moon of San Francisco docks, but his allies claim the companies regarded him as a dangerous agitator and did not want to give him employment.

Today, Bridges shows the result of those years. He is wary of everyone. He makes no secret of his mistrust of labor leaders. That is why he demands referendums among the union members on all important questions. He contends no union is secure unless it keeps a vigilant watch on its officials. Bridges is also intensely suspicious of politicians, even those who profess friendship for labor. "We use a politician as long as he goes along with us," he explains. "After that, we're through with him."

Several of Bridges' adherents frankly admitted to me he was not an able executive. "Too careless," they said. Twice he has allowed his citizenship papers to lapse. He has now taken them out for a third time. Thus, although he came to the United States eighteen years ago, he still is not a citizen. This is why the government is bombarded with resolutions and letters urging that he be summarily deported to Australia.

A Seattle banker told me it was an ominous portent when men followed, so devotedly and blindly, a leader as radical as Harry Bridges. "He's thoroughly in sympathy with the Communist program of the class struggle, admits it himself," the banker warned. "He's the most radical labor leader in this country. Yet those longshoremen would follow him into a fiery furnace."

A German ship steamed into San Francisco harbor flying the Nazi flag. Bridges told the stevedores not to unload the vessel until the swastika was hauled down. They obeyed. At the time of Italy's invasion of Ethiopia, Bridges ordered his union members to refuse to load scrap iron in the hold of an Italian freighter. Again they obeyed. When Bridges was rushed to St. Francis Hospital for an emergency operation for stomach ulcers, hundreds of tense and nervous seamen lined the corridors to hear the report from the surgery. More flowers than had ever before been received by any patient were sent to the leader of the Longshoremen's Union.

The men who sent him flowers recognize in Bridges a

"man with a mission." His mission, he tells them, is to improve the lot of labor, and he is determined to let nothing stand in the way of its fulfillment. He has been denounced as a fanatic, zealot, agitator, and Bolshevik, but everything he does and advocates is conditioned always by the one question: What effect will this have on the workers?

Beck does certain things because labor, business, and he himself will benefit. Bridges does things because labor will benefit. However shortsighted the latter course may seem, the men Bridges leads approve it heartily and he commands their loyalty.

"Get well soon," Tom Mooney wrote from San Quentin penitentiary when Bridges was in the hospital. "The working class needs you."

-3-

Although not a member of the Communist party, Bridges sympathizes with the Communist program and doctrines. His University of Washington speech about the class struggle was far more extreme, in fact, than most declarations of the regular spokesmen for the Communist movement in this country. Bridges is also an alien who for nearly a generation has been remiss and negligent in establishing American citizenship. He is as vulnerable as cheesecloth. More criticism is aimed at him than at any other ten people in the West. Yet he has the fidelity and adherence of large numbers of workers. The longshoremen follow him implicitly. They annually reëlect him their leader by preponderant majorities. And the brawny men who load ships along the Pacific coast are not proletariat-conscious laborers to whom Communistic tendencies and lack of American citizenship are without odium. They are college students forced to quit school or farmers foreclosed off their farms or just run-of-the-mill labor grist. They are considerably more radical than the average worker, but they certainly are not Communists. A large number of them are Catholics. Why, then, do they place such confidence in a wiry little Australian who believes in the ultimate dissolution of the employing class?

George P. West recently wrote in the New York *Times*, "Harry Bridges has led the maritime workers in a fight that already has won better wages and better conditions than maritime workers ever enjoyed before." Business men want bigger profits and workingmen want higher wages. Neither group is likely to be choosy about who gets these rewards for them. A mackinaw-clad young Communist distributing handbills on the Seattle docks said to me: "Let's even admit it's bad to have radical ideas and be an alien like Bridges. Surely the shipowners and big business have no right to holler. For years they've hired Ku Kluxers, ex-convicts, and thugs to break strikes and keep down the wages of the workers. People of that stripe certainly aren't privileged to wave the American flag."

West also wrote in the *Times* of Bridges: "Facing the shrewdest of corporation lawyers, he makes them seem soft and a little helpless by contrast, and this not only because Bridges is a master at repartee and quick thinking but an implacable presser for advantage and a scorner of amenity." Bridges has won strikes and deadlocks because he is shrewd, ruthless, and resourceful. These qualities he shares with Beck, although he employs them along a different route. Across the bargaining table, employers have found the pallid-cheeked longshoreman as unyielding and uncompromising as a time clock. Pompous lawyers and powerful business men hold no awe for him, and he openly sneers at their platitudes. Polite-

ness and courtesy are not words in Bridges' lexicon. He
frankly believes the workers and their bosses are locked in a
grim and bitter battle, and he treats a conference as a temporary truce between rival armies. Most labor leaders shun
strikes. These hold no terrors for Bridges. In fact, they help
sharpen the class struggle. He is always ready to throw down
this ace card of the unions, and frequently employers in no
position to stand a walkout accede to his demands.

I remember a longshoremen's meeting in Portland which
I attended. A conservative adversary of Bridges was lambast-
ing his leadership. He cited "Red Harry's" indolence regarding his citizenship status. He discussed his Communistic advocacies and the large number of Communists who constantly
surrounded him. The speech was making somewhat of an impression—that was obvious. Then one of Bridges' adherents
jumped to his feet. He uttered only three sentences.

"What are you guys kickin' about?" he hollered. "Harry's
gotcha better pay and conditions than you ever had before.
Ain't he?'"

A roar of approval filled the hall. It was apparent the longshoremen were more concerned with financial realities than
political abstractions.

One reason for Bridges' influence with the maritime
workers is that he came into power on the waterfront when
injustice and exploitation were rife in the shipping industry.
Men sat for days in the company-controlled hiring halls waiting for jobs. The belligerent and independent stevedores generally got a few hours' work in smelly holds. The sycophants
of a handful of bullying straw-bosses received the choice as-
signments. Defiance of the petty tyrants running the hiring
halls meant a man would be out on the streets. The longshoremen had as little independence as the subjects of a despot. This in itself, while not winning them to the class war or

a belief in economic determinism, made them the most radical segment of labor in the West. They were ready for Bridges when he began his tumultuous but inexorable ascent to labor power. Few of them understood or agreed with his Communist aphorisms about solidarity and struggle, but all of them recognized his ability to get concessions or win gains.

The cries in the Promised Land of the Far West that Bridges should be deported nearly shake loose the spring avalanches on Mount Hood and Mount Rainier. Newspapers like the *Oregon Journal* and the Hearst press will open their columns to anyone willing to say the leader of the longshoremen had better be returned to Australia. The basis for these demands, of course, is that Bridges is allegedly a Communist. Every bull-necked police sergeant along fifteen hundred miles of seaboard purports to have conclusive proof that the stevedore boss is about to overthrow the American form of government. These shouts and claims are extremely embarrassing to the C.I.O. in the region, and they are doing the labor movement in general no good. But Bridges will probably not be deported.* *Time* reported not long ago, "Government authorities have dutifully checked charges of false identity, of subversive activities, of a criminal record in Australia —and have given Harry Bridges a clean bill of health." A hearing on Bridges' citizenship standing was to have been held this summer. Then a Federal court in Louisiana ruled that membership in the Communist party does not provide a conclusive basis for deportation. The Department of Labor now announces that the Bridges case will not be investigated further until the United States Supreme Court passes on the

* Mr. West has noted in the *Times*, "Critics have been unable to find anything wrong with his [Bridges'] immigration record. Nor have those who accuse him of connections with the Communist Party—which he neither affirms nor denies—been able to discredit him with, for instance, the strong Catholic element in the rank and file of Coast unions."

Louisiana verdict. If the high tribunal concurs in that decision, the charges against Bridges presumably will be dropped. It is likely the strutting, Cockney-voiced longshoreman will eventually become an American citizen and will have to be combated on grounds other than that he is a foreigner. However, influential forces are working to make that likelihood as remote as possible. The latest development in the incessant attempt to deport Bridges has been the charge of the Dies committee that he once said "to hell with the President of the United States" and even suggested the sinking of American warships. More credence might have been attached to this claim had not the committee earlier insinuated that among the Communist "dupes" in the country were—Mrs. Roosevelt and Shirley Temple! Yet the commotion has done Bridges and his cause no good, and it is reasonable to wonder why after nearly two decades in the United States he is still without citizenship.

The fact that Bridges is an alien has been used throughout the West as a stick to beat Secretary of Labor Perkins, in whose department the immigration service is located. The lashing is premised more on politics than on fact. The Australian's tempestuous career as a labor agitator began in 1921, shortly after he had quit the *Ysabel*. That year he was arrested and jailed in New Orleans for picket duty during an I.W.W. strike. Harry Bridges was an alien then. He was also a radical. Republican secretaries of labor had a dozen years, before Miss Perkins took over the department, in which to send Bridges on his way. That the highly hysterical denunciations of the only woman cabinet member in the New Deal have been more noisy than effective is indicated partially by the circumstance that the West continues to be a principal stronghold of the Roosevelt administration.

There is an inherent danger in the antialien commotion attendant on this particular case. "We believe Bridges' Australian citizenship and alleged Communism would never have been mentioned," said the *Quest* of Reed College,* "if he had been just another longshoreman. But because he is the militant leader of the wide-awake union—whether we agree with him or not—deportation proceedings have been brought." No one doubts that, if Bridges had not been an aggressive and radical labor organizer, the alien cry would never have been raised. Many liberals in the Northwest, most of whom totally disapprove of what amounts to Bridges' slavish following of the Communist line, are afraid that deportation activities because a man is a union leader may some day become the precedent for shipping a man out of the country because he is a rabbi or a priest or an evangelist or even a banker.

A white-haired widow of means and education, who lives in an old home set back on a magnolia-dotted lawn in the hills west of Portland, said to me, "You know, I went to see a movie the other day. There was a foreign actress in it. She was the temptress who tried to lure the hero. I also notice in the papers that a young lady advertised as coming from Cuba is dancing without any clothes on at one of our local night clubs. It seems to me, if foreigners can corrupt the morals of our youngsters or exhibit themselves in the nude, that other foreigners ought to have a right to organize a labor union.

"I don't approve of Mr. Bridges," she continued, as she looked out toward the Willamette, shimmering in the spring sunshine, "but I would think that this great land of ours can

* This school, in Portland, is probably the foremost educational institution in the Northwest. It has an unblemished reputation for freedom for both faculty and students. Its president is Dexter Keezer, who formerly was associated with the Baltimore *Sun*. Reed's student paper is uncensored. The papers at such schools as Oregon State College and the University of Oregon are closely supervised.

survive a foreigner like him if it can stand some of the foreigners who perform in the movies or entertain at night
clubs."

-4-

Workers should be well off in the Pacific Northwest. It is
the country's treasure-trove of plenty. It also has a liberal
tradition, and the people are generally tolerant and progressive. Yet monopolistic practices and cruel exploitation have
largely denied labor the abundance that should be its lot. A
strong, healthy labor movement in the Columbia River basin
is needed. Grave doubts exist as to whether Bridges and his
coterie of immediate followers are traveling in that direction.
Certainly, the obese and reactionary Beck is not the inspira-
tional leader to show labor in the West the route to a new
standard of living. The chances are that neither is Bridges.

Most of the men close to the boss of the maritime workers
are either Communists or sympathizers with the objectives of
Communism. The party line is followed obediently. Radicals
who deviate even slightly are excoriated as "phonies," "Trot-
skyites," and "company stooges." It is almost as great a crime
to endorse the Ludlow war referendum or a speech by Nor-
man Thomas as it is to acquiesce in a wage reduction. Oliver
Carlson has claimed in *Common Sense:*

It is no secret that Communist Party members and close followers have been given preference in appointments as organizers,
secretaries, and attorneys by Bridges and his group, ever since they
took hold of the West Coast waterfront; and this policy has been
extended since he took over the C.I.O. directorship. Now it must
be admitted that many of these appointees are capable and ener-
getic, nor can their sincerity be doubted; but all issues and problems of the C.I.O. are likely to be considered by them primarily

in terms of advancing the Communist Party and its numerous auxiliaries.

I covered one of the conventions of the Maritime Federation. It went on and on interminably, and not all the proceedings concerned the supposed purpose of the meeting. There were resolutions pledging help to Loyalist Spain, condemning the Rome-Berlin axis, urging collective action among the democratic powers, demanding the pardon of Tom Mooney and other political prisoners, deploring the rise of fascism, advocating a boycott of Japan, and seeking more government relief appropriations. Funds were sought for the International Labor Defense and similar organizations, and enthusiastic young Communists circulated about, handing out circulars and leaflets amplifying various phases of the party's manifold activities. Some of the delegates privately inquired whether the convention was to discuss the peculiar problems and issues confronting the men on the Pacific coast whose work touched the sea or to extend the policies of the Comintern to the American hinterlands. Few of these skeptical doubts were voiced publicly. To do so would have been to risk immediate vilification as a "phony."

Some of the most conscientious and sincere trade unionists in the West receive the label of "phony" the instant they actively stray from the switchbacking path blazed by the Communist doctrinaires. Many of Bridges' henchmen are more anxious to convince their followers they should again cross the ocean to make the world safe for democracy than they are to promote a greater measure of democracy on the docks of the West Coast. "Let's bring back unionism into the C.I.O.," complain hundreds of workers who are not especially interested in the long harangues of Communist functionaries. Consistency is a quality which seldom hampers the

emotional free play of Bridges' satellites. In one breath they
can explain why union referendums distinguish the liberty
enjoyed in the C.I.O. from the despotism endured in the
A.F. of L., and in the next they can fretfully cry that endorsement of the Ludlow war referendum would in reality
be a subtle blow at the Soviet Union and a boon to Hitler.
These individuals are against union wrecking and for labor
unity; but let them find a union in which they think Trot-
skyism prevails or "subtle red-baiting" is taking place, and
they will strew carnage from one end of the union hall to the
other. "Tolerance in any society," Harold Laski once said,
"depends upon the degree of security felt by those who govern it." This is precisely the case in the unions dominated by
Bridges and his lieutenants. They permit rank-and-file control so long as the rank and file obediently accept their leadership. Dictatorship begins when insurrection starts. Edward
Levinson of the New York *Post*, a sympathetic observer, recently charged that Bridges helped break up Local 34 of the
C.I.O. office workers when that union became critical of its
international officers. This is a serious charge. No labor leader
in America talks more about industrial democracy and rank-
and-file supremacy than Bridges. That he frequently fails to
put these lofty sentiments into practice weakens faith in his
leadership. Beck makes small pretense of giving his dues
payers the whole say. Imperious mandates from him occasion
little surprise.

Harry Bridges pays no attention to the amenities required
of a man active in the arena of public affairs. He either ig-
nores or sneers at the prejudices latent in a large segment of
the population. At a mass meeting he said, "When agreements conflict with labor's solidarity, agreements must go."
There is something sacred to a lot of people about contracts
and other legal legerdemain. Many of these same orthodox-

thinking individuals were further antagonized when Bridges remarked, "You have to work with Communists because Communists make good trade unionists." The alien furor was increased in intensity the day he blithely ignored it by letting another foreigner become second in command of the C.I.O. in the West.* John L. Lewis is no Communist adherent. Neither is he asleep to the undesirability of having two aliens in charge of his organization on the sundown side of the Mississippi. Benjamin Stolberg contends Lewis has regretted the lofty position to which he has permitted Bridges to ascend in the C.I.O. The wiry longshoreman is actually so far to the left of Lewis that the latter can scarcely observe him with the Lick telescope. But Bridges is a competent organizer, and he wins new crests in wages and conditions for his men; and these facts are believed to counterbalance, in Lewis' judgment, his party-line fanaticism. Politically, Bridges is thoroughly inept. His endorsement is a liability, yet he insists on endorsing many New Deal candidates. Some of the New Dealers in the Northwest contend that Bridges, when he does this, is more concerned about his own prestige than about getting liberals into office. Two days before the Oregon primaries he was begged not to issue a blast at the arrogant Governor Martin. But he did so, jeopardizing the chances of Martin's progressive opponent.

Some people think Lewis is trying to devise a way to shake Bridges. More than anyone else, the Australian has made the C.I.O. stagger under the weight of the Communist bogey in its dual race with big business and the A.F. of L. Several observers have suggested that Lewis might purge the troublesome Homer Martin of the Automobile Workers as a conces-

---

* Harold J. Pritchett, president of the C.I.O. sawmill and timber workers, and a citizen of British Columbia. For a complete analysis of this situation see Chapter 10.

sion to the leftwingers and at the same time liquidate Bridges as a sop to the red-baiters. This sounds simple, but there are a lot of longshoremen such a move would drive right out of the C.I.O. Their first allegiance is to Bridges, for it was he who came onto the docks of the Pacific coast when the bosses held undisputed sway. Lewis does not want to lose these men; neither does he want to lose the organizing ability that has enabled Bridges to improve working conditions where the mountains touch the sea. Yet the chairman of the C.I.O. probably will not hesitate once he should decide that the longshoremen's leader is more of a hindrance than an advantage. Lewis and his henchmen used to throw radicals bodily out of the United Mine Workers. A few flinty observers even suggest that the deportation of Bridges would relieve an embarrassing situation all around. To the credit of Miss Perkins, she has stood against a fusillade of propaganda to insist that the case of the Australian be tried by facts and not hysteria. Many open-minded people in the West attribute the abuse of the Secretary of Labor over the Bridges' affair to a studied political plot to confound the New Deal.

With Beck on one firing line and Bridges on the other, the labor situation in the Far West has become a messy hodgepodge. To Mr. Roosevelt the Columbia basin is the country's Promised Land; but it is an inferno of verbal bombardments so far as labor relations are concerned. Anyone not subscribing to Dave Beck and his "voluntary NRA" as enforced by the notorious "goon squad" is castigated as a Communist and a recipient of Moscow gold. For those who disagree with them, however infinitesimally, Bridges and his left-wing allies have a variety of epithets, of which "social fascist" is the least and "scabby fink" is among the worst. Beck's lieutenants use such organizations as Americans, Incorporated, which almost endorse fascism in their tirades against all persons with liberal views. The Bridges faction never lets a Communist newspaper go to press without rabid indictments of everyone not participating in the follow-the-leader requirements of the party line.

These opposite extremes have impelled many onlookers to suggest that both Beck and Bridges should eventually evanesce from the scene, leaving the establishment of labor peace to others. The antagonisms attaching to the two men—as well as the hostility between them—may endure for a decade. Their bitter rivalry is the most serious threat to the continued standing of the New Deal in the nation's Promised Land. As these words are written, the President is more popular than ever in the Northwest. The voters in overwhelming numbers continue to register Democratic. The one grave menace to his prestige is the grim and deadly labor combat that ranges from Puget Sound to Mexico. Beck with his "goons" and Bridges with his Communist tendencies and allies accentuate that combat and make it far more grim than the internecine labor difficulties elsewhere in the country.

The main battle line of this warfare splits the Northwest's leading industry—lumber. It is in the tall timber and green-mantled foothills of the Columbia basin that the struggle most closely approximates an actual conflict.

10. The Labor Titans at the Barricades

LIKE a great carpet of green, the tallest trees in North America cover the hills of the Columbia River basin. From the uplands of Montana southwestward through the ranges of Idaho and Washington and Oregon, the region is blanketed by forests. Groves and windfalls as thick as hedges and as old as the discovery of the New World dominate every scenic vista. Here there are 917 of the 1,688 billion board feet of lumber in the entire country. The National Resources Committee has said that "no attempt to improve the social and economic status of the people of the United States can leave out of consideration this important industry in the Pacific Northwest."

From the forests which converge on the Columbia River will, in the opinion of the President, come most of the wood for the government housing program. Yet the fact that these forests are by far the nation's greatest supply of timber is not their principal significance. They have another and more cogent meaning. They are the battleground on which the American Federation of Labor and the Committee for Industrial Organization are met in the fiercest and most bitter internecine labor warfare in the history of the country. For two generations these forests have been the scene of a grim struggle between conservative and radical unionism. A quarter of a century ago the old "wobblies" of the I.W.W. scrambled through their leafy defiles. There also were heard the first militant protests against the lassitude and inactivity of the A.F. of L. And perhaps fifty years from now, when the A.F. of L. and the C.I.O. are mere historic initials, the workers who want to organize cautiously and those who want to socialize the nation will still battle with peaveys and axes where lofty fir trees line the Columbia's shores.

The clash between the A.F. of L. and the C.I.O. in the East is a mere verbal foray contrasted with the direct action ensuing in the timber groves of the Far West. There the conflict is an actual one. Mills with an A.F. of L. charter one day operate under a C.I.O. agreement the next, and *vice versa*. Heads are broken and eyes gouged as lumberjacks fight with fists and knives and hobnailed boots. Union officials carry blackjacks—and use them. Lumber with an A.F. of L. imprint is met with glowering glances by Harry Bridges' longshoremen. That with a C.I.O. stamp finds Dave Beck's teamsters standing by obdurately with folded arms. Beat-ups and combats are frequent, and each side has a growing hospital list. The jurisdictional tiffs that are settled in the East by conferences are decided in the lumber camps by pitched battles and grim sieges. Literally as well as figuratively, the A.F. of L. and the C.I.O. have confronted each other in the timber region. They are fighting it out there, with no holds barred and no quarter given.

The lumber industry has become the amphitheater of a passage at arms of showdown proportions between the conservative and radical forces in organized labor. The struggle is salient and decisive, and both the A.F. of L. and the C.I.O. have rushed organizers and finances and other reinforcements into the region. Victory is essential to the labor faction that would be supreme west of the Big Muddy. Lumber dominates the industrial economy of the Pacific Northwest and supports more than one-fourth of the population. A triumph in the forests for the C.I.O. would leave the A.F. of L. on the Pacific rim with only the teamsters, the building trades, and a few limp craft unions. An A.F. of L. conquest in the woods would limit the Western strength of the C.I.O. to a thin cordon of longshoremen.

Prestige is also a factor at stake. Nowhere else in the country have the rival labor organizations clashed so dramatically. The public mind grabs at the spectacular. To the nation at large, the battle in lumber epitomizes the cleavage in the ranks of labor. Other breaks between the A.F. of L. and the C.I.O. are circuitous and cushioned with qualifications. The warfare in the sawmills is direct, open, and savage. The public can see precisely what is happening. The eventual outcome will be easy to understand. Conference room bickerings awaken none of the attention and interest aroused by two hostile bands of flannel-shirted lumberjacks meeting in the Oregon pine woods. The side that loses the lumber campaign will lose more than the workers in the Far West's major industry; it will also suffer tremendous losses in national estimation, for it will have been vanquished in an outright test of force and sinews and power.

"Here are the real facts in the lumber industry out there in the Northwest," Daniel J. Tobin, the elderly international president of the Teamsters' Union, told the A.F. of L. executive committee.

"In reality it is not a fight between the C.I.O. and the A.F. of L., but it is a fight whether a communistic type of organization shall prevail in this all-important lumber industry or whether an A.F. of L. organization, believing in the American principles of justice and democracy, shall prevail."

This statement was made at almost precisely the time that

a host of teamsters belonging to the "organization believing in the American principles of justice and democracy" were arrested for offenses in the lumber struggle ranging from simple assault to the alleged burning of an $80,000 sawmill. The bitterness underlying Tobin's remarks and the grim reality of the deeds of some of his members indicate the reckless nature of the battle. Lumber camps have gone up in billows of smoke, and men have been cruelly beaten. The timber clash has nearly amounted to civil war. The C.I.O. is frankly determined to drive the A.F. of L. out of the woods. The A.F. of L. is retaliating by starving the C.I.O. loggers into submission. It is a feud that William Green and John L. Lewis cannot settle three thousand miles away by signing pieces of paper. The combat in lumber is too intensified by hatred and fury to be ended summarily. It has the elements of actual warfare—warfare that has endured since the "wobblies" fought the company unions in the wilderness more than twenty-five years ago. The present conflict is merely a phase of a longer struggle which has lasted from the time puffing little narrow-gauge locomotives replaced snorting ox teams in the timbered uplands.

"We are in this fight to a showdown," recently challenged Abe Muir, the Brotherhood of Carpenters' conservative chieftain in the Northwest. "We will continue to battle until we win or the Brotherhood itself is destroyed."

That utterance is a fair approximation of the anger and obstinacy behind the country's most malevolent labor combat.

-2-

From the ramparts of the Cascade Mountains the traveler looks out across a vista of never-ending forests. Only in occa-

sional spots is the expanse of timber broken by clearings—
patches of brown above which pillars of smoke float upward
in the clear air. They come from clattering donkey engines or
compact cookhouses, and they mark where logging crews are
at work.

They represent what is still one of America's big businesses
—almost the very oldest. They also symbolize the scene of
an internal labor battle that as much as any other single struggle may help to shape the destiny of the Far West. The
burly, weather-tanned men who convert trees into lumber are
found at the outposts of civilization. They swing their axes
or pull their saws high in the Oregon mountains or deep in
the redwood valleys of California. Yet they are playing the
same role in an epic labor fight as the men who work in mammoth factories near the population centers of the East.

The men in the woods are picturesque individuals, and they
toil in a picturesque setting. Drab, indeed, are the strikes of
subway employees and factory workers compared with the
angry battles of the rough-and-ready men who cut trees into
lumber on America's last frontier.

On the slopes of the Cascades, the Coeur d'Alenes, the Bit-
terroots, the Olympics, and the Rockies is a vast stand of timber that covers ridges and uplands for thousands of miles.
President Roosevelt calls it "the greatest reserve of virgin
timber in the United States." From a peak in any of these
ranges, an argonaut might imagine himself riding the front
of an immense ship plowing through a sea of green. Viscount Bryce once wrote that nowhere else were woodlands
and forests so blended with the landscape as in the Far West.

It is in this setting that loggers and lumberjacks transform
trees as tall as fifteen-story buildings into shingles and two-
by-fours, or material for pencils, desks, paper, or sailing ships.
Sometimes the men who work in the woods are literal pio-

log jams—immortalized in movie thrillers—occur, and then
the men must risk their lives to break them with axes and
dynamite. In some camps in the Northwest the water from
rivers is diverted into troughlike flumes, built on stilts above
the mountainsides, and the logs are floated through these to
the planing mills and factories. The transportation problems
of the logging industry illustrate its difference from most
other American businesses. Many enterprises build up hus-
tling villages and thriving cities—communities that find a
place on the map, and endure. But the logging industry goes
deeper and deeper into the forests. It must take its rails and
roads and flumes along with it. When one stretch of timber
is cut, the loggers go on in search of another slope of virgin
trees. Behind them they leave what F. A. Silcox, chief of the
United States Forest Service, describes as "ghost towns."
Bend in central Oregon is now a busy community. But the
timber around it is thinning out, and in time, Silcox says, it
may be silent and almost deserted, like the ghost towns that
worked-out gold-diggings have left behind them.

Against this wilderness background, the loggers and lumberjacks of the Northwest, woodsmen with heavy labor to do,
live and work in the open. The logger's day is crammed with
action and splashed with color. He is roused in the morning
by the beating of a crowbar on a huge circular saw, and from
then until the sun goes down behind the ranges, he matches
his skill and strength and tools against trees that were standing before Drake's frigate cruised along the Western coast.

After a logging camp has been established and a line of
communication secured, the most spectacular of all the tasks
connected with logging takes place. The high-climber scales
the tree—the highest and straightest on the highest patch of
land, chosen beforehand and marked with an X—which
serves a purpose as vital to lumbering operations as that of a

mast to a sailing ship. Indeed, loggers sometimes call it "the mast," though the right name is the spar tree. It is usually a fir or pine towering three hundred feet into the air. The high-climber's job is to get up it with spiked shoes and safety belt, saw off its needled top, lop off its branches, and fasten up there, aloft, the block and tackle and the lines and cables of the donkey engine. The great moment is just as the saw cuts through and the top crashes. Then the long trunk sways and buckles like a ship's mast, indeed, lashed by a gale. The man must cling for his life and he must still be dexterous enough, swinging at that dizzy height, to use ax or saw.

The purpose of the spar tree is to keep high above ground the lines that drag the logs to the loading platforms. When it is full-rigged the lumberjacks set to work bringing down the trees marked for cutting. In some camps power saws are used. But in many, the men still swing long double-headed axes—just as did the old woodsmen who came with Lewis and Clark and Captain Bonneville to invade for the first time the tall timber areas. In that case, brawny, sinewy fellows swing their axes alternately at a tree older than the Republic. It begins to topple. "Timber!" they shout. It crashes to earth in a spray of branches, bark, and wood.

This also is an expert's job. The tree must fall either parallel to the spar tree or at right angles to it—which is called "falling to the lead" or "across the lead"—in order that afterward the logs may be moved handily by the tackle. "Falling" a woodland giant as thick as an ocean liner's funnel takes experience, care, and nerve. One that topples in the wrong direction may cost the lives of its "fallers" and account must be taken of wind, undergrowth, foliage, and other things. Some men can fall a tree almost on an arrow line.

Other men cut the fallen tree into sections. They always have at hand an empty beer bottle filled with kerosene—to keep the saw from sticking to the pitch. The logs are either hauled by tractors or pulled by the cables of the donkey engine to the railway, motor road, or flume that will take them to the sawmill. The men consider all this part of the same process. "Sawmill and Timber Workers" is a common name for their union.

Living so much to themselves, the lumberjacks have developed a jargon of their own, like the soldier or the sailor. The superintendent of the logging camp is the "bull of the woods." A "hoosier" is a man unfamiliar with his work. Spotty and thin timber is a "bum show." The "whistle-punk" signals to the men who operate the donkey engines and locomotives. "Gyppo" is the term scornfully conferred upon the system of paying workers by the piece instead of by the hour. The foreman of operations is the "push." Horses are "hay-burners." Teamsters are "hair-pounders." The "bull-cook" does not cook at all but is the chore boy who does odd jobs around the camp.

Because so often logging camps and sawmills are in the deep woods, the issues between employers and employees include conditions of living. Primarily, this means food. In the days of the "wobblies" this was especially the case. Much of the resentment of the workers was over the burned johnny-cakes and greasy salt pork served in the mess halls. Like an army, a logging crew functions on its stomach. Today, mill and camp operators have recognized this fact—after years of agitation and struggle on the part of their more courageous employees. Beverly Smith of the *American Magazine* visited an Oregon lumber camp not long ago and ate a typical noon-day meal with the loggers. He reported wonderingly that the lunch consisted of chicken-tomato soup, veal chops, braised beef stew, fresh asparagus, baked beans, German-fried potatoes, rye hardtack, white bread, rolls, milk, tea, lettuce salad, stewed gooseberries, lime jelly with cream, assorted fruit, three kinds of cookies, and two kinds of cake. Smith said the lumberjacks did not eat veal chops *or* beef stew. They ate veal chops *and* beef stew.

In other respects, as well as food, the modern logging camp is different from the camp of a generation ago. The bunkhouses in which the men once slept in tiers, like sailors in a ship's fo'c'sle, have been replaced in many areas by rows of iron beds. Almost every camp has its radio, and many of them show motion pictures several nights a week. Years ago the only recreation of the loggers was gossiping with their friends on the job or reading paper-backed novels; collection boxes in various Western cities solicited old books and magazines for "the men in our forests." Now many of the men own dilapidated automobiles and drive to the nearest settlement after their evening meal.

These advances were not won without sacrifice. Men were blacklisted, beaten, and terrorized as the lumber industry was gradually civilized. In the Loyal Legion of Loggers and Lumbermen, the workers confronted one of the most skillfully organized company unions in the nation. Yet aggressiveness and tenacity forced even the "Four L" to seek improved living conditions and better safeguards. Logging has always been a perilous occupation. Falling trees, log jams in the rivers, grinding saws, forest fires, and runaway lumber trains take a tax in life each year. It once was far worse than it is now. Hours were longer, and the men consequently less alert. Dangerous machinery was unprotected. The lumberjacks worked in all sorts of weather. Drenching rain did not keep high-climbers off three-hundred-foot Douglas firs; and "fallers" swung their axes in gusty wind storms. Here is an analysis of one phase of the logger's task, as it was in 1917, from the staid *Sunset Magazine* for February of that year:

Shingle-weaving is not a trade, it is a battle. For ten hours a day the sawyer faces two teethed steel disks whirling around 200 times a minute. To the one on the left he feeds the heavy blocks of cedar, reaching over with his left hand to remove the heavy shingles it rips off.

Hour after hour the shingle-weaver's hands and arms, plain, unarmored flesh and blood, are staked against the screeching steel that cares not what it severs. Hour after hour the steel sings its crescendo note as it bites into the wood, the sawdust thickens, the wet sponge under the sawyer's nose fills with fine particles. If "cedar asthma," the shingle-weaver's occupational disease, does not get him, the steel will. Sooner or later he reaches over a little too far, the whirling blade tosses drops of deep red into the air, a finger, a hand, or part of an arm comes sliding down the slick chute.

Such hazards as this, the "wobblies" helped to eliminate. Unpopular though these wilderness agitators were with the public at large, they drove barbarism out of the woods. Their demands for decent living conditions and edible food constituted the first move in changing the logger's diet from burned batter and blubbery meat to the veal chops and fresh asparagus that Beverly Smith ate and sighed over. "Little enough it was they asked," the Rev. Robert Whitaker of Seattle has written, in discussing the turbulent raids of the I.W.W. "They sought reasonable hours of labor and exemption from that excessive toil which always takes fearful toll in the increase of industrial accidents, decent foods with which to maintain their strength, decent quarters in which to dry their rain-soaked bodies and clothes, and to get the sleep so fully earned and so indispensable to their safety and health."

The wobblies practiced sabotage and violence. They filled the hinterlands with wild threats of revolution. They made mortal enemies of the cautious middle class. But they were

stubborn and tenacious, and they got clean blankets and nour-
ishing food for the men in the forests. Even John F. Dore,
the most vehement denouncer of Communism ever to be
mayor of Seattle, once said:

Now, whatever you may think of the I.W.W., the I.W.W.
made one of the greatest contributions to the welfare of the timber and sawmill workers in the Northwest and on the Pacific coast
that was ever made to the welfare of any working class.

Their methods were methods of violence, but it may have been
possible that the conditions that existed could not at that time have
been cured by any other method than the violent methods that
they used. But when they got through, the logging camp that, up
to that time, had not been a fit place even for a dog to live in,
much less a human being, became somewhat a decent place for the
worker to live in.

As the wobblies fought the timber barons in the Promised
Land of the Columbia River basin, some of the ghastliest
labor tragedies in the chronicles of American unionism occurred. There were bloody massacres at Everett and Centralia, and in 1919 Seattle was gripped by a general strike.
A certain amount of vigilantism followed all these happenings. Civil liberties were placed in jeopardy and injustices
occurred in both seaport cities and backwoods villages.

Yet, despite the ferocity of the labor warfare that had en-
sued, the public temper was astonishingly calm and unruffled.
The people did not get hysterical. Much as the middle class
feared and detested the wobblies, it refused to run berserk in
persecuting them. Oregon succumbed briefly to K.K.K. fanaticism, and Seattle put the virulent Ole Hansen in the
mayor's office; but time quickly shifted these scenes. On the
whole, public feeling was remarkably stable. Even the sympathizers of the wobblies said it might have been far worse
in any other part of the country. The one *cause célèbre* was

not nearly as atrocious as the cases elsewhere in the nation that originated in far less bitter labor struggles.

Ray Becker, the lumberjack son of a Lutheran minister, is the most famous political prisoner in the Promised Land. He still looks out at the distant woodlands from his cell in the Washington State penitentiary at Walla Walla. He has been there eighteen years, ever since the grisly gunfire battle between wobblies and war veterans one tragic day in Centralia. Becker is the Northwest's Tom Mooney. Many influential people have urged that he be pardoned. His cause has won adherents among Legionnaires and other conservatives. He is inflexible in his faith in his own innocence. John Dos Passos calls him a martyr to the principles of abstract justice. The governor of Washington has proffered Becker a parole, but he consistently rejects it. He thinks acceptance would be an admission of guilt. It will have to be a pardon or nothing. Becker works in the penitentiary storehouse. He also studies law in the jail library and prepares innumerable briefs on his case. All are printed painstakingly in his own handwriting. He likes to see, far away though they are, the forests where he sawed fir logs so many years ago.

-3-

These incidents and background are part of the legacy of the labor movement in the forests. And with most of the prime causes of the disputes in the lumber camps a decade or so back removed—unsavory food, unsanitary bunkhouses, and the lack of adequate safeguards on the job—the issues there now are much the same as in the population centers of the East. Recently seventeen thousand loggers paraded on picket lines in the timber groves of Oregon, Washington, and Idaho.

They demanded wage increases and a closed shop in the hiring halls. Their employers countered with the American Way of Life and the right to work. The questions of Detroit and Akron and Weirton had been transported a continent westward.

Like other workers, town and country, the men who labor in the lumber camps are of various origins. No particular nationality predominates in the Northwest's great timber area, as do the Scandinavians in the woods of Minnesota. Most of the loggers were born in the United States. Some come from Canada. But they differ from other workers, especially factory hands, in one notable respect.

Lumbering is a migratory business. It moves about as the timber is cleared off and exhausted. Logging crews change continually. They are recruited from the farms and villages of the new locations, while on the other hand workers in a camp will sometimes stay on after the outfit moves away. They become "stump ranchers," raising patches of vegetables and pasturing a few cows on the land just cleared by their fellow lumberjacks. During the depression many men from farms took to logging to reinforce their depleted incomes. Very few of them in the Pacific Northwest lacked experience in falling trees, at least; practically all the farmers in the Promised Land of the Columbia River country know the rudiments of logging. An organization of thousands of men in British Columbia was once called the "Agricultural and Lumber Workers' Industrial Union," and the connection between the two groups is still close.

Loggers who work near agricultural countrysides often join Granges and farmers' unions. "Loggin' is half farmin', anyhow," some of them explain. When forest fires roar through the woods, it is frequently the farmers who join the loggers on the blazing line of defense. The social and economic view-

point of the lumberjack is as much agrarian as it is urban.
This tells why the I.W.W. could win only a minority of followers even in camps that were a shambles of filth and dirt
and bad food. Its leaders did not thoroughly understand the
men they were exhorting to action. The solitudes have a definite influence on people, and it is under this influence that the
lumber worker comes. The loneliness and beauty of the countryside rather than the turmoil and steel of the cities shape
his viewpoint. He practically considers himself a farmer, and
he is quicker to participate in a protest against mortgage fore-
closures than he is to denounce Fascist aggression. These loggers who are also agriculturists have helped to bring together
farmers and laborers in the Northwest. Nationally, the Grange
is a conservative, staid organization. But its Washington, Oregon, and Idaho chapters are big, active, defiant—and aggressively liberal. They have felt the effect of the men toiling in
the timber belt, and the men toiling in the timber belt have
felt the effect of the farms. The National Grange condemns
the New Deal and pleads for prudence and caution. The
Granges in the vernal Columbia River basin, with their lumberjack members and neighbors, solicit the New Deal to go
ahead. They have been the principal bulwark against the incorporation of labor unions. This farm allegiance the loggers
reciprocate. The men who work in the forests are radicals,
but their radicalism is of the Populist rather than the Marxian
brand. They favor public ownership, want higher wages, and
hate big business. But they pay little attention to class credos,
do not desire to go to war to punish the bandit nations, and
shun demonstrations for the sake of demonstrating. William
Jennings Bryan and "Fighting Bob" La Follette, instead of
Marx and Lenin, are their idols. This vexes the brash young
Communists, who worship their courage and belligerency but

far from the last outposts of civilization. The lumberjacks held defiant meetings in mess halls and bunkhouses, and also in the backwoods when those places were closed to them. Strikebreakers encountered heavy fists and hobnailed boots.

The owners of the timber industry became panicky. The year 1932 had been the worst for lumber since 1869. It had been less than a third of 1928. The industry seemed to be on its way into limbo. New substitutes for wood crammed the markets. Metal alloys began to replace lumber in thousands of construction jobs. Manufacturers advertised that certain products contained no wood. Lumber operators visioned a complete loss of their investment. The housing boom had not yet occurred to prod a stricken industry back toward normalcy. Before the frightened timbermen the labor activities of their employees loomed as the climax to disaster.

So the strikes were grim and bitter. Not much was won by the lumberjacks without hunger and bloodshed and violence. Little was conceded by the owners until mills had been silent and incomes slashed. The governor of Washington called out the national guard and established martial law in Tacoma. The governor of Oregon ordered the State police to use their clubs and "paddle" the pickets away from the camps. Detectives and labor spies augmented the work of these agencies. Feeling, for the moment at least, was tense and rancorous. Angry farmers clustered around mills and camps in Oregon and shook their fists at the smartly uniformed State troopers. Tacoma was dazed and bewildered; martial law was new to the neighborly Northwest. Vigilante societies had a brief but lively field day. They flourished like tumbleweed. Business men in Portland filled out questionnaires which asked, among other things, "Have you had any experience with gas bombs?" and "Do you own any firearms?" Law-and-order groups indexed by blocks and districts and neighborhoods the stout-hearted citizens with "military experience" who could be depended upon to defend the American Way of Life.

The tension would not have been unique in a strike-bound manufacturing area in the East, but it was extraordinary for the largely pastoral Columbia River country.

In this atmosphere the organizers and officials of the Brotherhood of Carpenters were strangely out of place. They had little in common with the determined men they were supposed to be leading. Their outlook was that of the man who had appointed them to their jobs: William L. (Big Bill) Hutcheson, the carpenters' international president, and the one person in the A.F. of L. hierarchy upon whom the Republicans could always rely for faithful service. Hutcheson's organizers quavered like aspic as the loggers and farmers lined up on one side and the employers and vigilantes and police on the other. They had not expected this when they admitted the lumberjacks on a nonbeneficiary basis. A struggle of such intensity was new to these labor bureaucrats. They urged the men to proceed cautiously. The inevitable happened. The loggers began ignoring their ostensible spokesmen. They took over the conduct of the strikes themselves. What gains they finally made were in spite of their organizers and not because of them. In some lumber camps where animus was at a high pitch the boss would have been far safer than the Brotherhood's officials. Contempt and mistrust among the loggers for the leadership provided by Hutcheson comprised by far the most significant result of the series of timber strikes that followed the commencement of the New Deal.

The rapid expansion of the C.I.O. made it merely a matter of time when the lumberjacks would secede from the carpenters' union. Philosophically, they never had belonged under the Hutcheson aegis. "As out of place as boiled cabbage at a cocktail party," one of their sympathizers described the paradox. The loggers were only nonbeneficiary members, paying Class B dues but having a negligible voice in the Brotherhood's activities. Woodland bunkhouses and lean-tos continually buzzed with anathemas against the Brotherhood. In many of the timber workers' locals, especially those near the cities and towns, there were small minorities of Communists. These men were generally the most vocal and aggressive members. They passed up no opportunity to assail the lethargy and reaction of the Brotherhood officials. Sentiment against the A.F. of L. gathered momentum. Populists and Marxians collaborated in vindictive accusations directed at the Brotherhood's regional organizers.

Hutcheson did not relinquish one hundred twenty thousand loggers without a final struggle. He scuttled the carpenters' craft guild principles and turned to the industrial unionism of John L. Lewis, who had hit him in the jaw at an A.F. of L. national convention. In the spring of 1937 Louis Stark wrote in the New York *Times:* "These sawmill and lumber workers are being organized as little industrial unions, so that the carpenters' union is in a fair way to become more industrial than the United Mine Workers of America, which is regarded as the peer of American industrial unions." Stark pointed out that the Brotherhood had asserted control over the whole lumber industry and made itself the dominant A.F. of L. affiliate. This control gradually weakened. The summer of 1937 witnessed the formation of the Federation of Woodworkers and the emphatic decision of its members to join the C.I.O. All the men who worked with wood, from high-climbers to furniture workers, were included in this body.

The West's basic industry was on its way out of the A.F. of L. and left-wingers confidently predicted C.I.O. domi-

nance from Puget Sound to San Diego and from the Golden
Gate to Pikes Peak. Already the longshoremen had followed
Harry Bridges into the ranks of the new organization. Now,
the additional departure of the timber workers from the
A.F. of L. would leave the old-time labor leadership on the
Coast in a demoralized condition. All over the country A.F.
of L. officials had accepted these secessions with not much
more than oratorical resistance. Dave Beck decided he would
set a different example. He would not succumb so easily. He
might be conservative in economics but never in action. So
Bridges wanted a fight, did he? Beck would give him a real
one.

"Some of the lumber boys seem to have joined up with
'Arry and his Communists," Beck ominously observed, as he
pounded his ornate mahogany desk. "Well, let 'em try to
move or sell that lumber—just let 'em try!"

Beck and the other A.F. of L. leaders in the West took in-
ventory of their resources for what would be a showdown
struggle. They had the truck drivers, a big, tough union that
was more solidly organized along the Pacific seaboard than
anywhere else in the nation. They had the carpenters, the
men who would have to hammer and plane a large proportion of whatever lumber the C.I.O. loggers produced. They
also had a fairly sizable group of timber workers who disputed the majority mandate to abandon the A.F. of L.—men
who were more conservative than their fellows, or who foresaw the hopelessness of the battle that lay ahead. These lumberjacks, although not as numerous, were little less formidable than those who had gone over to the C.I.O. They could
fight hard at the barricades.

The strange conflict began. It immediately became apparent that the A.F. of L. embargo was effective. The C.I.O.
could fell and saw the trees, but there the process stopped.

The yards clogged with lumber. Beck had established a rigid boycott. Teamsters would not truck the lumber, and carpenters would not use it. The industry slowly folded up. Axes and saws rusted in the autumn rain.

This ugly stalemate, continuing for month after month, has botched the timber industry in the Columbia River basin. The woodlands are a snarl of closed camps and idle mills. Thousands of men have been thrown out of work and onto inadequate relief. Valuable orders that may never be recaptured have gone to the Canadian market. The loss in wages and production has been cautiously estimated at twelve million dollars. Guerrilla warfare has taken place incessantly. C.I.O. workers have been beaten up and intimidated by the teamsters' manhandling "goon squads." Longshoremen with calloused fists have hurled the scornful cry of "Scab!" at the lumberjacks loyal to the A.F. of L. It is an internecine labor struggle far grimmer than any that has ever occurred in the forests between employer and employee. President Roosevelt has cited the lumber situation as one of the most flagrant examples of "abuse" of power by organized labor.

The embargo against C.I.O. timber has not been impenetrable, but it has been sufficiently tight to harass an already staggering industry. Beck and his allies have concentrated their forces in San Francisco, where much of the lumber from the Northwest's limitless woodlands is unloaded. Refusal of the teamsters to move it has resulted in chaos and confusion. Added to this is the boycott on the part of the carpenters, as well as the various subtle pressures that the A.F. of L. can apply to prospective lumber buyers. Mill after mill operating with C.I.O. crews has had to silence its saws. The embargo hurt the lumber business just enough to convert a slender margin of profit into an operating loss. For a while left-wingers in the timber belt maintained that the camps were shutting down not because of the embargo, but because of collusion between the employers and the A.F. of L. to force the lumberjacks back into the Brotherhood. This contention evanesced when Bridges himself told the San Francisco Business Men's Committee of Forty-three that the boycott was hampering the C.I.O. in the Northwest lumber war. He intimated that the longshoremen, in retaliation, might decline to load or unload the products of the mills and camps where a majority of the loggers had stayed with the A.F. of L.

In the autumn of 1937, a few months after the founding of the Woodworkers' Federation and its almost coincidental affiliation with the C.I.O., the National Labor Relations Board made a detailed survey of the lumber mess in the region near the juncture of the Columbia and the Willamette River. The Board's investigators found the bulk of rank-and-file sentiment decisively favorable to the Woodworkers and proportionately hostile to the Brotherhood. Hutcheson's organizers were in as bad repute as when they wilted in the 1933 and 1934 strikes. At the West Oregon Lumber Company, for example, the Board announced that 88 per cent of the men had signed C.I.O. petitions. The Inman-Poulsen Lumber Company reported 81 per cent. Other results were only slightly less emphatic. Yet most of these mills were either forbiddingly silent or running in desultory fashion. What the A.F. of L. could not do at a Labor Board election it was able to accomplish with a boycott backed up by the "goon squads." Raymond Clapper has inferred that in the combat in the forests the A.F. of L. has been willing to sabotage the whole principle of collective bargaining to beat the C.I.O. This is largely correct, but the situation is not as elementary as that. The few progressives still left in the A.F. of L. maintain that had the bulk of the progressives not gone over to the other union, together they might have ended the domination of Hutcheson and his stooges. Now there are two factions; bitter warfare stirs the woodlands; the reactionaries have tightened their grip in the A.F. of L., and the enemies of labor have an excuse for trying to hamstring both outfits. Nor is it an answer to label all the A.F. of L. survivors as traitors. One of the main targets for C.I.O. criticism in Oregon is Kelley Loe. Yet this A.F. of L. leader has put practically all his savings into a magazine called *Everybody's Business*, one of the few outspoken journals ever published in the state. When he was exposing corruption and bigotry that the daily papers dared not touch, many of the present spokesmen of the C.I.O. did not give him even perfunctory financial help. So despite the indefensibility of the A.F. of L. position in lumber, the dilemma is of many elements, and epithets will not solve it.

Even the sources of public opinion rabidly antagonistic to the C.I.O. seem agreed that in the fierce battle at the forest barricades the A.F. of L. has adopted a strictly dog-in-the-manger strategy. If it cannot control the timber workers, then the mills and camps must be prevented from operating. The *Oregon Voter*, a weekly magazine voicing the sentiments of that State's most conservative business interests, has declared, "Here in the Pacific Northwest, the A.F. of L. has denied to employees the right to choose their own bargaining agency unless they choose a union designated by the A.F. of L." Beck does not recognize the privilege of the C.I.O. to exist in the Promised Land of the Columbia River basin. With the possible exception of Tom Girdler of Republic Steel, the pudgy leader of the truck drivers has proved the most redoubtable foe yet encountered by Lewis' unions. "In Portland," according to the *Voter*, "the C.I.O. lumber workers are being starved into submission; the plight of their families is tragic." Spokesmen for the C.I.O. have appeared before the Portland School Board and pleaded that money be provided so that their children can have milk and graham-cracker lunches. Many of these lumber workers' youngsters have gone through an Oregon winter with tattered clothes and worn-out shoes. During all this the loggers have been told that the boycott will be lifted and they can go back to work as soon as they return to the A.F. of L. The owner of the West Oregon mill wrote a letter to his men that began: "As matters stand today, we cannot continue in business. The condition of the market is bad enough, but when you add to that a boycott that drives us out of one of our principal distribution points [San Francisco] and threatens to drive us out of others, we throw up our hands and howl for help. What are you going to do about it?"

Some of the men have capitulated. That more have not done so is surprising. Hungry mouths at home are a powerful influence. "The big pressure that is bringing the C.I.O. members back into the A.F. of L. one at a time," the *Voter* has contended, "is the need of milk for babies. The prospect, or the necessity, of going on relief to get food, fuel, and shelter is an acute personal problem. They feel very bitter over being compelled by A.F. of L. ruthlessness to give up the union of their own choice and resubmit themselves and their rights to earn a living to a control which by vote they discontinued."

When the woodworkers organized their Federation and moved, like a migratory tribe, out of the Carpenters' Brotherhood, twilight seemed to have set in on the day of A.F. of L. domination in the Promised Land of the timber area. Now the old-line labor leadership sees the gleam of continued control. Beck's embargo has saved the A.F. of L. on the Coast. What once appeared to be a runaway for the C.I.O. in lumber has become a closely locked stalemate. The timber boycott has been the hardest blow dealt the C.I.O. since Little Steel.

Unfortunately, it also has been a blow at democracy in organized labor. Even the bitterest enemies of the C.I.O. admit that the A.F. of L. embargo has reduced to a nullity the principle of industrial self-determination. The closing and harassing of the mills that voted to abandon the Brotherhood have tested the formula by which resourcefulness and ruthlessness can be combined to destroy majority rule in the American labor movement.

-5-

The warfare in the forests is tremendously significant. As goes the lumber showdown between the C.I.O. and the A.F. of L., so will go the labor controversy in the Far West. As the Far West goes, so may go the nation. Yet the timber strife has an extrinsic significance of almost equal consequence. What effect is it having on the social and political perspective of the great area on the sundown side of the Mississippi—the area that the President regards as a Promised Land and which some day may be colonized by ten million Americans from beyond the plains? Is it prejudicing the people of the Pacific seaboard against labor's efforts to organize?

Few situations have had so many elements calculated to antagonize the general public. There is Beck, obese, domineering, and crafty. His "goon squad" is full of thugs, prize fighters, and other plug-uglies. Opposed to him is Bridges, who symbolizes to the whole country the zenith of radicalism and class animosities in the forces of labor. The president of the Woodworkers' Federation is a fiery young Canadian named Harold Pritchett. Shrewdly timed attacks by the A.F. of L. have terminated his visitor's visa on numerous occasions. Both he and Bridges are constantly in the head-

lines because of their interminable efforts to resist deportation. This has attached the "alien" stigma, a sure target for
execration. Throughout the entire month of February, 1938,
the front pages of the newspapers of the Northwest were
monopolized by two stories—the antialien drives against
Bridges and Pritchett, and the police round-up of a horde of
teamster beat-up gangs. The association of the C.I.O. lumber
leadership with un-American activities and the identification
of the A.F. of L. lumber leadership with terrorism and racketeering seemed almost an automatic outcome of these events.

The timber combat has additional ingredients not condu-
cive to popularity. The very nature of the conflict tends to repel
the public. It is not a struggle of labor for better working conditions and a higher standard of living; it is an attempt by one union to thwart the endeavors of another. Some
employers paying union wages and willing to accept a closed
shop have been innocent victims. With the tyrannical Beck
and his pugilistic "goons" on one side, and the radical Bridges
with his Communist allies on the other, the scene has appeared propitious for a surge of antilabor vigilantism without
parallel in recent years.

The surge has not materialized. There have been sporadic
law-and-order commotions and a few revivals of the class
bitterness that was prevalent during the lumber strikes in the
early period of the New Deal. But these manifestations have
been only a flicker of the holocaust of animosity that the chaotic lumber hurly-burly might arouse in any other part of
the country. Even an inferential indorsement of Fascism by
the governor of Oregon failed completely to kindle the fires
of reaction. "These gangster leaders are brutal and selfish in
spirit, and their hands are bloody as those of the pirates of
old," said Governor Charles H. Martin in assailing labor
strategists "who want to do away with the capitalistic system.

"The Italians wouldn't submit; they organized their black-shirts," the governor declared. "The Germans wouldn't submit, so they had their brownshirts and Hitler. I don't believe Americans will submit."

That such outbursts as this have not stimulated a series of antilabor insurrections is largely attributable to the type of territory in which they have been uttered. The Far West is the newest part of the United States. It is the outpost of the nation. Is psychology and thinking habits are different from those of the rest of the country. Its people accept crises with greater stoicism. They are not so jittery and hysterical as their fellow citizens on the other side of the Mississippi. This attitude of the Far West toward apparently crucial occurrences is a major factor in the lumber struggle. It is the principal reason why America's bitterest labor warfare has not resulted in America's most frightful period of antilabor violence. Any consideration of the knock-down and drag-out interunion battle in the Northwest's tall timber must be accompanied by an analysis of the regional psychology which accepts the episode without widespread hysteria and fanaticism.

The whole of the United States is young as nations go, but the East is venerable compared to the great area west of the Plains. There had been settlements on the Delaware and Hudson rivers almost two centuries before the first white men paddled down the turbulent reaches of the Columbia. New York is almost two hundred twenty-five years older than Seattle.

In the same way, the East had many of the complex problems of modern society before the West was carved out of the wilderness. The Tweed Ring was already in power when settlers in the Oregon Country were still battling Chief Joseph and his Nez Percé warriors. New York was already constructing the Brooklyn Bridge when Custer made his last tragic stand on the Little Big Horn.

This discrepancy in maturity and development has existed through the years and still exists. The East is an area of tradition. It has a past. The Promised Land of the Far West is still a frontier. A number of Eastern States trace their political history back to such statesmen as Jefferson, Hamilton, and the Adamses. In the West there are States represented in Congress by men who have been in office practically ever since those States were admitted to the Union.

All this adds up to a sharp difference in mood as well as background. The West has not settled down. It still has the buoyancy and optimism of a new land, and tradition means little. In the East an old inn is a landmark; in the West it is just another building. Whatever thought the West may give to its past is largely superficial. There are frontier festivals and celebrations, and there are occasional tablets and markers; but the past can hardly be called venerable, nor is the attention paid to it exactly veneration. The West dwells largely in the present, seldom looking for long either behind or ahead.

It is the frontier way to live from day to day, concerned primarily with hard, tangible realities, not with problems remote in time or distance. So if, for example, changing numbers on a board or a paper tape in Wall Street fail to cast gloom in the West, there is a reason. Of course, it is another matter when those numbers are reflected in dwindling shipments of cattle or in unemployment in the silver mines; then the problem becomes immediate and tangible. But until such an effect is felt, there is little worry.

Another factor in the frontier way of life is the willingness to take a chance, to strike out boldly in new directions. Out of the West, therefore, have come such movements as the Single Tax League, the initiative and referendum, the Production-for-Use clubs, the Townsend Plan, the demand for public ownership of power. But note that all these movements have been concerned with definite economic aims of interest to the day in which they were born. What more definite than the idea of cutting electric rates, or paying two hundred dollars a month to everyone past sixty years old? There is objectivity in the West; no such theorizing as the East indulges in. The organizations to protect civil liberties and to preserve the Constitution or the American system of government are Eastern products.

And if society in the West is practical—at least in its aims—and organized on a day-to-day basis, it is so because individual life is that way. Life is less complicated in most of the West. The great bulk of the Westerners live close to the land. They feed and clothe themselves with what they produce, or they are so close to the producer that they feel their nearness to the land. The myriad of intermediate exchanges which results in the entrepreneur-to-customer relationships of the East are surprisingly lacking out West. Life is more complex than it was when Senator Borah was a young man, but still far simpler than it is across the Divide.

There are general stores in the Northwest, hundreds of them. Farmers bring in their eggs and cream, their poultry and their produce, and they trade, literally, for overalls and shoes and dress goods, for coffee and sugar and salt. The farmer in timbered country cuts a few extra cords of firewood and trades it for a receipt for a payment on his mortgage. The banker may eat beef "fed out" by a farmer who borrowed money from the bank to finance his feeding.

Transactions have more directness and fewer middlemen out West than they have in the East. And since such dealings

are less subject to the vicissitudes of business and fluctuations
of the stock market than are most transactions in the East, a
slump in Wall Street makes little difference. The economic
machinery of the West is neither so intricate nor so compli-
cated; it is not so likely to be jarred out of kilter or brought
to a standstill by vibrations in the business structure.

Even beyond this, there is a psychological assurance in
living close to the land. The mere sight of wide acres and
ripening fields and fattening herds makes the beholder less
reluctant to believe that all is lost when some one in Europe
talks of war or some one in Detroit warns of revolution. In
such a region as the Far West, of more importance by far
than a Wall Street slump are grasshoppers or hail or drought
or dust. The West watches the weather while the East
watches the ticker tape.

Perhaps this condition operates largely in another factor of
difference—the time-lag. The East, so greatly industrial or
dependent on industry, suffers first in any depression. Business declines, production slows up, men are laid off. It may
be months before the effects are felt acutely in the West.
Fewer families depend directly on industry for their daily
bread. More families have resources in land and the products
of the land, which are less affected by trade trends. And just
as depression strikes less swiftly and less severely in the West,
so does recovery come more easily. The whole region moves
along at a steadier pace. If there are not so many severe
depressions, there are also fewer frenzied booms.

With increasing frequency and force since the World War,
international events have been reflected in Eastern business.
This is natural, since trade routes are the nerves along which
an industrial country senses the import of events abroad.
Japanese planes drop bombs on Shanghai, and Wall Street
worries. Hitler and Mussolini exchange visits, and a new

agreement is signed among the dictators. Eastern business is nervous; the markets are slow and irregular, and the man with a job begins to worry.

In the West such news is read and passed by. The amphitheater of international happenings is far away from the rancher in Wyoming, the farmer in Oregon, and the fruit grower on an Idaho irrigation project. Strangely, this is true even when the most significant foreign events are taking place in the Orient, to which the West is closer geographically than the East. But so far as the West is concerned, wars have always been remote. The battle fields of France were twice as far from Oregon as from New York. It was no mere accident that, of the six United States Senators who opposed our entering the World War, four were from the Middle West and Northwest.

So while the industrial East sees an effect on its markets when shells burst in China or a new *coup d'état* is organized in Berlin, the West refuses to worry. It lives largely unto itself—or thinks it does—and it looks to the hinterlands rather than the ocean lanes for solution of its own economic problems.

A contributing factor to this Western indifference to international affairs is the great distance between the West and the national capital. It is in Washington that diplomats are interviewed, and it is from Washington that aggressor nations are officially censured—even though the President may speak in Chicago. And while Washington is only a few hours from the great cities of the East, it is a continent removed from the West. A Senator from New York can talk face to face with his constituents at night and be back in Washington in time for the next day's session. Few of the Western Senators make any attempt to get back home while Congress is in session. Six thousand miles is a long way to travel.

Most Westerners have yet to see their national capital. Washington to them is symbolized by the buildings they have seen pictured in magazines and newspapers—the Washington Monument, the Lincoln Memorial, the dome of the Capitol, the White House. But to the Easterner, the capital is not only real but near. It is the place where conferences are held when the business machine skips a cog. It is a sounding board for labor leaders who want relief funds for their striking followers. It is a loud-speaker for industrialists who want government troops to open their strike-bound mills and factories. It is the place where pacts are invoked and navy appropriations are approved and wars declared.

These are all factors in the psychological differences of East and West. But perhaps they can all be added up and defined as a fundamental difference in spirit and background which is an inevitable result of environment and history. The pioneer spirit of individualism and self-sufficiency and daring still prevails in the West.

In the West are people still living who suffered hardships in reaching the new country and found little of ease when they got there—men and women who crept across the plains and mountains in wagon trains or were buffeted around the Horn in fever-ridden sailing ships. They fought against great odds, and they won out; and they still scoff at the "easy life" of the East. And their children and grandchildren are of the same strain.

Depressions and stock-market panics and union battles are minor matters to men who hacked a civilization out of a wilderness and battled Indians to save their own lives. They have settled a vast empire in a lifetime, and they are proud of the job they have done. Some day they, too, may begin to worry and take their emotional cues from the ticker tape and calamity howler, but not while the memories of their tangible triumphs over the major forces of nature are fresh in their minds.

Many of these unique features of Western life seem far afield from the labor movement. But they explain why the fiercest labor warfare in American history can occur in the Columbia River basin without inciting the populace to vigilantism. The massacres in which the wobblies and their enemies fought were grisly and bloody. But they did not arouse hysteria among the masses of the people, for a few years after the general strike in Seattle and the I.W.W. raids in the woods "Fighting Bob" La Follette beat out John W. Davis in every State in the Northwest. The underlying factors of Western psychology are remote from the conflict between the A.F. of L. and the C.I.O. for the control of the lumber industry. This remoteness, however, does not prevent them from being important factors in that conflict—factors which protect organized labor from extinction on its most barbarous battle line.

To be sure, there have been discursive episodes of oppression and intolerance in the nation's richest woodland area. But those incidents have not been sustained. Oregon fell momentarily into the clutches of the Klan; then it shook loose and overwhelmingly elected a Jew as governor. Alarmed business men in Tacoma and Seattle might hold target practice in their basements, yet they could snap out of this Fascist frenzy in time to boast that their cities had the best publicly owned power plants in America. Most of the reaction and vigilantism in the Northwest have been relatively mild; the severe episodes have been brief. Not long after the passage of the abortive initiative bill closing Oregon's religious schools, a Catholic became the most popular Democratic politician in the State.

The charitableness of the public toward the grim lumber

warfare has been proof of these qualities. What bloody circumstances might such a situation arouse elsewhere! The overbearing Beck with his "goons," the radical Bridges with his doctrine of eliminating the employer class—perfect targets for a Mohawk Valley formula! The people of the Northwest have resisted these temptations. They have let the labor rivals fight it out. They have been far more tolerant, in fact, than their public officials. Governor Martin of Oregon told the farmers to grab their pitchforks and march against the labor agitators. The officials of the State's most respectable and powerful farm organizations immediately rebuked him for trying to incite the populace to violence. The Associated Farmers, a vigilante organization seeking to hamstring A.F. of L. and C.I.O. alike, has not been able to get a fraction as many farm members as the progressive and dependable Grange.

In recent labor difficulties the governors of Eastern States have trembled lest vigilantism get out of hand. Yet under far more exasperating circumstances in the Columbia basin, the people have warned their officials against giving vigilantism encouragement. The outpost spirit does not become hysterical so easily.

If the forces of conservatism and radicalism in labor had to come to direct grips anywhere, they were wise to do so in the Promised Land of the Far Northwest. The psychology of the frontier is less likely than that of the metropolis to destroy the labor titans while they struggle at the timber barricades.

11. Cockeyed Politics in the Hinterlands

OVER the desolate ridge of hills lying between the States of Idaho and Washington, a big monoplane streaked at 7:52 on the morning of April 20 of this year. Sitting fretfully in one of the upholstered seats was a thin-faced man with high cheek bones, Clarence D. Martin, the governor of Washington. The plane was specially chartered, and he had just spent $1,380 out of his own pocket for it to speed him westward from Chicago.

At 8:05 on the same morning a barrel-chested individual in a breezy suit arrived breathlessly at the Washington capitol in the little town of Olympia. He slammed a certified and pompous-looking document on the counter in the Secretary of State's office. "I want to call a special session of the legislature," he announced with a flamboyant twist of his waxed mustache.

The woman secretary of state looked at the clock. "You're too late, Lieutenant Governor Meyers," she said imperiously. "I have official notice that the governor has just returned to the State."

Victor Aloysius ("Just Call Me Vic") Meyers, erstwhile master of ceremonies and leader of the band at Seattle's most popular night spot, the Club Victor, struck a defiant pose.

"I'll carry this to the highest court in the State!" he cried. Then he strode dramatically from the granite-pillared capitol.

The next day the Washington supreme court, after hearing the great entertainer and statesman argue in surprisingly eloquent fashion, decided that by the scant margin of thirteen minutes had the governor retained sovereignty over his supposed second-in-command.

These scenes climaxed a series of weird and bizarre events without precedent in the annals of American public life. Anywhere else than Washington, such events would have been a nine days' wonder. That they were accepted in the Evergreen State in comparatively matter-of-fact manner proves that extraordinary and unbelievable politics have become an old story along the continent's sundown rim, where Puget Sound washes the ramparts of the Cascades.

Governor Martin's aerial version of John Gilpin's ride came after several years of boasting by Howard Costigan, the volatile, rumple-haired secretary of the left-wing Washington Commonwealth Federation, that the governor was "virtually a political prisoner." Just let him dare leave the State, challenged Costigan, and Lieutenant Governor Vic Meyers would put through a program of liberal and radical reforms that would make Martin's conservative brain reel like a log in a whirlpool.

The governor stuck closely to his hinterland principality and refused to risk this venturesome threat. Then President Roosevelt outlined the Federal government's second pump-priming foray. Governor Martin decided he had to go to the national capital to shove his State's receptacle under the money spigot. A Congressional committee also was holding hearings on a proposed new national park in the Washington wilderness, and the governor had some emphatic ideas on that. Where was Vic Meyers? The governor's aides made a search.

Vic was fishing off the coast of California! At last Martin could quit his outpost exile. He piled hastily into an airplane and began his first trip east in five years.

While the governor soared over the frontier and out across the plains, the bandmaster's left-wing adherents got busy. Their hour had come, too! "Has anyone seen Victor A. Meyers?" flashed over innumerable radio hook-ups. Sheriffs, patrolmen, posses, and newspaper reporters searched the seaboard for the lieutenant governor of Washington. The greatest political fantasy of the century was imminent. Seattle's celebrated night-club impresario had a chance to take over the whole State. After twenty-four hours of terrific effort, Vic was finally located. Northward up the Pacific coast he started a pellmell dash. Patrol cars were commandeered and trains held. Vic arrived in Seattle with only a pair of sandals covering his bare feet; he had not had time to change the clothes he wore on his interrupted fishing excursion.

While the lieutenant governor munched sandwiches and his advisers told him why a special session of the legislature was necessary at once, Governor Martin on the other side of the continent read big, black headlines implying he was about to be dispossessed from control of his State. He dug into his wallet and chartered a special plane. He had to be on the western side of the Washington-Idaho border before the bandmaster called the legislature into action. Once the call was issued it would be irrevocable. In Martin's balanced-budget scheme of things, there was no place for a legislative jamboree presided over by Vic Meyers and devoted to such notions as larger old-age pensions, more generous relief handouts, and new public power plants and housing projects.

By thirteen slender minutes the governor thwarted the great entertainer's *coup d'état*—although the State supreme court had to listen for several hours while Vic, with the same gestures that once heralded the Terpsichorean feats of the chorus or the playing of the latest fox trot at the Club Victor, insisted that his brief reign as governor was legal anyhow, and that the proclamation for the special session should be allowed to stand.

This unhappy incident in the chronicle of a great commonwealth in the West is ended, but its effect and influence survive. Before Governor Martin risked his hurried dash across the continent, he had an idea that he was a political prisoner in his own State. Now he knows he is. A short time ago he crossed the Columbia River and went into Oregon to inspect Bonneville Dam. After nervously looking at his watch every few minutes for half an hour, he rushed back to Washington to cut Vic off from any shenanigans he might attempt. The governor insists he does not dare leave the State now until the legislature enacts a law enabling him to do so without danger of the national guard being called out, the legislature convened, or the penitentiary gates allegedly opened. He does this insisting with a wry face and a grim jaw. The furious, $1,380 cross-country dash that canceled Vic's special session has not increased the governor's political popularity. Shortly after the spectacular hegira he rode in almost ghastly silence in a Blossom Festival parade in the Wenatchee valley. But the night-club harlequin returned to Seattle as a hero. He had tried to perform for the old folks, the left-wingers, and the reliefers—and the airplane argosy that spoiled it was the governor's fault, not Vic's.

-2-

Eugene O'Neill, who lived for a while on the shores of Puget Sound when he was gathering material for his new

cycle of eight plays,* is said to have once jestingly compared
Washington politics with a Gilbert and Sullivan operetta. The
comparison was appropriate yet circumspect. Politics in the
State that is the nation's upper left-hand corner prove that
perhaps George S. Kaufman's farces are not exaggerated,
after all. Not many novels on American political life describe
happenings as seemingly farfetched as those which actually
occur within the borders of Washington. In addition to being
the country's principal storehouse of timber, Chinook salmon,
apples, and hydroelectric power, the Evergreen State is also
the citadel of cockeyed and fantastic politics.

For years in the drama of national affairs, Washington has
provided the comedy relief. This caldron of boisterousness
and hilarity began to boil long ago.

Bushy pompadoured Isaac Stevens was the first governor of
the Washington Territory. At the provisional capital a great
reception and dinner had been arranged in his honor. He arrived tired and dusty and badly mussed after a long horseback ride through the wilderness. The men at the dining hall
refused him admittance. They thought he was some raga-
muffin adventurer from the timberlands. The hungry governor knocked at the kitchen door and asked for something to
eat. The head cook was a kind-hearted soul. So government
in Washington got under way officially as the guests ate roast
beef in the dining room and wondered if the governor had
been ambushed by Indians, and the governor voraciously gob-
bled up stew and other trimmings in the kitchen.

Lieutenant W. A. Slaughter was an heroic army officer
slain by savages during the frontier period of the Northwest.
A town midway between Seattle and Tacoma was named in

---

* The locale of several of these plays is expected to be the Pacific Northwest
in the early days of the Oregon Country. O'Neill has done considerable research
on the dry-farming disaster near Grand Coulee, the tragic fate of the Donner
party, and other memorable incidents in the history of the region.

his honor. Even from this tribute the carefree inhabitants of early Washington twisted a grisly jest. They did not want the town called Slaughter. To persuade the legislature to change the name, they applied it to the local hotel. "Right this way to the Slaughter House, folks!" chanted the baggage boys who met the first chugging trains from over the divide.

The legislature renamed the community Auburn.

Half a century ago Washington's garish unconformity amused a young English newspaperman from India. "They are all mad here, all mad," Rudyard Kipling wrote facetiously at Tacoma, forty miles down the choppy Sound from Seattle.* The Washington of today has all the slapstick tendencies that induced Kipling to write this quip and forced the first governor to eat his welcoming banquet on a kitchen stool. Jim Farley is supposed to have referred to "the forty-seven States and the Soviet of Washington." Twice Vic Meyers has been overwhelmingly elected lieutenant governor of this uproarious State, but he tells his constituents he does not know how to spell "lieutenant."

Washington is a curious combination of the hinterland and the metropolis. In all seven States wholly or partially encompassed in the basin of the Columbia River,† there are only five cities of any size. Three of these are in Washington: Seattle, Tacoma, and Spokane. The other two are Portland and Salt Lake City. So Washington, more than any other commonwealth in the country, merges the frontier and the modern industrial community. It has the zest and simplicity and newness of an outpost region, and it also has the technological and social problems incidental to urban life. Wash-

---

* The essays which Kipling penned when he visited the Northwest appeared originally in the *Civil and Military Gazette* and the *Pioneer*. Along with Mark Twain's *Roughing It* they gave the world at large some of the first intimate glimpses of the vast American hinterland beyond the Mississippi River.

† Idaho, Washington, Montana, Oregon, Wyoming, Nevada, and Utah.

ington is featured both by the frontier that is still primeval and by the frontier that has developed and expanded into civilization. It has the spirit of the hinterlands, and at the same time the contacts and functions and interdependence of an urban area. The first settlers where Seattle is now located called their stockaded hamlet "New York *Alki*," which in Indian jargon means "New York by and by." This flame of exuberance and recklessness has not flickered out in Washington's cities as it has in most American communities. It has been kept glowing by the omnipresent influence of the vast frontier that distinguishes the Northwest from the rest of the nation. The basic institutions of mankind in the cities are different from those in a self-sufficient rural society common to the frontier, declares the National Resources Committee.* The Committee also observes:

"In depicting the characteristics of city dwellers, therefore, and in distinguishing them from their rural fellow citizens, it is essential to recognize that they are by no means of uniform type. . . ."

The complete strata of society—the hinterland as primitive as when the first white man came, the thickly farmed countryside, the little crossroads community, the great American city—all are merged in Washington as in no other State. One result has been a species of politics unique even to a region which specializes in queer and unorthodox performances in the arena of public affairs.

Two years ago the Democrats of Washington held a State convention without parallel in the annals of orderly government. The delegates endorsed production-for-use and demanded a national referendum on Supreme Court decisions. Some one introduced a resolution advocating government

* *Our Cities: Their Role in the National Economy*, National Resources Committee, 1937.

ownership of all natural resources; but a flustered stenographer typed it "national resources," and the convention passed it that way. The session was so boisterous that the chairman splintered four gavels, and the sergeant-at-arms had to hack a limb from a fir tree to use as a club. Virtually every left-winger in the Northwest tried to attend as a delegate, with the result that many of the participants in the convention cast twenty-nine one hundred sixteenths or seventeen one hundred forty-fifths of a vote. Approximately sixteen hundred delegates were crowded into a high-school gymnasium built to accommodate about four hundred fifty people. The hall sounded like a locomotive works and looked like Times Square on New Year's Eve. No one was certain what was happening, and although the convention condemned capitalism it forgot to endorse President Roosevelt for reëlection.

This wayward gathering would have been a public curiosity in any State except the one where a burly amateur aviator named John C. Stevenson could become a political power. Not so many years ago Stevenson showed up in Seattle and achieved fame as the official orator for a chain of painless dentists. He started to advocate bigger and more frequent old-age pensions and soon got himself elected a King County commissioner, appearing on the ballot as "Radio Speaker John C. Stevenson." From this point of vantage, he began to put together a powerful political machine. Then Governor Lehman of New York, in an extradition request, alleged that Stevenson actually was John C. Stockman, wanted in Binghamton for grand larceny. Governor Martin of Washington refused to grant the extradition. At the last election Stevenson turned on his asserted protector and carried the city against Martin in the Democratic gubernatorial primaries. The *Argus* has referred to this unique political manipulator as "Mr. Stockman, alias Stevenson." Some day Stevenson may be a

had condemned the frequent epidemics of anti-Japanese jingo-ism that sweep through the Puget Sound region, and he was virtually the lone Democrat who dared to protest when Jim Farley suggested for postmaster of Seattle a man who had failed to obtain a rating in the civil service examinations. Zioncheck tried to read every bill introduced in the House; he also drank excessively. The combination of overwork and liquor probably resulted in insanity. He was an immigrant from Poland, and his original name was Marjan Antoni Sajaczek. He worked his way through the University of Washington peddling fish, and was elected president of the student body by the campus groups opposed to fraternity snobbery and football professionalism. He immediately ob-jected to a series of extravagant expenditures for athletic equipment, maintaining that they would delay the construc-tion of a much-needed study and recreational center. A troop of behemoth football players, angered by such outrageous interference with the "gravy-train," dressed up one night in hooded robes, and after shaving off Zioncheck's hair threw him into Lake Washington. The *Post-Intelligencer* was privy to this campus vigilantism, and a photographer was on hand to make a flashlight picture of the incident.

But Zioncheck was no mere college rebel. As soon as he became a member of the bar in 1929, he began defending de-portees and others in danger of losing their civil rights. With Jack R. Cluck he argued a succession of cases for the Civil Liberties Union. He was an enthusiastic admirer of Senator George Norris, and in 1931 interested himself in the public ownership fight in Seattle. He led the successful recall cam-paign against Mayor Frank Edwards, who was opposed to the municipal power activities of J. D. Ross.*

In 1932 Zioncheck was the spearhead in two victorious

* See Chapter 4. Ross, incidentally, was a pallbearer at Zioncheck's funeral.

forays at the polls. He aided in the election to the Senate of
Homer T. Bone, relentless crusader for public ownership,
and he himself was sent to the House. In Congress he joined
with the progressive bloc. He supported production-for-use,
and continually raised his voice against excessive military expenditures. He made an exhaustive analysis of the use of
various national guard units in labor disputes, and declared
that the people were paying taxes to enable the guard "to see
to it that scabs get in there and break strikes." He supported
the New Deal power and labor measures, but consistently
opposed any administration gearing up of the war machine.

Zioncheck had a plentiful supply of moral bravery. He was
not afraid of the power of the Seattle *Post-Intelligencer* and
frequently attacked Hearst. He scored the attempts to build
up a Nazi, anti-Semitic movement in his district, and he was
one of the first congressman to expose the Townsend agitation as an alleged money-making racket. A distressingly large
number of pseudo-progressives chimed in with the $200-a-
month pension chorus, hoping thereby to hold the crackpot
vote. Zioncheck refused to collaborate in this intellectual chicanery. He said the Townsend snare was ruining the chances
of a sane old-age pension program. He put in the first resolution to investigate the Townsend financial set-up.

Political courage and intellectual honesty—those were Zioncheck's outstanding virtues. He also had faults. He was arrogant and egotistical. He needlessly antagonized people by
discourtesy or downright rudeness. Frequently he was vulgar.
Many of his vituperative remarks in the House overshot the
limits of good taste and decorum. Against these shortcomings,
he had an attractive personality when he chose to be amiable.
Small and wiry, he seemed to have boundless energy. His
collapse was at least partly due to overwork.

It is difficult to say whether Zioncheck would have been

reëlected if he had lived. There is no doubt that many of his active supporters had been alienated by his behavior. But the workers and unemployed still had faith in his integrity, and they might have pulled him through the election. Before his collapse he was a possible gubernatorial candidate, and it was considered certain that he would one day be promoted to the United States Senate. His breakdown and death must be set down as an American tragedy, for Marion Zioncheck typified many of the best traditions of the Republic. An immigrant boy—the son of a family fleeing from oppression abroad—he took advantage of the opportunities offered by the great democracy of the West. He became the champion of oppressed and unfortunate people, and even until his garish end they retained unshakable confidence in him.

To millions of Americans Marion Zioncheck was a rambunctious young politician running wild, a haywire alcoholic who waded in fountains in downtown New York. Few episodes so illuminate the irony and incongruity of Washington's political harlequinade. Before his mental collapse the slender young Congressman was afraid of neither pressure group nor economic interest. He defied the threats of the Townsendites and the abuse of the Hearst newspapers. He refused to follow the devious trail imperiously mapped by the Communists, and he would not wear the yoke of Farley's patronage harness. Today he is more remembered in Washington for his intellectual integrity than for the lunatic behavior which preceded and led up to his suicide. The most complete collection of economic and social literature in the Northwest is the Marion A. Zioncheck Memorial section of the Seattle library. Each year people add to it more books of Laski, the Beards, Bowers, and Duranty.

Just before the body of the Polish boy who peddled fish to help a struggling immigrant family survive in the pull-and-haul of Western society was lowered into the grave at Evergreen Cemetery, the Reverend Fred Shorter said, "Marion was a shell-shocked comrade who died at the barricades fighting to the very last for the poor and dispossessed." Seconds before he threw himself from his office window Zioncheck scrawled in incoherent fashion on a piece of Congressional stationery, "My only hope in life was to improve the condition of an unfair economic system. . . ."

-3-

The buffoonery, waggishness, and clowning of Washington politics have their most uninhibited expression in the person of Victor Aloysius Meyers. Since 1932 he has been lieutenant governor of the State. His career would be practically unbelievable on the stage or between the covers of a storybook.

Running a night club has put men in a variety of spots—in jail, in clover, in bankruptcy, and in the movies. Vic Meyers is the first it has landed in high public office and political power.

Today, in his sixth year as lieutenant governor of the State of Washington, Vic, once proprietor of Seattle's liveliest night club, is putting on the best act in the nation's political circus. Managers of motion picture theaters in Olympia, the capital, are complaining that Vic has made the State senate, over which he presides, a better show than they can afford to offer, and that customers pass up the box offices for gallery seats in the senate chambers.

A born entertainer, an orchestra leader, and a gifted wisecracker, Vic Meyers with his gags has become one of the most successful vote getters in the Northwest.

Visitors to Washington go around to see Vic in action as

dutifully and expectantly as visitors to New York seek out Rudy Vallee. "Watch me make these babies strut," says the lieutenant governor, with a grandiose wave of his hand, and ascends the dignified rostrum. Then he raps for order with a tum-tiddy-um-tum of his gavel, and the fun begins. When the debate becomes bitter and acrimonious, Vic sometimes runs in the official senate quartet, whose *Rock-a-bye Baby* and *Sweet and Low* soothe the august but enraged senators back to smiles. And one night, at a late session, the senate cheered him enthusiastically when he recruited a troupe of singers and musicians to entertain them when they were waiting for conference reports to be brought over from the House.

Sometimes the gallery is favored with a wisecrack as choice as the one he pulled recently when the senate clergyman failed to appear in time to give the opening prayer. The senators had just finished scratching out the lieutenant governor's committee appointments, and he was in a chastened mood. After glancing about cautiously several times and not finding the minister, he said solemnly: "The senate will have to go without an opening prayer today. It hasn't been doing much good around here lately, anyhow."

But Vic Meyers is a successful politician today not merely because he is a good night-club host. Since the voters lifted him hilariously from the Club Victor into the statehouse, he has studied parliamentary law with such success that an old-line Republican leader rose after a lengthy debate on an involved revenue measure, and said:

"I congratulate our presiding officer on his parliamentary procedure during the consideration of this bill. It was as good as we have ever had in this senate."

Lieutenant Governor Meyers beamed. "I will entertain a motion," said he, "to spread the senator's remarks upon the journal."

"I make a motion—" began another Republican senator, and a chorus of ayes silenced the rest of his statement.

"It's unanimous!" cried Vic, and began to hum *Happy Days Are Here Again*.

Vic Meyers was not taken very seriously six years ago when he went bustling into the office of the Secretary of State under the towering dome of the Washington capitol and shouted: "Hurry, everybody! I want to run for governor."

A clerk sprang to the desk. "The filing fee will be sixty dollars, sir," he said.

The chubby face of the ambitious aspirant darkened. He twisted his diminutive waxed mustache perturbedly. "Sixty dollars!" he gasped. "It's too much. What have you got for twenty?"

"Well, there's the lieutenant governor's job. That's only twelve dollars," the clerk replied.

"Fine! I'll take it," cried the ebullient Mr. Meyers. "But I'll have to find out what he does." He paid the twelve-dollar filing fee, and went bustling away.

A few months later he was back—as lieutenant governor of the sovereign commonwealth of Washington, an area larger than England and Wales.

Not long before he was elected to be second in command of his State, folks were predicting a glowing future for Victor Aloysius Meyers. Why, it would be no time, they said, before he had his name in lights along Broadway. Had he not made Club Victor the gayest night spot in Seattle? The girls were prettier there, the entertainers more entertaining, the food tastier, the customers merrier. And of course the music was superior, for Victor Aloysius Meyers himself conducted the band. Already this thirty-three-year-old proprietor and master of ceremonies had won a Pacific coast radio popularity contest, and his band had been one of the first in the Far

West to make phonograph recordings. Vic might even become a second Guy Lombardo.

People remarked that his thin black mustache, round face,
and expansive smile gave him a striking resemblance to Paul
Whiteman. Surely the hour was near when Vic's name in
neon tubing would face the Great White Way in New York.

But there was one place where not even the most imagina-
tive reveler at Club Victor thought the name of his jovial host
would be—on a glass-paneled door in the massive statehouse
at Olympia, with the lettering:

STATE OF WASHINGTON, SENATE CHAMBERS
VICTOR A. MEYERS, LIEUTENANT GOVERNOR

Destiny struck up an acquaintance with Vic one spring
morning in 1931 when his night club was at its peak. Vic had
gone downtown early to Club Victor to assist in the removal
of some lighting fixtures. His nervous, active temperament
would not permit him to stand by idly while the work was
done, so he climbed a stepladder himself. A minute later he
descended in a crash of broken ladder rungs, splintered glass,
dented metal—and a fractured left arm. Vic did not know it
then, but, as he sat there painfully in the debris, he was on
his way to fame.

Naturally, the episode received some attention in the Seattle press. Vic was already regarded around town as a sort of
local prankster, and the slapstick comedy touch of the stepladder incident augmented this reputation. A few weeks later,
the United States government stepped in and closed Club
Victor as a "nuisance." Prohibition agents claimed that the
patrons were drinking openly at the tables. (Remember, that
was still before repeal.) With his fractured arm in a sling,
Vic stood under the canvas canopy at Club Victor and grinned

sheepishly while a deputy marshal pasted up a huge paper sign:

PADLOCKED BY THE FEDERAL GOVERNMENT

As Seattle's premier comedian, Vic met these disasters with good-humored quips, which won more press notices, and soon he was engaged to lead orchestras at two smart hotels and a cabaret. Club Victor was opened again—in less convivial fashion—and Vic planned to establish a branch in near-by Portland.

Then a local mayoralty campaign came along, and one winter afternoon a group of newspapermen sat in the editorial room of the Seattle *Times*, deploring the inferiority of the candidates. It was pretty bad, they declared, that the only big city on the frontier produced so mediocre a field of aspirants. Some one suggested the entire election ought to be scoffed at and ridiculed. Another proposed a series of stunts to parody the whole affair. Why not a candidate able to make Seattle laugh until election day? Doug Welch, the State's cleverest newspaper humorist, thought of the happy-go-lucky orchestra leader, and reached for the telephone. "Hello, Vic!" he called. "If you'll hurry over to the city hall and file for mayor, we'll spread your name all over the first page."

The events which followed are probably without duplicate, anywhere or at any time.

One of the first indications to Seattle voters that there was a new entrant in the mayoralty race came on a chilly February morning in 1932. Up Fourth Avenue strolled a chubby-faced man leading a goat on a chain. A raw wind was sweeping in off Puget Sound, but the man was clad only in a sheet and sandals. His bare legs looked blue with cold. Under his arm he carried a voluminous dictionary which he studiously consulted from time to time. Now and then he turned to eye the goat, which ambled along amiably behind him. The man paid no attention to the crowds lining the street, and he did not utter a word. Occasionally he adjusted the little gold-rimmed spectacles on the end of his nose. He entered a large hotel, sat at the speakers' table at a Shrine luncheon, and refused all food except goat's milk and raw carrots.

Dressed as Mahatma Gandhi, Victor Aloysius Meyers was launching his campaign for mayor of Seattle.

The Gandhi burlesque was part of an elaborate repertoire of skits fostered by his journalistic privy council. Seattle never knew what to expect next. Every afternoon Vic and his band toured the business district on an old brewery wagon, loaded with beer kegs and pulled by four draft horses. "WATCH 'ER CLICK WITH VIC," signs and banners blared. One day, while serenading the Washington Athletic Club with *Ta-ra-ra Boom-de-ay*, the band was sprawled into the street when the beer kegs rolled off the wagon. Vic's high silk hat was crushed flat by a rampant beer keg. "Okay," he grinned as he picked himself up off the car tracks. Incidentally, one of Vic's campaign planks was that he knew Walter Winchell and had taught Walter how to say "Okay."

Vic's opponents were making all sorts of promises regarding what they termed Seattle's antiquated transportation system. He went them one better. He promised to alleviate unemployment among women by placing a hostess on each streetcar. Then Laura La Plante, the movie star, came to town for a theatrical engagement, and Vic ceremoniously installed her on one of Seattle's lumbering old orange-colored trolleys. He and the blonde Miss La Plante rode all over the city, asking passengers if they were comfortable and happy.

Vic said the hostess experiment had proved so successful that he planned to serve cracked ice on the owl-car runs. He also intimated that down-and-out wrestlers and prize fighters might be employed to open jammed streetcar windows.

Here are a few of his other campaign cracks:

The only intelligent way to solve the liquor question is to pass an ordinance forbidding the singing of "Sweet Adeline" after eleven o'clock at night without the permission of the copyright owners.

I don't believe in daylight saving time. Seattle should have two-four time, allegro.

Rumors that I have sold out to the bicycle trust are false! Habitually I go without a vest so that I can't be accused of standing for the vested interests.

I'm not very economical and thrifty myself, but you ought to see my wife! As soon as I am elected, I will turn over the city to her. In two weeks' time Edinburgh, Scotland, will send a commission to Seattle to study the economies my wife will put in.

There's going to be no cheap chiseling at the City Hall. I intend to take it all myself.

I am not going to be a "yes man." I will be a "maybe man." I have noticed that mayors who say "Yes" have a lot of trouble, and that those who say "No" have more. So I am just going to say "Maybe."

Seattle has always been famous for eccentric politicians, but it had never seen anything to match this vivacious young night-club proprietor who conducted a campaign for mayor like the Marx brothers making a movie.

All the candidates were wrangling about who should be chief of police. Vic said he would settle the row by elevating to the position the one man really qualified for the job: Gus Hasselblad, the star piccolo player of the force.

Most of the mayoralty aspirants were harping on tax reduction. Vic declared he had a better idea. He would establish a Department of Worry to console poverty-stricken taxpayers.

Several candidates contended that Seattle should be beautified. Vic suggested flower boxes on water hydrants, and decorated grandstands for excavation watchers.

The candidates dressed as plainly as possible. Everyone was a "man of the people." Vic said it was up to some one to give the campaign a little class. His official costume, when he was not garbed as Gandhi, was tuxedo, silk scarf, top hat, velvet-lapelled overcoat, and kid gloves. He dressed like this even in the daytime. His musicians wore circus band uniforms.

Finally the hectic jamboree ended. The voters of Seattle stopped it on the day of the municipal election. There were ten candidates on the ballot, and Vic finished sixth, forty thousand votes behind the winner. He made a few jests about demanding a recount and then faded into the background.

But obscurity did not sit well with Victor Aloysius Meyers. He had tasted the nectar of fame, and now his diet was incomplete without it. Spring merged into summer and a State-wide primary election neared. And Vic had an idea. He would run for governor! He telephoned the *Times*, which had staged his race for mayor. The newspaper was not interested. Vic decided he would run anyway. But at Olympia he found the filing fee was steeper than he had anticipated. He also discovered that the incumbent lieutenant governor had determined to run for governor, and that the race was wide open for the former position. So he filed for it.

This time the newspapermen did not give him much attention. Vic was becoming a pest, they decided. He had had his fling. They predicted his candidacy would result in failure. But they overlooked one fact: People frequently vote on

name familiarity. Vic's opponents this time were comparatively unknown, while his mayoralty campaign had been first-
page news in all the papers. Vic himself was not hopeful of
his chances, but he thought the venture would be good publicity, at least, for his musical enterprises. So he went ahead,
drawing crowds by playing the saxophone. He even thumped
tom-toms on the Indian reservations until some one told him
the redskins did not vote. Then he staged the Gandhi stunt
again, and the nomination was his.

Horrified citizens now stumped the State, warning the electorate that the farce had gone far enough. They reminded the
voters of the significance of the lieutenant governor's position: he presided over the august State senate; he represented
the State on official occasions; and on the death or retirement
of the governor he became the chief executive of the commonwealth. Did the people of Washington want in such a
key position a man who fell off stepladders, whose night club
was padlocked by the Federal government, who walked
through city and countryside garbed as Mahatma Gandhi,
whose campaign speeches were saxophone solos?

Apparently they did. The final returns were: Judson F.
Falknor, Republican, 243,479 votes; Victor Aloysius Meyers,
Democrat, 286,402 votes.

Under Vic, the Washington State senate has become the
best show on the Pacific coast outside Hollywood. Vic has
personality and dash and fervor. His chubby face beams enthusiasm. He is exuberant and lively, and he puts as much
of these qualities into the senate as he did into his night club.
In fact, he used to recognize Senator Kathryn Malstrom on
the floor of the Senate in the same manner that he heralded
the appearance of adagio dancers on the floor of Club Victor.
"Ah there, Kathryn!" the lieutenant governor would remark
debonairly, with a twist of his waxed mustache.

Vic regards his mustache as not only a private but a public asset. When he asked the legislature to raise his salary, his principal argument was that unless the increase were allowed, he would have to stop waxing his mustache and wear it "Warner Baxter style." Eventually it might become a walrus mustache, he warned.

When he appointed committees on taxation, labor, education, agriculture, and the judiciary, he named an official senate quartet as well. Nothing undignified about that, says Vic, when the senate itself is just an orchestra—a gang of fellows, each blowing his own horn. Despite this buffoonery, Vic has been an efficient president of the upper chamber of Washington's legislature. His ambition is to be a great presiding officer, like Uncle Joe Cannon.

When Vic was reëlected to another four-year term as lieutenant governor, he received, at both the primaries and the general election, the largest vote ever cast for the position in the history of the State. His slogan was: "Me and Roosevelt will win in a walk!"

They did.

Vic polled 437,062 votes. His Republican opponent received 197,615. It was more than a two-to-one victory for Vic. "They laughed when I sat down to run," he boasted. "But who's laughing now?"

In his last campaign Vic was as much the jester and clown as he had been in Seattle four years before. At Sedro Woolley he advocated the use of beer, rather than water, in the tumblers placed before public speakers, a sure road to eloquence. In Seattle Vic announced that he would give a coming-out party for all his creditors to celebrate his "coming out of the red." At Vancouver he said he was campaigning as hard as he could against his reëlection. And in Walla Walla he staged the prize stunt of all. He attended the Whitman

covered-wagon centennial, and leaped—clothes, shoes, and all
—into the watering trough provided for the horses in the
pageant. The populace of Walla Walla clustered about wonderingly as the lieutenant governor of their State splashed
and frolicked in the horse trough like a playful porpoise.

The politicians of Washington are frankly afraid of Vic. A
number of them have told me he is the hardest man on the
Coast to campaign against. He burlesques the activities of his
opponents, and when they attempt to answer him the audience merely laughs. Vic is the most widely known man in
Washington.

Where other politicians must take definite positions or assume embarrassing straddles, Vic can dodge crucial issues with
a jest or chuckle. When some one asks his opinion on a hot
question he never fails to get a laugh by shouting, "I'm okay
on that!" He is in constant demand as a banquet and luncheon speaker, and his orchestra-leading gives him an entrée
that other politicians lack. He is continually asked to wield
the baton at public bazaars and benefit balls. If the State Federation of Labor holds a dance to finance its welfare fund, or
if the Elks stage their annual "Purple Bubble Ball," the affair is not complete unless the lieutenant governor of Washington leads the orchestra.

Vic and Governor Clarence D. Martin were once allies.
The former's alliance with the left-wing Democrats ended
that and resulted in virtually confining the governor to the
State. Vic put in with the liberals for several reasons. A boy-
hood struggle to get a musical education has made him genuinely sympathetic with the underprivileged. And progressives
and radicals, usually noisy and flamboyant themselves, sniff
less disdainfully at his comic antics than do aloof and dignified conservatives. The left-wing sponsors of the bandmaster
find his buffoonery a mixed quality. It alienates some staid

and upright liberals who want economic reform but not political pranks. Yet it also provides a cloak for what might otherwise be embarrassing irregularities. The late Mayor Dore bitterly accused Vic of having Communist backing when the latter was the C.I.O. candidate in the mayoralty primaries early this year.

There seemed to be little doubt that the Communists in Seattle intended to vote for Vic, but the night-club impresario shrewdly laughed off the charge. "I'll bet I'm the first man in the United States named 'Aloysius' who's been accused of Communism," he said. The city grinned amiably—and Vic beat out the mayor for second place.

In 1940 Vic may possibly run for governor. His recently acquired radicalism will give him the votes of thousands of benefit seekers and poor people antagonized by the economy tendencies of his rival, Governor Martin. Vic will mouth a lot of platitudes about liberalism, old-age pensions, and reform. But his most effective campaigning will probably be the spontaneous quips and stunts and raillery that have made him unique in the country's political amphitheater. It is in this role that he best symbolizes the eccentricity of politics in his State and most appeals to the fancy of the voters.

-4-

The weather changes with kaleidoscopic swiftness on the frowning slopes of Mount Rainier and often traps unwary climbers. Politics in the State below this mountain fortress shift with equal rapidity and similar results.

In 1934 the Washington Commonwealth Federation helped elect a big, deep-voiced lawyer named Lewis B. Schwellenbach to the United States Senate. Two years later Schwellen-

bach declined to sponsor production-for-use at the Democratic
national convention. The Federation began a recall against
him. Then production-for-use was deleted from the organization's program, and it decided to string along with capitalism
for a while. Now the Commonwealth Federation partisans
are booming Schwellenbach for the Presidential nomination
in 1940 and, that failing, for the next vacancy on the Supreme
Court.

So far as adherence to the New Deal is concerned, Schwellenbach is the outstanding member of Congress from the
Promised Land of the Far West. He fights tenaciously and
is not afraid to invade the defiles into which other administration spokesmen even peek with timid reluctance. He personally broke one of the late Huey Long's pertinacious fili-
busters, roaring down defiantly a threat to come into his
State and defeat him. The appointment of Senator Black to
the Supreme Court, Schwellenbach actively defended, and he
delivered a sixteen-page speech muckraking the Hearst newspapers and their publisher. When Al Smith made his Liberty
League oration, Schwellenbach was the first New Dealer to
fire a counter bombardment at the 1928 nominee. While other
followers of the President fume and hesitate, Schwellenbach
moves ponderously but inexorably into action. He is a former
State commander of the American Legion, and the canard of
"Red!" caroms harmlessly off his wide shoulders. If any individual from the circus of Washington politics is destined
for lofty honors while Mr. Roosevelt is the dominant influence in American public life, Schwellenbach is that person.
"Double-duty Louie" his friends jestingly call him, and he is
always ready to risk his political career for the President. No
one in public life except Senator Norris ever has denounced
Hearst as vehemently as Schwellenbach has done—and the
Post-Intelligencer is the largest newspaper in his State. The

great wall of the Cascades separates Washington from north to south. The sections of the State thus divided are rivals for recognition. After having lived for many years in Seattle, the alert Schwellenbach bought a piece of land in the desolate bottom of Moses Coulee and moved to Spokane "over east of the mountains." He felt the change of residence would fortify his political position, because the State already had one senator from "the west side."

Some of the experiences of Schwellenbach's frail, pallid Senate colleague, Homer T. Bone, show further that there is both perseverance and slapdash in politics in the Evergreen State. Until his election in 1932, Bone had crusaded for a generation for public ownership of the countless idle kilowatts in the Western streams that tumble to the sea. He ran unsuccessfully for public office as a Democrat, a Socialist, a Progressive, and a Republican, and he carried his message of cheap power to every cranny in the hinterlands. Once he was on the threshold of election to Congress from Tacoma. Then the streetcar system broke down for the first time in many years, and the workingmen were unable to get to the polls in time to vote. Bone is not as consistent a New Dealer as Schwellenbach, and his close friendship for Senator Wheeler of Montana occasionally induces him to spend a few nights away from the Roosevelt bivouac. Public ownership is still the subject dearest to Bone, and he loves to tell the Senate about the great rivers that crash over cliffs and precipices in the Promised Land—"rivers that should forever be the heritage of the people."

Washington's extremely liberal delegation in the upper hall of Congress are a strangely contrasting pair. Bone, a wisp of a man with hunched shoulders as the result of an accident some years ago, looks like a chickadee. Schwellenbach with his horn-rimmed glasses and big eyes is an owl. They work effectively and have gotten their State more than its share of Federal appropriations, in addition to the mammoth projects at Grand Coulee and Bonneville. Together with a pair of hard-hitting liberal congressmen—John Coffee and Knute Hill—Bone and Schwellenbach make the Washington contingent, for all its slapstick origin, one of the most militant and progressive on Capitol Hill.

These men represent the best element in Democratic politics in the Evergreen State. But there are others on whom no such credit reflects. Many of the individuals in Washington seeking office by affixing to themselves the Democratic label are demagogues who hand out promises as easily as water flows down from the Cascades. Two-hundred-dollars-a-month pensions, plenty for everyone who asks for it, ample relief checks—these and similar bounties are pledged in wild profusion. Even more than in other States, Washington politics are premised on the "gimme" faith. The Republicans, regardless of the impotence of their affirmative ideas, have behaved with more honor than the Democrats in this respect. Most of them have refused to buy office by promising twenty-four hundred dollars each year to impoverished old people and a scotfree education to every lad who wants to strut across a campus.

In a few States politics can almost be called a vocation. Washington is one of them. Tempestuous elections and hippodrome campaigns are as much a part of the State as is Rainier's glacier-defended dome. Yet the people of the commonwealth view this hurly-burly from no unfavorable perspective. They proudly boast that President Roosevelt was in Washington last fall, and that after he had met some of the funny politicians and seen all the scenic wonders, he said in Spokane as his train began the pull toward the East:

"My friends, I am sold on the State of Washington!"

12. Inside the Far West

HITLER assembled a vast military force and rocked the world to become the political master of the 32,277 square miles of Austria. Senator Burton Kendall Wheeler of the American hinterland commonwealth of Montana may have lost political sovereignty over almost five times that much territory by saying a two-letter word. The word was his emphatic "No!" to President Roosevelt's plan to reform the Supreme Court.

Until he uttered that word, Wheeler was the dominant figure in the third largest State in the nation—a State so wide that it comprises a fourth of the distance across the continent. Now his supremacy is seriously challenged by a baldheaded young man who was not even out of Butte High School when Wheeler ran for the Vice Presidency in 1924 with the elder La Follette. The young man's name is Jerry J. O'Connell, and he is openly out to supersede the fifty-six-year-old Senator as Montana's controlling political influence.

O'Connell is a fiery, left-wing Congressman, and the threat he constitutes to Wheeler's leadership in the West is of national significance. Wheeler is an important man in American public life. For more than a year he has been the strategist of the only successful parliamentary opposition ever thrust in the path of the New Deal. President Roosevelt's forces do not fear the feints and parries of the archconservatives. Tories are of little danger to New Deal aspirations. The real peril to the plans of the President comes from liberals who agree with his objectives but disapprove of his methods. Wheeler leads this group, and he has led it with remarkable effectiveness.

This tall, lean Montana senator, who once was persecuted as a radical because of his wartime dissension, blocked the Supreme Court bill. It was he whom Vice President Garner finally faced over a congressional conference table, saying, "Burt, write your own ticket!" Wheeler outlined the maneuvers which thwarted the scheme to reorganize government bureaus, and he embarrassed the administration on such other proposals as the navy bill and the Indian reservation set-up. He has stung the New Deal many more times than all the Republicans combined.

How does the Senate's most effective Democratic insurgent stand in Montana? Can he resist the O'Connell challenge? After all, Burton K. Wheeler may be able to save the people of New York from tyranny and those of Kentucky from despotism, but all this will stop if his behavior is not approved by the people of Montana. They are the arbiters of his conduct. The vast State that sprawls from the Columbia basin to the Middle West may have fewer inhabitants than the city of Cleveland, yet those inhabitants are vital to the continued tenure in Congress of President Roosevelt's most resourceful adversary.

Men are shaped by their background. To understand Burton Wheeler and Jerry O'Connell and their grim political feud, it is necessary to understand the enormous State in which the feud is taking place. Montana is a commonwealth without a middle class worthy of the name. Only six of its towns have more than ten thousand inhabitants. More than three-fourths of the population live on ranches or in places of fewer than ten thousand people. Butte is the sole community that can

properly be considered a city, and it is built around the hardboiled proletarians who mine copper in what they call "the
richest hill on earth." These agrarians and workers have
formed the bulk of Wheeler's backing in the past. There is
no large group of shopkeepers and white-collar employees to
whom he can turn for new support in the future. If he is re-
elected in 1940, it must be mainly with the votes of the people
who were enthusiastically following him when he was a flam-
ing insurgent progressive far out on the left with the elder
La Follette and George W. Norris. In area Montana is the
third largest state in the country, but in population it is thirty-
ninth; nor is there sufficient variety in that population to enable a man to move about freely from one political corral to
the other without being lassoed at the polls.

Montana has great land, mineral, and forest wealth, but
its people are poor. They have always been radical in their
voting. For many years they kept the late Thomas J. Walsh
in the Senate, where he was a persistent harasser of monopoly
and corruption. Then Wheeler inherited the Walsh cape, and
now O'Connell is attempting to tear it from his shoulders.
The dominant economic interest in Montana is the Anaconda
Copper Mining Company. Its name is symbolic to the people. They envisage it as a serpent coiled around the resources
of the commonwealth. You cannot be in the State two weeks
without being asked whether you are for or against "the company." The wealth that the Anaconda Company extracts from
Montana's mountains goes back across the nation to the absentee owners in the East. Farmers' mouths are taut and
miners' eyes are angry as they see the private Pullman cars of
company officials on the sidings at Butte. The company is
hated in Montana. Politicians who fight Anaconda generally
survive. Those who capitulate are sooner or later repudiated
by the people. Tom Walsh represented Montana perennially

on Capitol Hill, despite the company's continual efforts to squelch his militant liberalism. Since 1922 Wheeler has served in the Senate under the same circumstances. Anaconda opposition has fortified rather than weakened him.

Now, many of the miners think Wheeler is no more an active foe of the company. They regard O'Connell as Anaconda's principal adversary, and are intensely suspicious of the favorable publicity Wheeler has been receiving in company-dominated newspapers. They reason: Senator Wheeler is against President Roosevelt; the company is against President Roosevelt. Therefore, Senator Wheeler must no longer be against the company, *quod erat demonstrandum.*

I recall a miner rugged and slightly stooped. A scar ran along one side of his face. His bare forearm bore a tattooed United States eagle. He wore soiled jumpers and carried a lunch pail off which most of the paint had been nicked. He was still spattered with dust from "the richest hill on earth" and he waited on the corner in front of the M. & M. cigar store for a lumbering old orange-colored streetcar to take him home. He was engaged in earnest conversation with a fellow worker in the mines, who also waited, carfare in hand.

"No, by gosh!" loudly declared the miner with the scar. "I wouldn't vote for Wheeler for dogcatcher. He's sold out labor and gone over to the A.C.M. I'm through with him for good, and I've voted for him every time."

The other miner's reply was lost in the clatter of the approaching trolley, but he nodded in ostensible agreement.

I remember another episode with similar implications.

Over in the Bitterroot Mountains the North Coast Limited was stopped by a freight derail up ahead. It was impossible to read in the evening dusk as the lights dimmed in the club car, and a bunch of the men got out and strolled back along the right of way to where the brakeman stood with his lantern and torpedoes. Most of the passengers seemed to be either executives and salesmen going West on business or business and professional men who could afford to take their families to see Yellowstone Park on first-class railroad tickets. The delay was a long one, and the conversation soon got around to politics. The group started talking about the great service Montana's senior senator had done the country by almost single-handedly beating the Supreme Court reform plan. Apparently his deed had saved the Republic. The lean and wiry brakeman listened silently to the discussion. When the locomotive whistled shrilly and the men hurried back to the train, he spat on the roadbed and remarked:

"Well, none of that crowd votes in Montana—but, by golly, I do! And they'll never get me to vote for Wheeler again. I'm through with that guy. The Supreme Court threw out my pension, and that's enough for me. Day after day on this run I listen to those fellows from the East boosting Wheeler. I wonder what Wheeler'd say if I told him I never hear that kind of talk from the people up forward in the coaches, the people who live in Montana."

The statement of the slender brakeman on the Northern Pacific is a pretty shrewd analysis of the political situation that confronts Senator Wheeler in his own State. In the lobby of the Finlen Hotel in Butte the traveling salesmen sit and bestow encomiums on the Montana citizen who, in their opinion, has kept Roosevelt from becoming a dictator. In the lobby of the Grand Hotel, which Wheeler himself owns, it is the same story. Each day six transcontinental trains cross Montana's expanse of uplands and mountains. From the club cars travelers look out admiringly on the State that has sent Burton Kendall Wheeler to Washington to preserve the American form of government.

In two years Wheeler comes up for reëlection. The Pullman-car passengers from the East will not be in Montana to vote for him, and neither will the drummers who lounge in the lobbies of the Finlen and Grand hotels. He will have to depend for support largely upon three classes of citizens, all angered by recent decisions of the Supreme Court: (1) farmers, who burned the conservative justices in effigy after the verdict on the AAA; (2) railroad men, who were deprived of their pensions by Justice Roberts' majority opinion in *Railroad Retirement Board* v. *Alton Railroad Company*, and (3) miners, who, although tunneling for copper, regarded the Guffey decision against their fellow miners in the coal fields as a blow to governmental protection for themselves.

-2-

The soul of the most spectacular public figure in the Rocky Mountain region must have been searched the February morning that he received this communicaton:

Hon. Burton K. Wheeler,
United States Senate
Washington, D. C.

Dear Senator Wheeler:

At its regular meeting February 16th last the Silver Bow Trades & Labor Council went on record as favoring the proposal of President Franklin D. Roosevelt for revision of the United States Supreme Court and other Federal courts.

The opinion of the Council seemed to be that the present Supreme Court is composed mostly of former corporation lawyers, who naturally are not in sympathy with legislation that would be for the benefit of the common people. Also that Congress is almost helpless to pass legislation for the benefit of the people while the present Supreme Court remains unchanged.

The Council instructed me to inform you of its action in this matter.

> Yours very truly,
>
> SILVER BOW TRADES & LABOR COUNCIL
> By THOMAS KENNEDY, *Secretary*

Since 1922, working people have been the principal operators of the political machine that has kept Wheeler in the Senate. Even before that—as long ago, in fact, as 1910—he was elected to the State legislature with the votes of laborers and their families. For more than a quarter of a century he has been in politics as a partisan of labor and the underprivileged. The Supreme Court question presented the first potentially serious split between himself and the bulk of his constituents. Yet he thus bravely concluded his reply to the Silver Bow County Labor Council:

> You don't agree with me now, but you will some time in the future.
>
> I regret exceedingly to disagree with those that I fought with, but I would sooner resign from the Senate of the United States than to vote for this proposition which I know is wrong, and which I know every liberal will regret if it should become an accomplished fact.

Some of Wheeler's friends and allies tell me he was genuinely surprised at the reaction in Montana to his militant attack on the Court plan. In first opposing the President's bill Wheeler carefully distinguished his position from that of King, Burke, and other outright conservatives. He made it clear he was assailing the proposal as a liberal and as one who still believed in liberalism. And in Washington it undoubtedly appeared as if there might be quite a progressive front against the plan. Norris was cool to it at first. Borah, just reëlected as a mild New Dealer, condemned it vigorously. So did Nye, Frazier, and Johnson of California. Bone was not enthusiastic over it. Among Wheeler's adherents are men who maintain that the senator believed opposition to the court measure might be considered in the same light as the vote to override the President's veto of the bonus. He had no idea, they say, that thousands of his constituents would interpret his stand as an outright break with the New Deal. Their anger took him by surprise.

Undoubtedly there was a difference in shading between Wheeler's condemnation of the Court proposal and the attacks from men like Tydings, Vandenberg, and Copeland. But the mauves and heliotropes of the picture were not discernible to the farmers and miners of Montana. They saw only that Senator Wheeler was against the President. He was in the company of the Liberty League and the National Manufacturers Association. Mayor Hauswirth of Butte said the senator had gone over to the du Ponts. Both the A.F. of L. and the C.I.O. indorsed the President's bill. The miners in Silver Bow County, heretofore the citadel of Wheeler's strength, manifested unmistakable sympathy with the Court proposal. Wheeler found himself branded a reactionary.

This is the background of what has since become a deep schism between Wheeler and the New Deal forces in Congress. The Senator's friends deprecate the rumors that he has broken with the President because he was not tendered the vice presidential nomination in 1932, or because he was edged out by the reactionary Bruce Kremer in the dispensing of Montana patronage. They claim that Wheeler had many better opportunities to draw his sword during Mr. Roosevelt's first administration, when the President was far less militant than now, and when he flirted with the conservatives much more frequently. Many of Wheeler's old supporters insist that he attacked the Court plan because he sincerely believed it was perilous to American institutions. They also say that he completely misjudged what the Montana reaction would be, that he never dreamed he would be rebuked by the miners, who had supported him so long. But once he realized what had happened, they explain, he concluded that he had already crossed the Rubicon and moved against other acts of the New Deal.

In his own State Wheeler today is, like Mohammed's coffin, suspended between heaven and earth. He is bitterly hated by the New Dealers and he is still regarded by the conservatives as too radical to be supported. One newspaper editor I spoke to went into a state of verbal ecstasy over Wheeler's leadership of the anti-Court-bill forces but showered imprecations upon him in the next breath for sponsoring a measure to forbid newspaper control over radio stations. Whatever support Wheeler has won in Montana because of his recent behavior is largely of a passive variety. This is not true of the antagonism he has incurred. Miners and railroad men vigorously insist they will never vote for him again. One mine union leader carried around a clipping from the New York *Times* describing a speech by Wheeler before the Maryland Bar Association. "He'll be takin' dinner with the du Ponts next," the union man said. The statement that has lost Wheeler the most ground in Montana was his mawkish observation after the death of Senator Robinson that the President had better drop the Court plan lest he appear to be fighting against God. This demagogic remark disgusted many of the Senator's erstwhile supporters and definitely created the impression in Montana that his opposition to the New Deal had moved out of the liberal perspective within which he had promised to confine it.

The Bonanza State voters aroused to anger and indignation because Wheeler was largely responsible for the bogging

down of the President's judiciary legislation are voters who
otherwise would be militant Wheeler followers. A ragged
fellow selling a labor paper near an A.C.M. shaft said he
had distributed Wheeler's literature in 1934. "But I'd roast
in hell before I'd do it again," he cried vehemently.

President Roosevelt epitomizes to the voters the cause of
the underprivileged. The workers in the A.C.M. shafts gave
him more than a four-to-one majority in Silver Bow County
in 1936. His margin in the whole State was nearly three to
one. Copper has been up around 14 and 14½ cents and Montana has boomed again. Butte is wide open; faro games and
roulette wheels entice men in from the main streets. Girls
have packed the cribs along "Venus Alley." Prices are high,
and the men in the mines are earning $5.75 a day. A recent
Department of Labor survey showed wages to be higher in
Butte than in either Denver or Portland. This prosperity and
bustle and hilarity are attributed by the workers to Roosevelt
and his policies. Their present bitterness against Senator
Wheeler emanates largely from the fact that they believe the
President has helped them personally.

Relatively few people ever thought they would see Burton
K. Wheeler on shaky political ground in his home State. He
is a tradition in Montana. Persons talk about what he wears
and what he likes to eat. A ranch near Missoula achieved
fame when it became known that Wheeler occasionally
stopped there for bacon-and-egg breakfasts. During the War
the United States Attorney's office in Montana was occupied
by Wheeler, and he ran squarely into the belligerents by refusing to prosecute members of the I.W.W. and other social
nonconformists. The bitterest and most vituperative gubernatorial campaign in the history of the country's principal copper State took place in 1920, when Wheeler was the candidate
of the forces opposing the Anaconda Company. He was de-

feated, but the publicity attendant on the election enabled him to go to the Senate two years later.

Now, Jerry J. O'Connell may replace Wheeler in the Senate. A Representative at twenty-eight, O'Connell is the youngest individual in Congress. Besides being a militant New Dealer, he is a champion of the Spanish Loyalists and a defender of the C.I.O. O'Connell also sponsored a Congressional memorial petitioning Governor Merriam of California to pardon Tom Mooney—a popular move in Montana, where year after year the miners have clamored for Mooney's freedom. O'Connell's father died from a combination of silicosis, contracted in the mines, and a wound suffered in a strike, all of which gives young O'Connell a closer bond with the miners than Wheeler ever had. There is little doubt that the chubby, blue-eyed congressman is rapidly superseding Wheeler as Montana's dominant figure in liberal politics.

Another potential aspirant to Wheeler's office is youthful Joe Monaghan, a member of the House until 1936, when he ran unsuccessfully for the Senate against James E. Murray, a New Deal Democrat. Monaghan dabbles in progressive politics but is far to the right of O'Connell. He was a Townsend enthusiast at the crest of the two-hundred-dollar pension hysteria. Indicative of the change in Wheeler's position in his home State is the fact that, although Monaghan entered politics as a confirmed Wheeler adherent, when Wheeler came to Great Falls recently Monaghan challenged him to a debate on the Roosevelt Court plan. Wheeler declined.

Other factors are material in this frontier political hodgepodge that has attracted national attention.

Three transcontinental railroads twist across Montana's vast expanse.* One would be enough. Each day six limited

* The Great Northern, the Northern Pacific, and the Chicago, Milwaukee & St. Paul.

trains—three bound toward the Coast and three headed in the opposite direction—clatter across the State. Many of the coaches and Pullmans are as empty as culverts in August, and plenty of revenue is required to withstand the capitalization on right-of-ways that cross Montana; the State is an eight-hundred-mile stretch of mountains and canyons. Railroads must switchback over it. Transportation is a Montana industry second only to Anaconda's encirclement of Butte's copper hill. And it is a losing industry. Six sumptuous passenger trains, each traveling eight hundred tortuous miles, are too many to serve half a million people scattered in the hinterlands. This is a problem Senator Wheeler is in a strategic position to handle, because of his chairmanship of the congressional committee that has investigated the railroads so painstakingly for several years. He will see to it that the handling is done with the great State of Montana not out of mind. The gaudy, orange-striped Olympian, rolling along behind its electric locomotive, may be tearing out the pillars of the capital structure of the Chicago, Milwaukee & St. Paul, but trappers and sheepherders and cowboys in the Montana wilderness get a possessive thrill as it clicks majestically past their hinterland homesteads. If the distinguished Senator sees to it that this thrill is not entirely sacrificed in the interest of economy, his frontier constituents will be eternally grateful.

But Wheeler's closeness to the railroad problem will fail to offset Jerry O'Connell's closeness to the Roosevelt administration. That relationship is highly important in Montana. At the abandoned fur-trading post of Fort Peck on the upper Missouri River, the Federal government is building a massive $100,000,000 earthen dam. It will be for flood control and irrigation, and O'Connell and others want hydroelectric power added to its functions. Fort Peck Dam is Montana's prize project. The commonwealth is also one of the fifteen "irrigation States" in which a senator or congressman in administration favor gets credit for the reclamation undertakings on which depend the crops of thousands of farms. The tunnels below the great, earth-filled barrier at Fort Peck will divert into irrigation ditches part of the Missouri, Yellowstone, and Milk rivers. That water means the difference between desert and Promised Land to many Montana ranchers. The President wants the voters to know just who is responsible for this. At Fort Peck last year, he talked about conserving Montana's rivers. He referred to "Senator Jim Murray's interest" and he referred to "Jerry O'Connell's interest." But Senator Burton K. Wheeler's interest he did not mention, and from the Bitterroots to the plains the voters noticed the omission.

And, ominously for Wheeler, in the New York *Times* Warren Moscow noted at the time of the Fort Peck speech, "All over the State, the President still stands high in public esteem, with those who voted for him last year still for him."

O'Connell has another advantage. He is thoroughly consistent. A baldheaded bundle of left-wing tendencies, he goes around the country delivering the most radical speeches ever made by a congressman. He praises Harry Bridges, calls the conservative governor of California a "reactionary stool pigeon," enters the lair of Boss Hague, and makes demagogic utterances extolling the Townsend Plan. Wheeler, on the other hand, does not always travel on the same track. He sometimes switches routes, as on the occasion he called Mr. Roosevelt "the one President who has done more for the workers and the common people than any other." This may have been a sincere tribute to many policies in which Wheeler believes. But it annoyed his new-found conservative allies, and did not lure an appreciable number of liberals from the O'Connell forces.

In the national capital Senator Wheeler's opposition to the tendencies of the New Deal occasionally seems ribbed with granite. Sometimes in Montana the consistency of this opposition more closely resembles aspic. As the President traveled across the country in 1938 to the accompaniment of enthusiastic cheers from the Far West, Wheeler predicted better business conditions and defended Mr. Roosevelt's right to endorse Democratic primary candidates. Even the cautious United Press called his attitude an "about face" and his conservative friends stirred surprisedly. And when Jerry O'Connell claimed the President had urged him to "fight like hell" against Wheeler, the Senator did not accept the challenge. Instead, he wishy-washily insisted the President had never told O'Connell anything of the kind. This proved poor strategy. It weakened Wheeler with his new cohorts and did not reinstate him with his old ones. When the nimble-witted, prematurely bald O'Connell was renominated over a conservative Democrat, everyone in Montana predicted the scene was ready for 1940. And in that scene Wheeler will never be the knight of the New Deal, no matter how much he attempts to hedge and qualify the blunt philosophy and strategy that beat the Court plan. The Senator has one particular advantage, however; he is exceptionally able. That was shown in his manipulation of the fight against the Court plan. O'Connell is shrewd and daring, but lacks Wheeler's ability. He also is more of a crackpot and demagogue than such congressional liberals as Maury Maverick of Texas and Tom Amlie of Wisconsin.

In the final analysis, what happens to Burton K. Wheeler may rest almost entirely with Chief Justice Hughes, who of late has become such an intimate of Montana's illustrious Senator. More than any other person, Wheeler symbolizes the defeat of the Supreme Court plan. He, and he alone, was

actually responsible for the abandonment of the scheme. If
Hughes holds the Court on its present progressive course,
Wheeler may run the gauntlet of the 1940 campaign unscathed
by O'Connell's whip. But, as one mine workers' leader in
Butte said to me, if the Court again starts to nullify social
legislation popular with farmers and copper miners and railroad employees and frontiersmen, then Wheeler had better
"find that old law shingle and dust it off right handsome."

-3-

Practically all the notable public figures in the country's
Promised Land are members of Congress. Borah is the most
notable of all. Burton Wheeler and Jerry O'Connell belong
in the select category. So do Senators Schwellenbach, Elbert
Thomas, Pope, and Bone, as well as Senator Charles L. Mc-
Nary of Oregon, the Republicans' courtly minority leader.

Of eccentric and foolish politics, the region has far more
than its share. Some of the politicians in the Northwest are
the funniest in the nation. Yet, although the last frontier has
a disproportionately large number of crackpots and buffoons,
it is fortunately almost without the individuals who occasionally make politics so ominous in other sections. The vast domain of the Columbia basin has escaped the Huey Longs, the
Talmadges, and the Boss Hagues. Political shenanigans are
infinitely preferable to political tyranny.

Amidst all the harlequinades and tomfoolery, the Northwest has had few political despots at all comparable to Boss
Hague or one of the feudal governors of the South. One of
these autocrats was Governor Charles H. Martin of Oregon,
but his autocracy was mercifully brief.

A retired major general, Martin came to the Far West

after half a century spent in the rigid, authoritarian atmosphere of army cantonments. Virtually all his seventy-four
years had been lived in the economically secure caste system
of military posts. He never understood the hopes, aspirations,
and needs of struggling stump ranchers, sweating lumberjacks, and hell-for-leather cowboys. He thought those people
could be ruled like buck privates on a parade ground.

Some of the drought refugees from the scorched Dust
Bowl began to demand relief. Martin called them "alien
paupers" and told them to sell their rattletrap automobiles.
He got even more furious at the regular relief recipients. "I
believe in taking care of the old folks," he said, "but I'll be
damned if I'll feed the young ones. Are we going to feed
them for the rest of our lives? Hell! Let them work!" Martin's conception of taking care of "the old folks" was not distinguished for generosity. Although getting a $6,000 annual
pension himself, he observed, "I believe ten dollars a month
ample to care for them." Needy World War veterans in the
backwoods could not repay loans they had obtained from the
State. Martin said they were "skunks." He added that school
teachers who taught pacifism were "yellow-bellied," and he
intimated the inmates of the State home for the feeble-minded
should be chloroformed. A prominent Catholic priest described this as "cold-blooded murder."

The financial requests of the national guard and the State
police, Martin left untouched, but he reduced the requirements of the State Hospital, the Welfare Commission, and
the Humane Society. He also admonished Harry Hopkins
to keep his money out of Oregon, as the people would provide for the destitute by drinking more whisky at the State
liquor stores.

The racketeering in the A.F. of L. and the unpopular alien
leadership of the C.I.O. gave this aged militarist a chance to

be his most malevolent. He advised the sheriffs of the State to move against labor union gangs and "beat hell out of 'em!" At a public meeting Martin shouted: "Crack their damn heads! Those fellows are there for nothing but trouble—give it to them!" He also counseled the State police to apply third-degree methods to the men grabbed in antiunion raids, and grimly noted, "We have thirty-five hundred national guardsmen in the State, and each of them knows how to use a rifle!"

These crackling remarks evidently were not forgotten by the voters when they decided not to give the General a second term. Martin's militaristic behavior and his antagonism toward the New Deal were the determining factors of the campaign. He had ordered people around like lackeys, and one of his subordinates complained as she resigned, "I thought they freed the slaves in '63." Martin boasted that President Roosevelt told him at Bonneville, "You and I make a good pair," and a few days before the election the President denied any such statement.

The transient tenure of Martin's tyranny showed that the people of the neighborly and democratic Northwest have little patience with profane and autocratic government.

Conversely, the twenty-year tenure of Charles L. McNary in the Senate of the United States indicates that tolerant, sincere, and competent leadership they are willing to perpetuate almost *ad infinitum*.

"Charley Mac," the friends of the Republican spokesman call him, and he provides the minority party with its best strategy. Association with the farmers and ranchers of the progressive West has convinced McNary that the way to oppose the New Deal is not with reactionary bombast. When a group of conservatives drafted a seventeenth century manifesto against Mr. Roosevelt's policies, McNary refused to sanction it. He said it sounded like a Liberty League handout,

and he tipped off several liberal columnists to its origin. Mc-
Nary is extremely popular with the newspapermen. Affable
and mild-mannered, he plays no favorites and declines to
trade on his important position.

At home in Oregon, McNary displays the same qualities.
He lives at Fircone, the ranch in the timbered Willamette
Valley where he was born, and on its two hundred acres he
raises prunes, apples, pears, and filbert nuts. Many years ago
he organized the Salem Fruit Union, one of the first successful coöperatives in the Columbia basin, and for a generation
in the Senate he has promoted progressive agricultural policies. McNary works closely with the Grange, the most useful
and public-minded organization in Oregon, and the gates of
Fircone are perennially open to his rural neighbors. He likes
to sit on the rolling lawn in a wicker chair and talk about the
latest hinterland happenings. The minority leader's favorite
dish is baked beans, and a big pot usually bubbles over the
fireplace. McNary himself superintends the preparation of the
dish, and he prefers the beans richly sticky with bacon and
brown sugar and tomato sauce. He converses candidly, and
will stroll around Fircone with a gaunt and rangy farm neighbor discussing intimate political occurrences in Washington.
Wild-life conservation is another of McNary's hobbies, and
he has no patience with the Republican reactionaries who
want the uplands and ranges left vulnerable to exploitation
by manufacturing interests. On his farm the Senator has a
regular wild-fowl refuge. For years a flock of wild geese has
inhabited Fircone every season and eaten the food "Charley
Mac" never fails to set out. The minority spokesman is as
proud of those geese as he is of outlining the strategy that
has brought the Republicans the only victories they have enjoyed over a succession of lean political years. Even the constituents who do not approve McNary's social and economic

views like him personally, and he has a tremendous following among the farmers of the Northwest. This has been accomplished without delivering speeches; he is not an orator
and he hates the demagogy and panoply of politics. Most of
his campaigning is done through personal conversations. Mc-
Nary knows thousands of farmers intimately. He will drive
up to a lonely crossroads store far out on the frontier, walk
jauntily inside, buy a pound of coffee or a jar of peanut butter,
sit down on an upturned cracker box, and talk for several
hours with the farmers lolling around the stove or sawdust
tray. Then word will spread through the county that "Charley Mac" has been in the hinterlands, and everyone will want
to know what he had to say about crop conditions, the grain
market, the new farm bill, and President Roosevelt's latest
ideas. McNary refuses to help concoct the personal venom so
many Republicans spew at the President. He insists that the
New Deal be opposed on issues alone. In 1936 he would not
let his reelection campaign be conducted by the ossified and
bungling Republican State committee. He pointedly declined
the committee the privilege of signing his page in *The Voters'
Pamphlet*. The prominence in party councils of the editor of a
vindictive, little anti-Semitic newspaper in Corvallis finds no
favor with McNary. Tolerance is one of his qualities. When he
first entered politics after being dean of the law school at
Willamette University, he lost election to the Oregon supreme
court by one vote in a statewide campaign. He got to the senate originally by appointment; he was chosen to fill the un-
expired term of Harry Lane, who had voted against the War
and then been hounded to the grave.

A discouraging commentary on politics in the Promised
Land is that neither an open-minded conservative like Mc-
Nary nor a thoroughgoing liberal like Senator Pope receives
half the adulation in the press that is bestowed upon an oli-

garch like Martin. A member of the Oregon Board of Higher Education, Mrs. Cornelia M. Pierce, once said to Martin, "You, sir, are the creation of newspaper propaganda."

The newspapers of the Pacific Northwest are predominantly reactionary. The more tyrannical and encrusted a politician is, the more closely he approximates the ideal of a majority of the region's press. The *Oregon Journal* sets the tempo of this tune. Its front page is periodically turned into a conglomeration of editorials camouflaged as news. Its political writers smear the progressives and glorify the reactionaries. One week the *Journal* played up in big headlines Governor Martin's "triumphant" journey through a wilderness county he later lost overwhelmingly, but subordinated a dispatch from Washington that the President of the United States had rebuked Martin's bid for renomination. For a time the *Journal's* managing editor, Donald Sterling, hinted to his friends that he was the "political boss of the Oregon Country." Then the national administration discovered that the *Journal*, while hypocritically pretending to be for the New Deal, was knifing the President on major issues. Sterling's influence at Washington swiftly evanesced. He failed to prevent the appointment of J. D. Ross as Bonneville Dam administrator, and Mr. Roosevelt listened coldly to his entreaties not to oppose Governor Martin.

Unfortunately, the bulk of the newspapers of the Northwest follow the lead of the *Journal* rather than that of the few publications which represent the best traditions of the press. Those few merit mention.

The *Capital Press* at Salem defends civil rights and protests against dishonesty in politics, and the *Times* in the hills of the Coos Bay lumber area is not afraid to expose chicanery and corruption. These and the other newspapers in the Northwest which assume forthright and intelligent positions do so

against odds, because the bulk of the region's press is geared
to a dull and cautious pitch. There are some courageous
smaller periodicals in the Northwest, of both liberal and conservative tendencies. These include the Grange papers, the
Argus at Seattle, the *News* of the left-wing Washington Commonwealth Federation, and *Everybody's Business* in Portland.
The *Capital Press* takes delight in assailing the stodginess and
bias of the bulk of the territory's papers. Farmers aid in the
process by filling the *Capital Press* with advertisements telling of produce to barter. "Swap ads," the little displays are
called. The *Oregonian* at Portland, a fixture in the Columbia
River country before the last warwhoops sounded, is the newspaper stand-by of the region. An upright, conservative daily,
its news columns, more than any others in the West, duplicate the impartiality and objectivity of such national newspapers as the *Christian Science Monitor* and the New York
Times. The *Oregonian* does not use its news space to influence political opinions; and, although frequently oblique in
its editorial attitude toward the New Deal, it is a sturdy and
reliable champion of civil liberties. It helped force the judicial
test which led to the Supreme Court's outlawry of the oppres-
sive Oregon criminal syndicalism law; it has fought against
compulsory military training and the denial of the use of public buildings to radical groups; it has continually condemned
the suppression and intimidation of liberal students at Oregon
State College, and it led a crusade which resulted in the curtailment and exposure of Portland's singularly vicious police
"Red squad."

Almost alone of the many newspapers in the Far West
which attack the New Deal and demand liberty for big business, the *Oregonian* also seeks liberty for the little fellow and
the underprivileged. The fact that it has sharply passed the
Journal in circulation serves to indicate that the people of

the frontier prefer a consistent philosophy in regard to the Bill of Rights and want opinions and prejudices kept out of the news columns.

-4-

All over America, politics are a queer business. Men struggle, equivocate, compromise, and surrender to keep on sitting in the seats of power. The Pacific Northwest fits into this general pattern. But there is an exception. The politicians in the Promised Land have a greater opportunity to do something for the people they represent. Senator Wagner of New York must look at crowded slums, rickety tenements, and a back country jammed with factories and industrial towns. But Senator Wheeler and Senator McNary and Senator Pope see idle hinterlands ample to care for every destitute person in America.

The "plenty for all" advocated at meetings of the Oregon Commonwealth Federation may be farfetched, but it is by no means fantastic. It can be achieved in the Northwest, and politics is the route by which it must be attained.

I remember the girl hitch-hiker I picked up on the road between Portland and McMinnville in the green-tinted Tualatin valley. She was wearing shorts, and she told me sardonically that they stopped more cars than a "crossing bell." Her family owned a farm in eastern Oregon, and she had become tired of a prosaic existence on the lonely, brown ranges. She was drifting around the State, and she said she was enjoying herself. Down over her forehead her tawny hair straggled, and she chewed gum vigorously and talked in crisp, hardboiled fashion. Lithe brown legs ended in sandals, and her feet were dirty from the dust of the road. I asked her if she behaved herself. "When I feel like it," she said, and then added, witheringly, "And I feel like it now."

We neared the hamlet where she wanted to get out. A cardboard sign tacked to a telephone pole urged, "Reëlect Governor Martin."

"Humph!" she snorted. "I wouldn't vote for that old guy."

"Why not?"

"He said there was plenty of electricity in eastern Oregon, and us folks on the farms didn't need any. Bet he never did any washing or pumping by hand!"

Then, seriously, she said, "I'll tell you the politicians I'm for—the ones who really get you a few things. You can't eat hooey, you know."

I thought about more than her trim figure and casual nonchalance as she got out of the car, said blithely, "Thanks, darling," and walked unconcernedly up the little country street as several farmers viewed her brief costume with ill concealed wonder.

13. The Saints in the Promised Land

OUT along the interurban line in a tree-shaded section of Salt Lake City stands a sturdy brick-and-timber building. Deep bins in its basement hold five thousand sacks of potatoes, four thousand sacks of apples, and two thousand sacks of onions. Men in mackinaws and overalls trudge in all day long with additional sacks and crates. On the floor above, they leave heaping armloads of fruits and vegetables still moist with rain and dew.

In a spacious kitchen at the rear of the building, kettles of pears and peaches and tomatoes boil merrily as nimble-fingered women in white aprons preserve this array of products of the orchard and field. More than two hundred thousand jars and cans already have been stacked ceiling-high in countless rows. Up a flight of wooden stairs other women are sewing dresses, stuffing quilts, and cutting patterns. Above them on the wall hangs a hand-lettered sign. Here is what it says:

> It ain't the guns or armaments
> Or the tunes the band can play,
> But the close coöperation
> That makes us win the day.

Coöperation means a lot to these people, and to many others like them in two hundred twenty-one such storehouses throughout the Far West. Not so long ago most of the men carrying sacks and armloads of vegetables and the women canning fruits and stitching shirts were dependent upon government relief, or possibly on private charity. Now they have become self-supporting. They are doing useful work. The food they preserve and the clothes they sew provide not only for themselves, but for thousands of other persons engaged in the various phases of the Security Program of the Mormon Church. This program is America's most unique attempt to answer the grim question of unemployment and relief.

The plan was officially started in the early summer of 1936, but it had its indirect origin almost a century earlier. The first Mormons in the Utah wilderness dragged massive blocks of granite across twenty miles of uplands to build a lofty Temple on the shores of Great Salt Lake. When their supply of nails gave out, they whittled wooden pegs and cut cowhide thongs and with them held together a vast, domed Tabernacle that has endured since the Civil War. These first Mormons farmed the fastnesses diligently and erected what they called "Bishops' storehouses" to contain surplus goods distributed to the poor and unfortunate. On sagebrush flats and rocky slopes the pioneer followers of Brigham Young reared a new civilization beyond the Rockies.

This legacy of toil and independence and resourcefulness has come down to the Mormons of today. It is their greatest heritage. Two years ago their bearded president and leader, eighty-one-year-old Heber Jeddy Grant, whose frontiersman father helped build the Temple and the Tabernacle, decided that people with such a history should not have to look to the government for sustenance. That was the beginning of a new idea: the Church Security Program. The idea is of importance to the whole nation; it may be the eventual solution to the troublesome dilemma of relief, taxation, and Federal spending.

At the April conference of the church in 1936, the tall, patriarchal Heber Grant said that coöperation and hard work and the intelligent use of Nature's bountifulness could end the evils of the dole. Mormons from metropolitan Salt Lake City to the lonely foothills of the Uintas and Cascades voiced eager agreement. They eagerly helped set the program in motion. Idle church members were given a chance to harvest crops, cut trees, mine coal, sew petticoats and jackets, and provide other necessities. People once indigent and destitute became self-sustaining and independent. Work replaced idleness. Excess goods were stacked in abundance in bins, cellars, and storehouses.

This unique plan of the Mormons is based on the belief that every able-bodied person can do some useful task, if only given the chance. Why not make that chance available? There are plenty of natural resources in the Promised Land of the Far West waiting only work and development. The church, financed by tithes and "fast days," is obtaining farms, building storehouses, setting up sewing projects, and making other arrangements to provide the necessities of life for thousands of men and women. The work is done by the people taken off Federal relief rolls or private charity lists. Each Mormon is put at the job for which he is best fitted. The idle lumberjack fells trees or chops wood. The destitute farmer plows a loamy field. The housewife in a hungry family cans vegetables or patches clothes. The products of all these tasks are pooled in the storehouses. From there they are distributed to the people engaged in the program.

The work is done coöperatively. The supplies are given out on a coöperative basis, need rather than skill or ability determining what each individual receives. Yet the Church Security Plan differs from other coöperatives in one fundamental respect. It is a means to an end, whereas coöperatives of the Swedish type, for example, are ends in themselves. The Mormons' program is pointed toward the time when the coöperatives will cease to be coöperatives—when the surplus goods from the Security farms will enable the men tilling them to pay back their debt to the church and own the tracts outright. The ordinary coöperative does not have this objective. Its solitary purpose is to produce or distribute certain products coöperatively.

But although the Security Plan seeks to make its participants independent farmers and workers once more, it has a very definite principle in common with other coöperatives. It is for security and not for profit. No one makes any private gain from it, either directly or indirectly. Goods are produced to be consumed. Use and need are the standards. Profit is not a measuring stick. Wheat is grown on the Utah highlands and in the Idaho valleys, not for what it will bring in the Chicago pit, but for how many hungry Mormon mouths it will feed. Even when people outside the plan join in and help, there is no question of profit. A Latter-day Saint family in Denver canned eight hundred quarts of the fruit picked in Security farm orchards. The jars were distributed to the people working in the program who needed them. No one thought of seeking any profit for his labor.

Under this coöperative, nonprofit system wilderness fastnesses have been cleared, farms cultivated, storehouses built, and Temples erected. Thousands of men being given work and supplies by the Security Plan have helped add new buildings to the estimated $16,000,000 work of edifices already owned by the Mormon Church. Last year the Security Program encouraged a building outlay of $3,000,000, the greatest annual expenditure in the history of the Latter-day Saints. Much of the work and materials that went into this undertaking was provided coöperatively by once idle Mormons in

communities scattered all the way from the Coast to the
fringe of the Dust Bowl.

Exactly two years have passed since the plan was started.
In that time twenty-two thousand Mormons have been taken
off Federal relief rolls. More than thirty thousand others
have received aid and assistance in the form of food, clothing,
shelter, and fuel. Private employment has been found for an
additional twenty-four hundred. The program is still under
way. The ultimate goal is to make every able-bodied Mormon
self-sustaining. The church hopes to see all its members as independent and industrious as the undaunted Mormon argonauts of 1847 who raised orchards and wheat fields on ground
so caked and hard that at first their plowshares bent against
it. Each day that goal is nearer, as new numbers of Mormons
get an opportunity to perform useful tasks.

Unquestionably the church program has brought forth a
lot of exaggeration. Marc A. Rose rosily inferred that it had
taken *all* Mormons off relief. Charles Morrow Wilson used it
to jab at the New Deal, despite the fact that Utah is one of
the President's strongest States. Others have panegyrized
similarly. These exaggerations have hurt the program, rather
than advanced it. The Security Plan has been a good beginning, but there still are many Mormons on relief. The important thing is that the number is becoming less. Sometimes
men and women on relief are reluctant to quit the WPA, and
these have discouraged Heber Grant. One such discouragement recently was taken to imply that he had abandoned the
program. This was wrong, of course; a month later in Portland he restated his faith in the undertaking. Anti-New-
Dealers who have seized on the Mormons' venture as a thrust
at the Roosevelt administration miss many of its implications.
Surely it is not fundamentally a Tory enterprise to let people
produce for themselves. Is that not along the line of what

J. D. Ross and other New Dealers in the Columbia basin are proposing, when they urge that the farmers of the West form Public Utility Districts to distribute the water power from the great river on a nonprofit basis?

No doubt some of the leaders of the Mormon Church are bitterly opposed to progressive government. This is especially true of those with extensive holdings in beet sugar. They want high tariffs and low wages. Probably these men have regarded the Security Program as a happy slap at the WPA. But theirs is not the predominant spirit of the undertaking. I have talked with a lot of Mormons in the movement. Most of them told me they were for Mr. Roosevelt. Five or six of them called him "our President." A number of them said they hoped their efforts would help the President solve one of the many problems confronting him. Coöperation and brotherhood are doctrines of the Latter-day Saints. They are humanitarians. A great many of these people think they discern such qualities in President Roosevelt. National commentators may interpret the Church Security Program to the country as a sock at the administration, but the Mormons actually engaged in the project are adherents of the New Deal. "Sure I'm for Roosevelt," said a tall Latter-day Saint sorting potatoes in the cool basement of the Salt Lake City storehouse. "I hope this program of ours helps him with the relief mess. I think Roosevelt's the greatest President since Lincoln."

I asked the man if many other Mormons in the Security Program felt as he did. I told him the Republican newspapers were claiming the plan would show up the New Deal. "Listen, mister," said the Mormon to me, "Salt Lake County is the center of this program. Roosevelt carried it three to one in 1936. He'd carry it three to one right now. He'll carry it three to one in 1940. That stuff about us being against him is just bosh."

He turned back to his potatoes.

Getting Mormons off relief and helping them to use the natural resources of the hinterlands to become their own providers is the primary aim of the Church Security Plan.

Heber Grant and the other leaders of the program also have in mind a secondary objective. They want to keep stored away in well buttressed warehouses enough grain and other foodstuffs to carry the Latter-day Saints of Jesus Christ, as the Mormons are called, through any famine or drought that might grip the country. The produce for this purpose is harvested on scores of Church Security Program farms that dot the great region between the continental divide and the shores of the Pacific. The harvesting is done by Mormons who formerly relied upon WPA appropriations for support and livelihood. Part of the produce is eaten by these once idle people who have sown and cultivated it. The rest is preserved or dried or sacked, and put into the Mormon storehouses against a possible day of want. The early Mormons always kept a year's supply of wheat in their granaries. Lean years were not going to catch them unawares.

–2–

Exactly how is the Security Program being worked out? What methods and ways have taken twenty-two thousand Mormons off relief and made them independent citizens once more? How are the Latter-day Saints of the present applying to modern economic problems the persistence and vigor of their fathers and grandfathers who settled Utah's rough-and-ready frontier?

The Church Security Program is made up of a number of different phases. Here they are:

1. Keeping a complete index and record of all Mormons who are unemployed or destitute, and making an intensive effort to find jobs for these people in industry and business in their communities.

2. The prompt payment of tithes, the observance of special "fast days," and the contribution of volunteer work by every Mormon able to do so, in order that the church may carry on and finance the Security Program.

3. Investigating thoroughly the agricultural conditions in all sections of Utah, Idaho, Colorado, California, Oregon, and other States where Mormons are located, and placing needy families on farms that are productive and fertile—farms they can pay for in extra produce and surplus goods.

4. Promoting and planning church building projects, irrigation undertakings, mining operations, and similar enterprises, and letting the local communities supply their share in labor and materials.

5. Encouraging a coöperative spirit that will make possible the rehabilitation and recovery—spiritually, as well as materially—of many families through the aid and assistance of their friends and neighbors.

The whole country watches closely as this plan is put into effect on the eastern extremity of the mighty basin of the Columbia. Who knows but that the basic principles of the Mormons' idea may eventually be as useful in Kentucky or Pennsylvania as they now are in Utah and Idaho? For six years America has sought a route out of the bewildering relief labyrinth. Perhaps the Mormons are pointing the way.

Each part of the Security Program has proved important in providing work and the necessities of life for considerably more than fifty thousand people. The coöperation feature of the plan may not seem essential, yet several Mormon Elders assured me that revival of the friendly, helping-hand comradeship of the early pioneers had saved a large number of families from the relief roster. Vividly and dramatically, the

Security Program has brought back the coöperative and neighborly spirit of the old West.

In the rolling hinterlands of Utah a farmer was taken seriously ill. He could not move from his bed. More than one hundred tons of sugar beets lay in his fields, ready to be dug and picked. They represented a year's toil and livelihood for the farmer and his family. One of his fellow Mormons drove past and saw the beets ripening in the autumn sun. The neighbor called together the church members in the district and related to them their friend's predicament.

"What are we going to do about it?" he asked.

"We're going to pick those beets," an Elder replied.

On Armistice Day a score of Mormons plodded to the sick farmer's fields, and picked and hauled one hundred ten tons of sugar beets. Thus a family was spared the loss of its farm, and the Federal relief rolls for the county were spared five or six additional names.

Episodes like this have been plentiful since the Security Program was started. In a suburb of Salt Lake City a poor man's neighbors helped him renovate and modernize his house. The Mormons in another locality cut a cord of wood for a man with a broken arm. In the picturesque Raft River valley in Idaho, twenty-six Mormon families were given a new start on a big ranch they are now running coöperatively. When twenty-five families of Mexican Mormons faced poverty and destitution, the church purchased a four-hundred-forty-acre tract in the Colorado highlands and gave them a chance to farm it. Those Mexican families have become independent. They know how to get the utmost out of each beam of sunshine and every drop of rain. They harvest rich crops and pour into the storehouses what they do not use themselves. Their produce helps to feed hundreds of people engaged in work other than farming under the Security Program.

This plan that has taken so many Mormons off relief and made so many others self-reliant is a sort of combination of the Swedish coöperative idea and the common storehouse system used at Jamestown three centuries ago by the first English colony on the American mainland. There also is a generous dash of rugged individualism. The Mormons continually emphasize the evils of the dole. They do not want their people to be wards of the government. Brigham Young's words on idleness are often recalled:

"My experience has taught me that it is never any benefit to give out and out to man or woman, money, food, clothing, or anything else, if they are able-bodied and can work. Such a course would ruin any community and make them idlers."

Not only the unemployed and impoverished Mormons are participating in the Security Program. Virtually all the seven hundred fifty thousand Latter-day Saints throughout the world take part indirectly. The basic financing of the plan comes from the general fund of the church. This means that when farms are obtained and similar expenditures advanced to provide useful work for indigent Mormons, the church puts up the money. The church, in turn, is financed by tithes from its members. A tithe consists of one-tenth of the member's annual income. Mormons once negligent about tithing have become faithful again under the stimulus of a program designed to make their church the first large group in America to "take care of its own."

Money for the plan also is derived in another fashion. It has long been a tradition of the Mormon Church for its members to go without two meals on the first Sunday of each month and to contribute the value of those meals to a fund for the poor. A short time ago a special "fast day"—the first in fifty years—was observed. The proceeds went directly to the Security Program. In the vicinity of Great Salt Lake alone, more than one hundred twenty thousand people denied themselves two meals each to help give their more unfortunate fellow Mormons a new start. Clerks and truck drivers did without goulash and dumplings and contributed seventy or eighty cents apiece to the program. Bankers and railroad executives passed up *filet mignon* on toast and sent in checks for five or six dollars.

A few days after this remarkable event I had a chance to see exactly what it meant to a great many people. In the spacious kitchen of the Mormon storehouse at Salt Lake City, I talked with a slender woman who was watching a boiling kettle of tomatoes. She must have been forty-four or forty-five years old, and wisps of gray streaked her dark hair. Every now and then she picked up a wooden ladle and stirred the vat in which the tomatoes plopped and steamed like bubbling lava in some incipient volcano. Splashes from the kettle red-flecked the woman's white apron.

"Pretty hot work?" I ventured.

She smiled. "Sure, but I don't mind it. Don't you know it's fun for a woman to be in a kitchen—especially when it's the first kitchen she's been in for a long, long time?"

That was a lead. So I asked, "What do you mean?"

She told me her story. The depression had taken away her job as cashier in a tearoom. She had worked on and off in stores, but three months in a millinery shop had been the longest at any one place. Finally she had been forced to go on relief. Most of the time she had lived in rooming houses and dingy hotels. Occasionally she had gone hungry. The WPA had been a last refuge. Now, she was preserving fruits and vegetables in one of the Mormon storehouses. From the storehouse she also was drawing blankets, clothing, shoes, towels, soap, pillow slips—and even books and magazines from a little library that occupied part of the crowded upper floor.

I asked her if she was happy.

"Happier than I've ever been since the crash in 1929," she replied. "I lost my job right at the start of the depression. This is the first time in almost ten years that I've felt any security. All of us here who work in the kitchen"—she pointed around the big room where other women were peeling and boiling golden pears and ruddy apples—"feel that we have a real chance to come back. We're also much happier in our social life. The church is helping that way, too. Some of us are going to move into a home that a prominent church member has just given to the Security Program. Won't that be grand?"

And she turned back to her steaming pot of tomatoes— tomatoes that would feed the Mormon families whose mothers stitched the clothes and whose fathers chopped the wood that the slender woman at the kettle wore and used.

Preparing food and sewing garments are only two of the many tasks done by people engaged in the Church Security Program. Here are some of the others: logging timber, mining coal, shearing wool, stuffing mattresses, repairing furniture and toys, making shoes, providing medical care, digging irrigation ditches, building dams, planning gardens, and constructing storehouses, chapels, houses, and barns.

The products of all these varied labors—whether they be shingles for a leaky roof or a wool coat for a cowboy shivering on the range—are pooled in the two hundred twenty-one Mormon storehouses scattered throughout the West. There they are distributed on the basis of need. For example, each of two Latter-day Saint lumberjacks may cut precisely the same amount of timber; but, if one is unmarried and the other has a wife and two children, the latter will draw four times as many quilts and blankets and four times as much meat and vegetables. Profit has no place in this venture. At the top of the requisitions which the workers present at the warehouses is the all-important question, "Number in family?"

The Mormon Church is divided into one hundred eighteen sections known as "stakes." Every stake has seven or eight subdivisions called "wards." In each ward there is a committee concerned exclusively with the Security Program. When a person has done some work under the plan, he receives a receipt signed by the ward committee member in charge of the task. This receipt entitles him to goods at his local storehouse in accordance with his particular requirements.

There is no feeling of charity or donation about the procedure. The men and women who push "work receipts" across the warehouse counters do so as proudly as if the bits of paper were coin of the realm. What they receive they have honestly earned. The Mormon sheepherder exchanges his lonely vigil for the carpenter's homemade chair. The housewife trades her preserves and jams for the shoe cobbler's handiwork. The coal miner digs in the earth all day so that his family may eat the celery and carrots grown by a fellow Mormon who has farmed in the fields from sunrise until dusk.

-3-

I watched the distribution of goods at the amply stocked storehouse within sight of the towering spires of the Mormon Temple in Salt Lake City. There was scarcely any haggling. The workers got what they wanted. A man laboring on an irrigation dam left the big warehouse carrying in one hand a pair of children's sandals and in the other a pair of buck-skin-laced boots for himself. A farmer who had trudged into the basement with two sacks of potatoes asked for clothes for his "womenfolks." He went out with an armload of gingham dresses and cotton petticoats. A minute later he was back.

"Say," he stammered embarrassedly, "you give me a green dress here. Martha, she just hates green."

"All right, Campbell," said the Mormon officiating at the storehouse counter. "Supposing you make the choice yourself. Pick out whatever dress you think your wife will like."

The farmer groped through the folds of cloth. He stepped back, scratched his head quizzically, and surveyed the array of garments. Then off its hanger he gingerly took a printed housedress as crimson as a Utah sunset.

The bulk of the vast amount of supplies distributed by the Security Program is produced by the people participating in the plan. This includes even sprays, disinfectants, ladders, and brooms. However, there is a corner in most Mormon storehouses for such goods as coffee, tea, dry breakfast foods, canned fish, gelatine, crackers, matches, toothpaste, and blu-ing. A young woman with a baby in her arms asks for a clip of safety pins. An old man needs a wheel chair. These prod-ucts are not readily manufacturable with the equipment and materials at hand. They must be purchased. This is where the financing of the program, through tithes and fast days, becomes essential. Much of the plan takes care of itself, but some outside help is required. That help comes from the general fund of the Mormon Church.

The general fund also makes possible the financing of nu-merous building projects. This is one of the main features of the Security Program. Last year a record was set for construc-tion in the history of the Mormon Church. The result was 241 new buildings, 407 major programs of renovation and repair, and employment for many thousands of people.

The impetus for the building boom has originated in the headquarters of the church. The general fund will contribute 60 per cent of the necessary financing to any practical project. From the stake or ward in which the project is located comes the remaining 40 per cent. Generally, this 40 per cent is in labor and materials; both are usually provided by Mormons hitherto idle or on relief.

In the railroad division point of Pocatello, tucked away in Idaho's rugged hills, I talked with some Mormons who were planning the construction of a new Security Program storehouse. They told me that unemployed bricklayers, carpenters, painters, and loggers all were finding work on the undertaking. For example, the building required heavy timbers. Idaho is part of the forest belt that President Roosevelt calls the greatest lumber area in the nation. So Mormon lumberjacks went into the backwoods and got the logs required.

"The people doing this work," a young Mormon in Pocatello explained to me, "draw food and clothing prepared by the people working in the farm and sewing projects."

As its contribution to the Security Program, the Cottonwood stake in Utah decided to beautify its chapel. Cement walks were laid out, the building repainted, and the surrounding lawn landscaped. Shrubbery was put in, and trees brought down out of the hills and replanted. Even the bishop and the deacon of the local ward took a turn at the cement mixer to give enthusiasm to the job. Approximately 13,360 hours of labor went into the work.

Beautification of the various church buildings—temples, chapels, and storehouses—has given enployment to a large number of Mormons. Two vast new temples are under way, one in Los Angeles and the other in Idaho. Under the Security Program the Mormons are erecting buildings in every State on the sundown side of the Rocky Mountains.

The construction part of this plan to remedy unemployment and end the necessity of government relief has not been confined to buildings. On the plateau of eastern Utah, hundreds of Mormon farmers found themselves the victims of adverse weather. The melting snows of the spring washed away the loamy topsoil like a knife scraping frosting from a cake. This was followed by dry, arid summers. The answer? Build reservoirs and dams to store and control the freshets of the spring for use during the hot spells later on. So that became a Security Program project, and Mormons toiled and labored in the wilderness to protect the crops on which they and their families would live.

Several other Latter-day Saint irrigation and reclamation undertakings are now under way—little replicas of the mammoth projects the Federal government is constructing at Fort Peck and Grand Coulee.

The mainstay of the Church Security Program is farming. The coal mines, the timber groves, the carpentry shops, the sewing tables, the building enterprises: they all are important, but secondary to the farms. A venerable Mormon Elder in Boise said to me: "We have plenty of land out West. The Lord has provided it. Why shouldn't our unemployed brothers and sisters be cultivating that land, making good things grow? As long as we have idle land there is no need for idle people." The Mormons are putting into practice this bit of hinterland philosophy. On hundreds of Security Program farms, produce is being raised to feed thousands of families.

Potatoes and corn cover the farms in Idaho. The Utah tracts produce fruits, sugar beets, and garden vegetables. Lettuce and oranges come from Arizona and California.

Sheep and cattle graze on upland pastures in all the Far Western States. Mormon wards in Canada and Mexico grow great quantities of wheat and other grain. These farming projects vary in size from ten or fifteen acres to the huge thirty-five-hundred-acre Juab security farm near Great Salt Lake. Half the produce from the vast Juab tract goes into the storehouses. Part of the remaining half is consumed by the once idle people who have farmed it; the rest is used to help retire mortgages and debts on Mormon farms harassed by financial difficulties. It is a thrilling sight to watch these Mormons, once destitute and discouraged, zealously tilling fields in the mountain-ringed valleys of the West.

The average Security Program farm is about forty acres in area. The land is sold to settlers for as little as a dollar an acre; prices never go beyond thirty dollars an acre. Like trappers going into the Arctic from a Hudson's Bay post, these colonists of 1938 can draw supplies in advance from a church storehouse. The debt is paid back in farm produce. Generally the farms are taken up for an experimental period of a year. This trial system accomplishes the double purpose of finding out whether the land is fertile and whether the settler has the perseverance and temperament to succeed. Mormon Elders assured me that relatively few of their Security Program farmers have failed to make a go of it. In the Wells stake of the church some young men organized a coöperative farm and grew a crop of crunchy Utah celery worth $5,000.

The West's modern-day pioneers—for that is what the Security Program people actually are—get plenty of help from their neighbors. Tractors and similar farm equipment are loaned back and forth, and veteran farmers are quick to advise and help their friends who have turned to the countryside to escape the bread line and relief window. In the Juab stake the Mormons provided an example of this friendly co-operation. A frost-proof storehouse was needed immediately to protect fruits grown under the program. Shortly after sunrise one morning four hundred Mormons went to work. By nightfall the pits had been dug, the structure raised, and dirt packed all around to keep out the cold. The whole area had joined efforts to make the Security Program succeed. This happens in many Mormon communities in the Promised Land.

-4-

Hard work is the foundation on which the Security Plan rests, and hard work is a Mormon tradition. The beehive, which is the Latter-day Saint symbol for labor and toil, is to Utah what the crown is to England and the eagle is to the United States. A beehive appears on the State seal and the State flag. "Deseret" is the Mormon word for work and industry. It, too, is seen everywhere in the picturesque Western State where 90 per cent of the church members are Mormons. Dozens of business establishments are named "Deseret." One of Salt Lake City's leading newspapers is the *Deseret News*. And "Deseret" was the original name bestowed by Brigham Young and his followers upon the State they hacked out of the wilderness. The word appears many times in the Salt Lake telephone directory.

Herculean labor created a civilization in Utah, out on the sunrise flank of the Columbia basin. Salt Lake City is a community of monuments commemorating those early years. A stone shaft marks the spot where trail-weary Brigham Young led his wagon train over Emigration Pass ninety years ago. Below him he saw Great Salt Lake and the valley. He pointed westward. "This is the place," he said.

Many groups and sects raise monuments to their warriors and other heroes. The grateful Latter-day Saints are the only people who ever dedicated a stately granite column to a bird. The first crop in the Mormons' new-found Canaan would have been destroyed by crickets had not dense flocks of sea gulls flown in from the barren islands of the lake and devoured the pests. Today, a unique monument in America, the Sea Gull Column, gives thanks for those white-winged deliverers of the past—and it is against the laws of Utah to kill a sea gull.

The Temple is to Salt Lake what St. Peters's is to Rome and Independence Hall is to Philadelphia. It is a symbol of past achievements and present ideals. Epitomized in it are the untiring industry and rigid spiritual discipline of the Mormons of both yesterday and today. The fiercest kind of effort went into its construction. Men labored beneath the glare of the desert sun and in the grip of mountain winters. Straining oxen dragged blocks of granite out of the highlands and across the sagebrush flats. It took five days to haul the three-ton stones from the distant quarries.

After each sundown, modern flood lights throw the granite spires of the Temple into sharp relief against the darkness of the sky. The traveler who comes by night through Emigration Pass sees, in the land below, the illuminated stone towers of the Temple pointing upward toward the heavens. Outlined on the tallest spire is a golden statue of the Mormon angel Moroni. It is a man-made scene that compares in grandeur and impressiveness with the mountains and lake that the visitor can look upon by day.

The Temple is the actual as well as the religious center of the city. All street numbers are counted from it in every direction. The population of Utah and Idaho is largely Mormon, and so the lofty church building is the spiritual hub of an area more than three times the size of England. Entrance to this granite monument to forty years of persistence and toil can be gained only by Latter-day Saints whose daily lives fulfill certain religious requirements and principles.

High-powered lights playing on the weather-beaten stones of the old Temple are but one of the contrasts between new and old in Salt Lake City. Directly behind the Temple is the dome of the massive Tabernacle, still sturdy and durable, held together by the wooden pegs and cowhide thongs that the pioneering Latter-day Saints used in lieu of nails. On its spacious roof are splotched arrows to point the way to the Salt Lake airport to the aviators who come down out of the hazardous ridges of the Rockies—aviators of whom the Mormon frontiersmen never dreamed when with crude tools they built a massive meetinghouse in the wilderness.

To the pioneer Mormons who hewed the State of Utah out of the desert and mountain fastnesses, the family was the principal economic and social unit. This still prevails to some degree today. The Mormons are home-lovers and family people. They pride themselves on a low divorce rate. They also take offense when the polygamy of early-day Mormonism is mentioned. This doctrine, they claim, has no place in the church at present. It is significant that much of the literature distributed in Salt Lake City takes special precaution to refer to "wife" in the singular when discussing the pioneer Mormon families.

The Latter-day Saints are thrifty, self-sufficient people. They delight in pointing to the results of the energy and effort of their argonaut predecessors. They would rather help than be helped. The Mormons, they contend, have always been prepared to assist State and nation in a crucial hour. A cherished Mormon tradition is the first overland telegram ever sent in the United States—from Brigham Young to President Lincoln in 1861:

UTAH IS LOYAL. HAS NOT SECEDED FROM THE UNION.

In Salt Lake City these traditions of the Mormon Church and the customs of modern society are skillfully blended in a cosmopolitan atmosphere. The community is a landmark of history and at the same time a symbol of progress. It combines religious solemnity with commercial and social activity.

New hotels and modernistic office buildings stand within sight of the great Temple. Electric traffic signals jingle above the statues of Brigham Young, Joseph Smith, and other Mormon immortals.

These contrasts do not seem incongruous in Salt Lake. Despite its religious background, the community is gay and lively. It does not have the night life and animation of an Eastern city, but is as convivial as other places in the West. There are many theaters, two vaudeville houses, a stock company, and the old Salt Lake Theater. Like most of the other cities on the Pacific side of the Rockies, it has no saloons and bars. Liquor in Utah is sold under a State monopoly.

The Mormons are temperate people. But they also are tolerant and do not believe in foisting their views on others. They comprise a voting majority in Salt Lake and Utah, but have made neither city nor State hidebound and prudish. The Utah liquor control system is efficiently and soundly operated. The Mormons shun alcohol themselves, yet never attempt to deny the privilege to others. Sally Rand's nude dances do not find favor with the Elders of the church, but she was allowed to perform unmolested when she appeared in Salt Lake.

No censorship is imposed upon the city's fine public library.

When the first Mormon ox teams stumbled down from the pass, worn volumes of Shakespeare and Homer and Juvenal bounced in the bottom of the wagons. The University of Utah in Salt Lake is a modern educational institution, with all the atmosphere and spirit typical of a State university. The city eagerly follows the fortunes of the football team and other athletic aggregations from the school. The same is true of the Mormon college—Brigham Young University in near-by Provo. Occasionally even dignified Heber J. Grant attends Brigham Young football games and cheers for the "Saints," as the team is sometimes called.

In few respects, aside from its history, does Salt Lake differ from other Western cities. It has twenty-one parks and playgrounds and many places of scenic beauty. Public and private dances are held frequently, and the Mormon Church sponsors many parties and get-togethers for its members and their friends. The community has never been prudish. For many years the Mormons have practiced tolerance in regard to the religious, social, and political views of others.

The Mormons live in harmony and peace with the members of other churches. There is scarcely any religious bigotry or prejudice in Utah and Idaho and the other States where the Mormons are numerous. Utah's predominantly Latter-day Saint population not so long ago elected a Jew as governor. The Utah supreme court, in rebuking a jingo district attorney, has just ruled that Communism and other political tendencies have nothing to do with the guilt of men charged with rioting. This general attitude of tolerance and understanding has, if anything, been strengthened by the Church Security Program. The other people in the West feel that the Mormons are trying to solve a problem which confronts us all. As the number of Mormons on relief has gradually dwindled, the region has looked on with aroused interest.

The sole criticism that I heard directed against the church's program came from some adherents of the New Deal who insisted that the denunciations of the dole and relief were thrusts at the Roosevelt administration. I asked several Mormon leaders about this. They denied the contention and pointed out that in November of 1936—when the Security Program was well under way—Utah with its three hundred thousand Mormons gave the President the largest proportionate majority over Landon that he received in any State outside the South except Nevada. Church and State, these men assured me, are separate in Utah. A few years back Reed Smoot, high-ranking member of the Mormon Council of Twelve Apostles, was defeated decisively for reëlection to the United States Senate by a University of Utah professor of political science named Elbert Duncan Thomas.

The successor to the conservative Smoot has become one of the aggressively liberal supporters of the New Deal. He delivered the most scholarly Senate speeches in defense of the President's plan to renovate the Supreme Court, and he earned a place on the *Nation's* honor role by upholding the National Labor Relations Board against its host of vituperative critics. Placid, calm, and sad-faced, Senator Thomas has brought to Capitol Hill both the learning and the imperturbability of the typical college professor. He argues for civil rights and economic security with the mild demeanor of the pedagogue rather than the vigor of the politician. In Washington he represents the best and most humanitarian traditions of the Mormon religion and proves that, regardless of what anti-New-Deal tendencies may purportedly be latent in the Security Program, the Latter-day Saints of Utah enjoy being represented by a thoroughgoing disciple of the President.

-5-

The hope of every Mormon active in the Security Program is that some day no able-bodied Latter-day Saint will be dependent upon government relief or private charity. In his spacious office in the marble-columned Mormon Church headquarters building, solemn-appearing Heber Grant said: "Our primary purpose is to set up, in so far as possible, a system in which the curse of idleness will be done away with, the evils of the dole abolished, and thrift and self-respect once more established among the people. The aim of the church is to help the people to help themselves."

It is a proud boast of the Mormon president that the Security Program is steadily reducing the number of his followers on relief. "Some individuals are born tired and never get rested," he said with a wan smile. "Some of them seem to prefer government aid to the church's policy of work and economic independence for all its members. However, they are in a decided minority. For the most part our people welcome the chance to become independent and self-supporting again." Occasionally Heber Grant gets discouraged about the plan, particularly when he sees Mormons turn it down for Federal relief. But the general opinion throughout the Northwest is that in one respect the program of the church has been invaluable. The people outside the scope of the economic system cannot go on forever living off taxes paid by the people who are working. Some time they must start producing for themselves. Why not in the vast, unpopulated Columbia basin? The church's idea has enunciated these facts.

Despite fitful discouragement and Heber Grant's elderly impatience, the Church Security Plan has been headed in the correct direction. Why should people live off the government

—or off charity—when they can produce for themselves and live off the land? In sparsely settled Nevada, where there are scarcely as many people as there are in the huge concrete box of Radio City, President Roosevelt recently said there should be a much larger population. Divert water over the dry Nevada uplands, he said, and the State could support millions more people.* If a region can feed and house a much larger population than it has now, why should the indigent people there at present either exist on charity or putter around at artificial tasks? A Mormon school teacher in Twin Falls, where the Shoshone River crashes over a crumbling precipice, said to me: "I know our church plan has plenty of imperfections. But at least it's sane. I get a salary of $125 a month. I hate to pay part of it in taxes to support a family that could live much more adequately if it were given one of the thousands of farm tracts near here. I know we have to support the church plan by tithing now, but some day it can be self-sustaining. Then our people will be producing for themselves, instead of living off the government or a Community Chest."

The eighty-one-year-old president of the Mormons is himself an example of the hard work and tenacity he recommends to his adherents. When he was a young man in frontier Utah, his handwriting shocked the Elders. "Heber," he once was told, "your letters look like an ink bottle struck by lightning." Grant made himself sit at a desk hour after hour to learn how to write. Today, he writes with the most graceful flourish in the Rocky Mountain States. For a while he was a professor of penmanship at the University of Utah.

As a boy Heber Grant was messenger for an insurance com-

* Nevada, considerably bigger than the State of New York, has fewer people than one or two blocks in New York City. Much of Nevada is arid soil far from water. But some of it can be irrigated, and ground as dry as talcum powder can be converted into fertile soil. President Roosevelt advocated that this be done when he traveled across the State in July of 1938.

pany. Now he is the president of three insurance companies. He saw the Union Pacific's tracks laid westward. Now he is one of the railroad's directors. "I have three guideposts," the president of the Latter-day Saints said, "purity, punctuality, and perseverance."

Heber Grant has been president of the Mormon Church for three decades. Yet he is still active and vigorous. He thought of the Security Program in his eightieth year, and takes a direct interest in its management. He has seen to it, for example, that the various stakes and regions exchange surplus products back and forth. In the big Salt Lake City storehouse there was an abundance of canned fruits. The Kanab stake had an excess of mutton. So a trade was made. This takes place all the time under the bearded president's watchful gaze. He even helped arrange an exchange with the Mormon storehouse near Calgary in the Canadian province of Alberta. Utah strawberries and pears were traded for Canadian beef. The bartered goods were admitted free of duty and the railroads reduced freight rates 50 per cent.

"We're making progress," said Heber Grant as he gestured out the window toward the lofty Temple his father had helped to build so long ago. "Some day all our people may be doing useful work and none of them will be on relief. We make that our goal."

Outside, on the tree-bowered Salt Lake street, I met a couple of young Mormons who were volunteering their spare time to assist in the Security Program. They introduced me to a lad who, unable to get steady work in the city, was cultivating celery on one of the coöperative farms.

"How do you like it?" I asked him.

"Well," he said, "it's hard to get used to after living in the city so long. But I like it better all the time. I'll make a go of it!"

14. The American Wilderness

WHITE space on the United States census map means fewer than two people a square mile. The only white space east of the Mississippi River is a little rectangular patch indicating the swampy Everglades of Florida. On the other side of the Mississippi the map describes a different sort of land. White space nearly predominates in the great basin the Columbia River has carved in the Pacific Northwest.

The map shows half of Oregon as white, and almost the same proportion of Utah and Idaho. White is the color for two-thirds of Wyoming, one-third of Montana, and virtually all of Nevada. These vast, blank areas may be mere undotted expanses on the census map, but they actually symbolize the last American wilderness—the final part of the nation where there is still a frontier to be settled and colonized.

Few people realize the extent of this frontier. How many citizens of Ohio, for example, are dimly aware that Oregon contains as much land practically uninhabited as there is in the whole Buckeye State? It has become almost a truism to observe that the hinterlands of the United States have disappeared. Not long ago President Roosevelt declared, "Our last frontier has long since been reached." David Cushman Coyle believes that gone is "the old frontier of prairie and forest" and with it the "freedom of opportunity embodied in seemingly inexhaustible resources." The outpost regions, "always an avenue of escape" from the dilemmas of civilization, are closed forever in the opinion of Carl Dreher. With hundreds of other politicians and economists, similar expressions are axiomatic. A poetess penned a famous line: *

> Last league of water sailed, last island settled.

But *is* the frontier gone? Was the President correct when he said, "There is no safety valve in the form of Western prairie to which those thrown out of work by the economic machines can go for a new start"? Even as he uttered these words, the Bureau of Reclamation at his order was erecting a dam that will open to thousands of settlers a hitherto desolate region in the State of Washington ten times as spacious as all of New York City. Right now, Secretary of the Interior Ickes and lumber interests in the Northwest are bitterly arguing whether a new national park shall include a million or only six hundred thousand acres. Can the wilderness be gone when men in Washington, D.C., sit down over maps and blue prints and juggle chunks of hinterland as big as the entire State of Delaware? As long as there are five hundred and twenty-eight people to the square mile in Massachusetts but only five to the square mile in Idaho, the nation has a population outlet westward yet to be actually used. Crowded Connecticut with three hundred thirty-three inhabitants for every square mile is not even comparable to Wyoming with only two. They might as well be on different planets. In New England the cities are strung closely together like insulators on a wire. In the Northwest they are nearly a day's journey apart. A Vermont farmer lives within easy distance of his neighbors; the ranch family in Oregon must drive many lonely miles to see other faces.

There *is* an American backwoods, and the Pacific North-

* Marie de L. Welch in the *New Republic*.

west is it. People who have never been on a trolley car live in the Idaho forests, and a girl from the Utah uplands who won a national slogan contest has just had her first glimpse of a two-story building. In this wilderness dwell cowpunchers, trappers, sheepherders, lumberjacks, mountaineers, fishermen, and ranchers. I have heard these men talking about remote valleys no one has ever explored and secluded ranges no one has ever penetrated. There is a vast basin in the Sawtooth Mountains of Idaho that the Forestry Service contends is as wild and primitive as it was before the Pilgrims landed on the continent. Much of this frontier may be hedged around with rights and claims and deeds and easements; but it is a frontier nevertheless, and some day the country will spill the population surplus over into it. People are crowded in the East and lonely in the West, yet eventually the disproportion will be balanced. The property-interest barrier that hems in some of the wilderness is not insurmountable. At Grand Coulee the land speculators and mortgage companies will have to part with their holdings at prices fixed by the Department of the Interior. Otherwise their land will receive no water and will continue to be worthless.

The last session of Congress passed an act generally overlooked which will be of great significance in the development of the wilderness. It authorizes the Secretary of the Interior to open the vast public lands in the West, and permits him to sell or lease five-acre tracts. This will make available for settlement more than 259,000 square miles on the sundown side of the Mississippi River, an area as large as the State of Texas. Joel D. Wolfsohn, the secretary of the General Land Office, regards the act as extremely important. He contends that as the grazing, timber, and farming lands thus opened are put to use, small towns will spring up to provide the trading and service centers for the contiguous backwoods areas.

So, slowly, the population of the country will be spread out westward. The idea that Congress had in mind in the adoption of this act parallels Harry Hopkins' statement, when he was asked to explain why so great a proportion of the government funds for pump-priming have been spent in the lonely West:

"If I were to give one reason, I would say the development of great conservation projects in the Far Western States, looking forward to the time when millions of people will inhabit areas which are now sparsely settled."

Americans hear so often the frontier is gone that they have little conception of the enormous hinterland left in the West. Of the immensity and grandeur of this frontier, they have no notion whatsoever. I live in Portland. It is a growing city of three hundred twenty thousand people located where the Willamette River pours its pittance into the majestic Columbia. Fifteen miles eastward the Columbia pours out of the granite chute it has cut through the mountains. In half an hour I can drive my Buick from Portland's busiest street corner to the entrance to the canyon of the Columbia. The highway approaches the scene almost by stealth. The road twists past a tiny village, snuggles against a wall of fir trees for a hundred yards, and then the ground before it seems to fall away.

Three thousand feet below, the great river—dwarfing the Hudson and second only to the Mississippi—swirls seaward. Cliffs as precipitous as the wall of a tomb tower up from the water. The Palisades of the Hudson would look like an embankment down there. Across the river, the ground rolls away in billows of green. Ridge surmounts ridge, until the whole panorama culminates in the lofty snow-tipped summits of Hood, St. Helens, and Adams. "It's terrific!" Stuart Chase gasped when he saw this spectacle, and Otis Wiese, the editor of *McCall's,* said the same thing. People from the East are invariably impressed by the fact that in the vast scene scarcely anyone seems to be dwelling. "Gosh! It's the real stuff," a well known Washington correspondent remarked as he looked half a mile straight down to the flecks that were the Columbia's whitecaps. "This is a wilderness for fair."

Lewis Mumford stood on one of the huge basalt abutments above the Columbia. "I have seen a lot of great scenery in my life," he observed, "but the view in this gorge knocks me flat. It is one of the greatest in the world."

The endless vista of water and meadows and hills brought to life the sociologist and technician in the onlooker. "I have seen nothing so tempting as a home for man as this Oregon Country," Mumford said. "There is a basis here for civilization on its highest scale. This is one of the last places in the nation where natural resources are still largely intact."

Up through the hills and mountains the Columbia has cut its way. As the river narrows and runs more swiftly, the scattered farmhouses and little villages disappear altogether. Rugged peaks stretch toward the sky like unfinished towers built to reach to heaven. The cliffs are gaunt and grim, and the land is barren or dotted with sagebrush. The great waterway is a living force in a dead land. Coyotes and rattlesnakes and an occasional antelope are all that move on the plateaus that surmount the steep banks of the river. The Columbia seems to roar more angrily the farther back toward its upper reaches the traveler goes. It is joined by its principal tributary, the Snake, and now the two hurtling streams mark off the least explored area of continental United States.

Above the junction of the rivers looms the Seven Devils Range that spans the border between Oregon and Idaho. Seven serrated mountains stand in a semicircle like horned goblins at a council fire, and below them the terrain is a series of countless rock crevasses. This is believed to be the richest mineral region in the world. The only reason it is not honeycombed with copper and gold and silver mines is that transportation is practically impossible. No highway or railroad can get into it. Trails hewn out of granite and basalt by CCC workers are the sole avenue of entrance. The hands and foreheads of airplane pilots are clammy as they fly over this forbidding area. Engine trouble or a broken strut in the air means death below. There is not an acre of level ground in the ominous hinterland that the Seven Devils guard. Through one of the gorges that split the range the Snake River rushes. From He Devil Peak to the silvery strip of water in Hell's Canyon way beneath, the drop is a sheer seventy-nine hundred feet. This is more than two thousand feet deeper than the Grand Canyon of the Colorado. For grandeur and breathtaking immensity, there is no sight in the country to compare with the cleft the Snake has dug along the Oregon-Idaho boundary. It is relatively unknown and is rarely visited only because it is so inaccessible. Six Empire State Buildings could be piled on one another in the canyon, and still they would not reach to the brink. For four miles there is a sheer precipice four thousand feet high. A boulder dropped over it seems never to reach the river far below. Roaring falls and rapids in the Snake are mere wisps of spray from He Devil Peak. For many miles the stream surges through territory such as this. From the Oregon wall of the canyon there is a rutted automobile road constructed by the CCC. But not many people use it. Nerves and imagination cannot survive the experience. The road is wide enough only for one car. There is no railing. Beyond the running board, it is sometimes a precipitous half-mile to the rock-strewn river beneath. The ordeal is too hair-raising for the average person. Even hardened forest rangers come away from it with frail and wobbly knees. After the river's long course through this most rugged and wild of all America's outpost areas, the highlands fall away, and the Snake rolls between hills instead of bluffs. The Union Pacific spans the stream on a spidery bridge of steel latticework, and when a limited train from the East thunders over it with a hollow roar, the adventurous wayfarer is reminded that he is living in the twentieth century, after all, and that the immense gorge is only a final recollection of the continent that existed long before the Indians came upon it.

There are other mountain strongholds in the Northwest—not so wild and massive as the Seven Devils, perhaps, but formidable ranges just the same. They stud spacious flats and tablelands like turreted castles in the desert. The flats and tablelands are dry and arid now, but they could be checkered with farms and orchards. How? The water that has cut Hell's Canyon seventy-nine hundred feet into the earth's surface can also make the sagebrush regions bloom. Water! That is the magician's fluid to transform the blank spaces on the census map into mottled areas representing thickly clustered farms and thriving towns. Irrigation is the artery of life to thousands of Western farms. Not many Americans realize that the potatoes from Idaho that they bake or the peaches from Utah that they make into cobbler were brought up through the soil, not by water that fell from the heavens, but by water that flowed through an irrigation ditch. In much of the Columbia basin there is no rain. The ground is caked and hard, producing only sagebrush and weeds. But through these stretches, from the snow-laden uplands far away, flow rivers rich with surplus water. That water in irrigation canals and behind reclamation dams will make the Western desert green with life. It will make the Promised Land dream start to come true.

-2-

In his most eloquent manner Daniel Webster once proclaimed that the vast arid stretches of the United States were as worthless as the sagebrush and cactus that flourished in their arid soil. He said he would not give a dollar for all of Oregon.

The government which the great Senator from Massachusetts served has embarked upon a campaign which may prove that he was wrong. The recent Congress appropriated $41,731,000 for projects that will attempt to make grain and fruit and vegetables grow where only the grotesque foliage of the Western desert sways in the hot winds. This sum is part of more than $500,000,000 required to complete the most thoroughgoing irrigation and reclamation program in American history.

Some of the projects are of a magnitude never before undertaken by any nation. Boulder Dam, on the Colorado River at the Arizona-Nevada border, is the largest structure ever built by man; yet the Grand Coulee Dam, heart of the colossal irrigation project now rising on the barren flats of northwestern Washington, will be more than two and a half times as large. Casper-Alcova Dam will inundate dry lands in Wyoming, and the Vale-Owyhee Dam already is watering the crusty soil of eastern Oregon.

The area affected by the irrigation projects includes fifteen States—all large States by any man's measure. A glance at a map will indicate their extent. Start at the Canadian border with North Dakota. Go southward through South Dakota and Nebraska. Skip Kansas and Oklahoma and let your finger come to rest in Texas, on the Mexican border. The States you have touched and every State from there to the Pacific are included in the Federal enterprise. They constitute an area nine times as large as Germany. All the States in the Pacific Northwest and the Columbia River basin figure importantly in the undertaking.

The changing of arid waste lands into fertile valleys is one of the great dramas of the American West. Beyond the prairies of the Central States are millions of acres that require only water to become productive. Westward toward the Pacific the arid plateaus and hills roll away to the horizon. Often they support only desert weeds and bushes, and coyotes and rattlesnakes and prairie dogs. Given water, they will grow wheat and corn and apples, or become lush pastures for herds of sheep and cattle.

Here is a dry upland flat in Idaho. On it a man without a canteen or a knapsack soon would die of thirst or hunger— unless he could bring down with his rifle one of the coyotes that skulk by night from sagebrush to sagebrush. The area is grim and desolate. Nature seems to scowl. The automobile roads are dusty and dry. There is no sign of habitation. A breakdown without water might mean the death of a carload of people. Brush and cactus, here and there the skull of a perished animal—these are all the traveler sees. Yet the soil over which he drives is potentially fertile; moisture is all that it requires. And somewhere beyond the hills that shimmer in the distance is water.

Man diverts the river. By means of ditches that twist through the hills he brings it to the arid upland flat. Cultivation is begun. Poplar trees, tall and stately, wave in the breeze. Farmhouses stud the landscape. Fields of corn are green under the sun. Small communities spring up. A railroad spur is run in from the main line one hundred miles away. Warehouses are built. Long, yellow refrigerator cars are loaded with apples, peaches, berries, and pears, and they carry their freight to the distant cities of the East. Though, without water, much of the land of the Western third of the nation is as valueless as Daniel Webster predicted it would be, with water it becomes worth from $100 to $1,000 an acre.

Today irrigation is one of the most important functions of the government in the Northwest. Senator Borah says irrigation canals carry the region's lifeblood. The enterprise offers a contrast between the new and the old in the West. Irrigation at one time was an individual project. A farmer on one section might try to water his crops by digging a ditch from the nearest creek, like the Indians whom the Spanish conquistadors saw along the Colorado River in 1540. Irrigation, at present, starts in one of two ways. Either the Federal government surveys a certain region and finds it adaptable to a water-right program, or the farmers in an area band together spontaneously, form an irrigation district, and seek assistance from the Bureau of Reclamation. If irrigation is found to be practicable, the bureau advances the money and the project gets under way.

But first a careful analysis is made of the territory to be irrigated. How much water is needed? Does the nearest river maintain a steady flow? Is the terrain too rugged to be spanned feasibly by canals and ditches? Is the area a healthful one for those who will live there? Will the crops produced be sufficient to finance the irrigation project and at the same time support the farmers who harvest them? Is there a market for those crops? Is transportation available, or is the region secluded in one of the Northwest's far-flung reaches? The thoroughness of the analysis is occasioned by memories of early ventures which failed. All the questions must now be answered satisfactorily before the new project is begun.

A dam is built. It may be a small barrier no larger than that constructed by a miller for his water wheel or by beavers

felling saplings with their teeth. Or it may be a Grand Coulee, costing more than the Panama Canal and containing
enough cement to build a road completely around the United
States. Once the river is dammed, a steady supply of water
is assured. In dry seasons the reservoir behind the barrier can
be tapped. During high-water periods the dam controls the
river and prevents floods.

Then the irrigation ditches are dug. Over gorges, through
canyons, around mountains, the water is carried to the distant
waste areas. Occasionally, in hilly sections where lava rock
and pumice threaten slides, the ditches must be lined with
concrete. Seen from a peak, they seem to wind through the
countryside like fantastic serpents. They must be carefully
policed and tended, because a break might mean the loss of a
valuable harvest.

Up to the highest possible point on each farmer's land the
main ditches reach. Then it is the problem of the farmer to
use the water as he sees fit, digging his own subsidiary ditches.
In most irrigated areas the farmers hold frequent meetings
in Grange halls and country schoolhouses to discuss their
problems. When the water is used too freely, the crops are
flooded; when it is used too sparingly, they are scorched.
And the failure of one farmer is an additional financial burden on the whole district. His neighbors must prorate among
themselves the payments on which he has defaulted. Thus
irrigation is distinctly a coöperative enterprise.

An irrigation farmer in Idaho or Montana or Oregon has
vastly different problems from his fellow agrarian in New
York or Tennessee or Illinois. He must meet not only the
ordinary costs of farming. Above all, he has to keep up on his
irrigation charges, which are divided into two sections: the
charge to retire the construction costs, and the charge to operate the project. The first varies from 75 cents to $4 an acre.

The second is usually about $1.25 an acre. The size of the undertaking and the length and detail of the ditches determine the construction charge. No interest is assessed against the farmers for the money lent by the Bureau of Reclamation, and repayment periods are from twenty to forty years.

A farmer with 500 acres must pay about $1,650 a year for his water—and unless he pays, his water is cut off. This makes irrigation farming a determined affair. That $1,650 must be raised each year, or the farm will be as worthless as yesterday's wind. Sarah, the farmer's wife, needs a new sewing machine; Mary, the farmer's daughter, is crying for a doll; Bill, the farmer's son, yearns for the .22 rifle in the window of Abner Slocum's general store. These things are important, but they are never realized until that $1,650 is accumulated.

The irrigation farmer in the United States is less of an individualist than the average dirt farmer. The dirt farmer is largely the master of his own destiny. The irrigation farmer must conform to the rules and regulations of the irrigation district to which he belongs; he must raise a fairly substantial sum each year to keep water flowing onto his acreage. But in the face of these liabilities, he has one great asset: a steady, reliable supply of moisture. He need not look anxiously at the weather. The mercury reaches 115 degrees on the Umatilla irrigation project in Oregon, but each year the acres it waters produce corn, potatoes, melons, lettuce, and alfalfa, and support dairy herds.

Irrigation in the Promised Land of the United States is linked inseparably with the program of conserving the country's natural resources. Some economists foresee the time when there may be a food shortage in the nation. Thus the turning of arid wastelands into fertile valleys ranks as a major aim of the New Deal conservation program.

Last year, President Roosevelt said: "The tragic drought

of 1936 has reëmphasized the importance to the welfare of the nation of conserving the waters of our Western streams for use in stabilizing agriculture and strengthening the economic structure of the arid and semiarid States. Federal reclamation projects served to mitigate the effects of the drought of 1934 and are this year in many localities giving another demonstration of the wisdom and usefulness of our national reclamation policy."

John C. Page, the Commissioner of Reclamation, contends that without irrigation the West as it is today would be only a myth. "The large coastal cities," he says, "would be the small villages they were in pioneer times. It is doubtful whether, without the growth in importance of the West due to irrigation, the United States would have found the Panama Canal necessary, and it is almost certain that the transcontinental railroads could not exist except for the traffic created by the irrigated farms and the increased urban population supported by these farms."

Yet America's far-reaching irrigation program has many opponents. Some of them hold it absurd that the government which reduces crops in one locality should spend millions to increase crops in another. Proponents of the irrigation program answer that in 1934 the crop returns for the entire country averaged $16.60 an acre; on Federal irrigation projects the average was $42. They point especially to the success of the irrigation venture in the Yakima valley. Farmers who originally settled there abandoned their farms to the heat and dust. Then a dam was built across the Yakima River, a tributary of the Columbia, and irrigation ditches were dug. Water flowed onto the soil. In 1929 irrigated farms in the Yakima valley raised crops seven times as valuable as the gold mined in Alaska during the same year.

The Yakima project is the third largest irrigation enterprise in the nation. The largest is the Minidoka undertaking in Idaho, and next is the Salt River project in Arizona. Greater than all these combined will be the mammoth Grand Coulee development.

The thousands of farm families who have come west from the Dust Bowl have the greatest immediate stake in the irrigation program. Commissioner Page says the irrigation projects now under way can provide for a new population of approximately a million people. Upon these projects the victims of drought may find new homes, may have a part in developing a new land which droughts can no longer waste. There they may again become producers and useful citizens in a national economy of which Daniel Webster never dreamed.

-3-

Arid lands need water, and latent kilowatts need dams. But there is one resource in the wilderness of the Northwest which requires neither improvement nor development. That resource is the most majestic scenery on the continent.

Mountain ranges rear three miles in the air, and rivers fall so far they dissolve into plumes of mist. Foaming creeks are alive with trout, and each spring the Columbia is a broad expanse of salmon. Even the gaunt desert uplands have a grim and striking beauty, and the snow-capped peaks of the Cascades have a grandeur that matches the Alps.

This "garden-spot," as Charles A. Beard once called it, is the last reminder of the America that was. Cougars and bears still roam the hills and maraud herds and flocks. Indians camp on lonely streams in quest of fish, and trappers plod through the highlands setting their traps and snares. Civilization has not yet actually despoiled this region, although in some places its encroachments have meant exploitation and waste. "I have lived!" Kipling exclaimed many years ago when he fished the Clackamas for the fighting Chinooks; and the angler of today can still whip the river where the great writer stood and achieve the same results. David Cushman Coyle's warning that "the resources are shrinking" applies less to the Columbia River basin than to any other part of the nation. The great white spaces on the census map are yet to be developed—but, also, they are yet to be plundered.

An outpost society exists in the wilderness, and it has the characteristics of which Mark Twain and Bret Harte wrote in the early days of the West. There are old-fashioned rural church sociables, and there are primitive country hotels where watery noodle soup and thick slabs of beef go with a dollar room. At crossroads corners there are poker and checkers feuds as old as the State; and many backwoods hermits can remember when smoke signals dotted the horizon and the nearest cavalry post was five hundred miles away.

What sort of people live in this vast hinterland? How do they compare to their fellow citizens in the metropolises beyond the mountains? From what perspective do they regard recent political developments in Washington? How do they estimate the martial occurrences abroad? Do an Oregon rancher three days' travel from the nearest line of rail and a truck driver who wheels his machine through Times Square in New York City think similar thoughts on the Supreme Court and battleships and war referendums and a third term for the President? We have seen already that the mood of the citizens of the frontier is more placid and less turbulent than that of the people of the East. What are the contacts and relationships of the dwellers in the wilderness?

The people in the outpost areas encounter public opinion in different fashion than the inhabitants of such populous

States as Illinois, New York, and Pennsylvania. Lecturers on various topics and advocates of various causes seldom penetrate the frontier. Nor is there as much reading or listening to radios. Electricity is fairly essential to these pastimes; only about 6 or 7 per cent of the farms of Montana and Wyoming have power. Telephone lines are also comparatively rare in the backwoods.

A sheepherder in the McKenzie Pass of Oregon or a prospector in the Rocky Mountains of Utah does not get his newspaper the morning or afternoon of its date. Many times it is a week late. Hitler was in Vienna before trappers in the uplands below Mount St. Helens in Washington knew Schuschnigg had called a plebiscite. Frequently, treks to remote post offices are long and weary, and it would take a newsboy with the dimensions of Paul Bunyan to deliver papers to ranches and cabins and bivouacs separated from one another by miles of rugged hinterlands.

What effect does this comparative isolation have on people's opinions and outlooks? The men and women in the backwoods are voters, too. Do their beliefs weave into the quilt of general views—views on war and peace, capital and labor, conservatism and liberalism?

It is in the outpost regions that the answers to these questions must be found. Here is the little hamlet of Sandy, high on the steep Oregon hills that sweep from Mount Hood's glacier-barricaded pinnacle to the capes and promontories that extend out into the Pacific. The usual population of Sandy is 284, but on this day it is four times that.

The regular monthly Grange meeting for the county is being held, and farmers and their friends from all over Clackamas County have come. Clackamas County contains some of the wildest mountain grandeur in the nation. President Roosevelt drove through it last autumn when he dedi-

cated Timberline Lodge on Mount Hood, and the correspondents accompanying him said it was one of the most
primeval areas a President had ever visited.

The people at this hinterland Grange meeting live and
work in the open. One notices that first. They are tanned and
rugged, and their hands are hard and calloused from gripping
plows, swinging axes, churning butter, or pumping water.
Many of the men wear suits obviously donned for the occasion. The suits are not particularly new in style or cut, but
they are neat and pressed. A lot of the older men wear little
shoestring neckties. Against the wall hang long rows of the
wide-brimmed felt hats common throughout the Far West.

Most of the women wear linen dresses with conservative
print patterns. Those active on the Grange program have
come in dark dresses that are more formal. There are only a
few high-heeled slippers in the group, and scarcely any of
the men have wrist watches. From their vests dangle old-
fashioned gold watch chains. A lumberjack in a blue denim
shirt has a dollar timepiece fastened to his suspenders with a
big safety pin—"blanket pin," he calls it. A considerable number of the women have brought knitting bags, crochet hooks,
or embroidery hoops.

It is the noon hour, and the meeting has adjourned for a
time. Upstairs in the timber-built Grange hall, stout-armed
farm wives serve a dinner of chicken fricassee with all sorts
of fresh fruits and vegetables. The men stand about, talking
with friends they have not seen since the previous county-
wide Grange meeting three months before. Some of them
reminisce about old times, and one white-mustached farmer
looks for new faces to tell about the time he watched Kipling
fish for salmon in the roaring Clackamas half a century back.

Principally, these dwellers in an outpost land talk about
matters of direct and immediate concern. This means such

subjects as the weather, local crop conditions, the influx of drought refugees from the Dust Bowl, the lumber industry, and the discontinuance of the interurban electric line from Portland to Estacada farther down the river.

But other problems, more remote yet of greater significance, also interest the people at the Grange meeting. It is the first time in several weeks that some of them have left their ranches and farms. Stirring new developments have occurred both in this country and abroad—developments to be argued, discussed, and wondered about.

Japan continues its invasion of China, and a lean, angular man who grows celery on a Clackamas County river bottom says to one of his friends: "You know, I don't think those Japanese people give two whoops for what their army's doing. There's a little Japanese fellow who raises tomatoes down the road a piece from my place. He says he ain't got anything against the Chinamen."

Even more than city dwellers, the people of the hinterlands have the tendency to reduce grave national and international problems to terms of their own particular experiences.

A sheep rancher at the Grange meeting looked with favor on the Ludlow war referendum amendment because he happened to mistrust his particular Representative in Congress. A stout woman in a gravy-splattered apron was sure the national debt was not a serious matter because she and her family had made their way for a number of years with a heavy mortgage on their farm. "And we're still going," she said.

Most noticeable of all on the frontier is that opinions do not necessarily dovetail into the pigeonholes of thought customary in the cities. For example, one extremely articulate group of American citizens favors coöperative action with the other democracies against the aggressor nations, power in the

President and State Department to formulate diplomatic policy, and an increase in naval armaments. An opposite faction advocates strict neutrality, a national referendum on war, and a relatively small navy.

These lines of demarcation were not evident to me in Sandy. Many of the backwoods people who believed in the war referendum also said they approved of collective action. Many others in favor of neutrality also were in favor of increasing the navy. The so-called "schools of thought" were not divided along the lines apparent in many areas.

In the backwoods approach to the international scene, there seems to be less discussion of and familiarity with such terms as "Fascism," "Communism," "Nazism" and "totalitarianism." The people of the countryside condemn Franco when he bombs a town and his Loyalist foes when they sack a church. The conflicting philosophies of government at issue enter their comments relatively infrequently. The despots of the world are referred to mainly as dictators, regardless of whether they represent the fascist or communist type of economy.

There were few stereotyped attitudes at the Grange meeting here in this little rural hamlet of Sandy. One young farmer thought the sit-down strikers should be sent to prison, and another believed the Labor Board had stirred up rather than alleviated the labor situation. Yet both were for Roosevelt and thought he merited a third term. A couple of other tillers of the backwoods soil were against the sales tax and for public ownership of hydroelectric power. Yet they both looked forward to the time when the Republicans would supersede Roosevelt in the White House.

There seem to be numerous reasons why hinterland opinions do not fit into the general compartments of public thought. One is that the advocates, zealots, and crusaders of most causes seldom get beyond the outposts of civilization. Little indoctrination takes place on the frontier. Opinions are formed naturally, with a minimum of influence from propaganda. Beliefs are not grooved. A member of a C.I.O. timber workers' local is not necessarily sympathetic with the sit-down strikers. A farm wife who belongs to the American Legion Auxiliary does not let that fact put her on record for a belligerent policy of national defense. Opinions are developed more independently.

The people who live here in Sandy and in the hills and uplands near by are influenced principally by events that can be made to bear somewhat on their own lives. The news that Hitler seeks the timber preserves of Rumania has a tangible meaning here. The slopes around Sandy are covered with trees. The people of the village can almost imagine the Nazi war machine grinding up the steep slopes from the Pacific.

The Ludlow war referendum seemed to be popular at the Grange meeting, mainly because the inhabitants of the region long have applied the initiative and referendum to their own immediate problems. If Oregon can have a referendum on tax bills and farm legislation, why cannot the whole country hold a referendum before war is declared?

Much the same type of reasoning appeared to prompt them to be for President Roosevelt. Most of these hinterland dwellers spoke out against many of the advocacies commonly associated with the New Deal. But everyone liked the CCC camps in the area. The Federal dam at Bonneville has brought a promise of more electric power, and the President has promised a reforestation program. These matters are of vital and immediate concern to Clackamas County. They appear to be the determining factors in shaping the hinterland viewpoint. There also is the general, withal intangible, feeling on the part of the wilderness people that Mr. Roosevelt is their friend. "Our President," they call him, and they may not like all he does, but they are sure his heart is in the right place.

More than to the city dwellers, whose radios and daily contacts and newspapers on their doorsteps bring them close to the rest of the world, to the men and women in the backwoods Europe and Asia seem far away. It requires an occurrence applicable to their own lives to interest them vitally in events across the seas. For example, Hitler canceled the contemplated Austrian plebiscite at a time when Clackamas County was about to conduct a referendum in which a public power proposal was rejected.

"Supposin'," mused one overall-clad farmer, "that some dictator came in here and told us we couldn't vote on the power set-up."

"Or that we had better vote '*Ja*,' " another farmer interposed.

Immediately the whole group of farmers was heatedly discussing the situation in Central Europe, a subject they probably had not mentioned for two or three weeks.

The people of the country's frontier talk about things in terms of their own experiences and not with any preconceived ideas or notions. Perhaps that is why some of them are for Roosevelt and against the labor unions, and others are against business and for the Republicans. Their views may follow no chartered course, but at least they reflect the independence, freedom, and uniqueness of the majestic hinterland in which they live.

In my peregrinations through the wilderness that reaches almost to my backyard, I have had innumerable experiences indicating how the people on our last frontier reduce to terms of their own hinterland environment the questions that rock the planet.

Half a dozen men leaned on the counter of a general store in the Oregon hills, talking with the proprietor who slowly turned the wheel of a glittering, old-fashioned coffee grinder.

One of the men pulled a wisp of bunchgrass from the corner of his mouth. He spat into the sawdust box near the stove in the center of the little store. "Let me tell you something," he said reflectively. "If the League of Nations fizzles out, there'll be Nazis in these here hills." He gestured out through the smudgy window to where tree-blanketed ridges formed the sky line.

"And if we get in the League," another farmer retorted, "do you know where we'll be? We'll be over in the German hills gettin' bombed and shot at."

The storekeeper paused at the wheel of the cumbersome old coffee grinder. "You fellows better get organized on your ideas," he chid. "If we get in another mess, it ain't gonna be safe anywhere. They'll bomb the top clear off Zigzag Mountain up there. This place'll be under fifty thousand tons o' granite."

At breakfast a lean-jawed young member of a jackhammer crew at Grand Coulee Dam looked up from one of the Spokane newspapers scattered over the mess-hall tables. "H'm-m," he said, half to himself, "it says Franco's outfit has captured some power plants." He turned to the man eating hotcakes and ham beside him. "Wonder what'd happen if they tried that here?"

Both workers looked out of the window to orient themselves to their surroundings. Then they began speculating on the probable outcome should the legions of General Franco —or some other foreign militarist—suddenly appear in the last American wilderness and try to take over the country's biggest power project.

A potato grower in the Snake River valley liked the idea

of a national referendum on war, but was not sure it would work. The reason for his skepticism was unique. Idaho had just had a referendum on the sales tax. He thought the people had been confused about it. "If they get mixed up about a little tax here at home," he asked, "how can they decide about a lot of foreign plotting ten thousand miles away?"

Near a rural community in the State of Washington, a middle-aged orchardist brought to his own locale the other aspect of the war referendum question. "I got a congressman," he said, "who wrote me a letter about fruit raising that don't make a radish o' sense. If he hasn't got 'nough sense to know somethin' about apples, I don't see how he can know anythin' about dictators. I'll be darned if I want him to be able to send my boy off to war."

A few years ago I stumped my State for the independent candidate for governor. He was a farmer, and farmers put me up each night. I remember a big ranch I stopped at below the hump of McKenzie Pass. The people were descendants of Jesse Applegate, who had led one of the first covered-wagon caravans to the Oregon Country. "We're still for progress," the smiling farm wife told me, and over the big stone fireplace hung pictures of Senator La Follette the elder and President Roosevelt. The dinner we had that night was one of the best I ever ate. There was a roast beef as big as a mimeograph machine, and gravy that swamped froths of mashed potatoes and mounds of peas. The pear cobbler for dessert was inundated beneath a glacier of homemade vanilla ice cream.

Afterward we sat around the fire as it drove off the chill of the autumn night. Germany seemed far away from that ranch locked in the Oregon fastnesses, but one of the boys had read in the paper the day before about Hitler's rearmament program. He mentioned it. His mother looked out of the window, to where the moon loomed above the jagged sky line. "Don't worry, son," she said. "There's room enough in these hills for the whole German army to be lost. Rural Free Delivery hasn't found us yet. I don't see how the Germans can!"

She smiled, and poked the fire in the fireplace her pioneering father had built when the Oregon Country was very young.

-4-

There is no more conclusive proof that the Columbia River basin is still a frontier than the rambling shack villages that follow every great construction project in the region. Civilization is left far behind as man attempts to master the wilds of the Northwest. These hinterland outposts marked the Great Northern's boring of an eight-mile tunnel through the core of the Cascades a few years ago, and today they mark the great Federal dams at Fort Peck, Bonneville, and Grand Coulee.* Construction undertakings elsewhere are relatively close to cities and towns. In the Northwest they are hundreds of miles away. They must take a crude sort of society with them. This society generally takes the form of frontier villages strikingly similar to those in which the picturesque characters of the old West lived, sinned, and died.

Fly-by-night towns in the wilderness are not yet confined only to movie sets. There is one at Grand Coulee Dam as boisterous and melodramatic as any through which Tom Mix or Gary Cooper ever galloped. Jim Marshall of *Collier's* named it "Boom Town," and a newspaperman in Seattle once called it "the toughest place in North America."

Grand Coulee—as well as the other towns which merge

* See Chapters 3, 4, and 12.

with it—sprawls over the uplands above the great dam like a torn and ragged carpet. There is no order or planning. Shacks and cabins dot the hills as unevenly as marbles rolled on a rug. The streets are rut-strewn and sloping. In wet weather they are a series of ponds, and in dry weather they are prolific manufacturers of dust. If the gasoline pumps were hitching posts and the neon signs were oil lamps, Grand Coulee might be one of the mushroom towns which followed the Northern Pacific westward.

In contrast to the dam which, rising block on block in the river canyon, appears as permanent as granite, the town of Grand Coulee seems as ephemeral as a one-night circus stand. The buildings are of crude lumber or formed from tar-paper tacked to laths. Here and there is one of greater durability, but it is an exception. Tents, shacks, and lean-tos stud vacant plots of ground. Some of the houses resemble big packing boxes. A piano would fill most of them to overflowing. Everything bespeaks haste and hurry and carelessness.

Seven thousand men working on a giant construction project means seven thousand men to spend money on food, drink, women, clothes, and amusement. Five years ago this fact became apparent to many of the individuals who now inhabit Grand Coulee. They got out maps and discovered that the proposed site of the dam was two hundred fifty miles from Seattle and three hundred eighty-one miles from Portland. The law of supply and demand was put into operation, and these people headed into the wilderness. There was certain to be a demand, and they would provide the supply.

Barbers, cooks, taxi drivers, electricians, mechanics, newspapermen, manicurists, dishwashers, innkeepers, musicians, entertainers, carpenters, druggists, butchers, grocers, prostitutes, locksmiths, lawyers, doctors, teachers, dentists, dope peddlers, ministers, photographers, waitresses, tailors, jewelers—all trekked across the undulating uplands of eastern Washington to the scene of the government's most important PWA undertaking.

Every element—good, bad, and indifferent—that goes to compose a community in the hinterlands, joined the parade. Over the desertlike plateau of the Columbia a veritable caravan rolled. From trucks, wagons, and trailers protruded barber chairs, hand printing presses, and permanent-waving machines. Cooks dreamed of making fortunes out of hamburgers and custard pie and beer. Real-estate agents visioned lucrative returns on the quick turnover of lots and sections. Ministers thought of men to reform spiritually and morally. Prostitutes imagined ready dollars.

Today, Grand Coulee contains all the paradoxes of the more complex civilization beyond the mountains. There are churches where some of the workers go to worship on Sunday mornings, and there is a tiny newspaper office where several enterprising young men strive to tell the world the progress on the biggest dam ever planned. Along B Street brothels operate wide open. On one side of the rutted road an evangelist cries out that he is saving souls; on the other a wizened little fellow with a whisky breath whispers that he knows of a shack where, for the modest price of one dollar, you can watch a young lady dancing in the nude. The city hall is an old dancing pavilion.

This is Grand Coulee: a mushroom town of the sixties and the nineties reproduced in 1938. Here salvation and sin stroll opposite boardwalks on the same street. Here past and present meet in front of a beer parlor. An Indian sheepherder, down from his lonely vigil in the hills, peers wonderingly through the smudgy plateglass window. Inside, a score of taxi dancers stumble about in the arms of workers from the dam. The radio on the counter has picked up a national network pro-

gram, and the Indian listens to a jazz band spanning the
ether from New York City, twenty-five hundred miles away.

From hopes and visions and dreams, Grand Coulee was
built on the hills. It grew like a mushroom and flourished
like a weed. Sagebrush flats one day became the sites of taverns and general stores the next. The first shelters were
scarcely larger than tents. Ferd Warner's barber shop was so
small he had to step outside to strop his razor. But swiftly
the trek increased. The original cluster of shacks and cabins
expanded into a sprawling agglomeration of lumber and paint
and gaudy signs.

Social disease is one of the most distressing problems at
Grand Coulee. The prostitutes undergo periodic examinations,
but this does not apply to the taxi dancers, some of whom are
claimed to part with their virtue for the price of a ham sandwich and a glass of beer. Many of the women in the brothels
complain that the pseudo-amateur competition from some of
the taxi dancers has made prostitution a submarginal occupation in Grand Coulee. "There's no more money here in this
racket," said one prostitute. "The damned dames who chippy
for thirty-five cents have wrecked it."

Signs with little red-cross symbols indicate the presence of
prophylactic stations; but just how widely these are used is
debatable. The prevalence of venereal disease in Grand Coulee is a hotly disputed question. That it is fairly rampant,
there is no doubt. Some of the men at the dam are so cautious
that, when they go up on the hill to one of the shack towns,
they order bottled beer and will not drink out of glasses filled
at the tap.

How widely the taxi dancers cut into the prostitution business is also an intangible question. One woman running a
dance hall at which the girls get ten cents a dance and give
the house half of that, contended that the taxi dancers are as

virtuous as any other young women. But other people claim that the taxi dancers, too, should undergo regular examinations, and that a regular check should be kept on where they live.

B Street is where most of the revelry in Grand Coulee takes place. There the men dance, play cards, drink beer, gamble, quarrel, pick up women, and loll along the sidewalk. Once in a while there are fist fights, but not many. Most of the magazines sold are pulps or else slick-paper periodicals filled with photographs of young ladies of the stage and screen in various degrees of nudity.

There are some pretty tough people on hand, and I watched in goggle-eyed amazement as a big-jowled bartender threw out of his establishment a redheaded taxi dancer who insisted on taunting him. There was neither restraint nor chivalry in the manner in which the young lady was induced to leave the beer emporium.

It is likely there is nothing at Grand Coulee which does not exist in Seattle or Portland or Des Moines or Denver or any other city. But it prevails in highly concentrated form, and this is why Grand Coulee is notorious throughout the United States as a citadel of wild living. In defense of whatever exists in the shack towns surrounding the great dam, an engineer said to me:

"After all, constructing the largest edifice in the history of mankind is no kindergarten picnic. Men who can hew down granite cliffs and walk on girders five hundred feet above the Columbia River are not nice Nellies. They are men who need diversion and amusement.

"The nearest city is nearly a hundred miles away. If the entertainment and hilarity available at the Grand Coulee shack towns were not there, many of the men would quit. After working eight hours with a jackhammer or cement

mixer, you cannot expect men to go home and read disserta-
tions of a high moral character. The mushroom villages are
where they blow off steam. The conditions there are necessary
and essential."

So Grand Coulee squats on its hills and is a definite social
phase of a great engineering project in the wilderness. In it
live wild and dissolute individuals, and in it also live decent
and respectable and upright Americans who are trying to
make a living on the country's last great frontier. On one side
of B Street you may find a crooked gambler or a shameless
woman; and on the other you may find a sun-tanned worker
from the dam, a typical Irishman with a broad smile and
sharp jaw, who stands in a grocery store with one of his little
children on either hand and buys veal cutlets and string beans
for their supper.

Grand Coulee is a page from the past. If it were not for
a few technological developments such as radio repair shops
and automobiles, it might be recognizable to Buffalo Bill and
Jim Bridger and other heroes of pioneer days in the West.
With her low-necked dress, heavily rouged cheeks, and forced
smile, the taxi dancer in the Silver Dollar might be a character from a Jack Dalton serial of the Klondike.

Whether they trekked across the barren uplands to peddle
dances, to mix prescriptions, to fry T-bone steaks, to remove
tonsils, to save souls, to provide sexual intercourse, to sell
groceries, or to write newspaper dispatches, most of the inhabitants of Grand Coulee arrived there with a single dominant thought. Seven thousand men were about to be put to
work at fairly high and steady pay. Those seven thousand
men meant money to be spent. Grand Coulee is the maw into
which the money pours—that is, all except that which is spent
in the contractor's camp for food and lodging.

The model communities at the dam of Mason City and

Coulee Dam are contributions to progress. They represent a vast forward step from the tents and shacks and huts in which the movers of the frontier once lived. Half a century ago the laborer who pounded spikes on the railroad slept under canvas at night and ate a starchy, monotonous diet. Today the carpenter or riveter at Grand Coulee Dam lives in a cottage or dormitory heated and lighted by electricity, and eats vegetables and fruits kept cold in the largest ice plant in the world.

Yet on the hills above the dam is a scene that would be familiar to the laborer of railroad days. There in Grand Coulee is the boisterous, tense crowd—drinking beer, eyeing the dancers, quarreling, looking for entertainment and revelry. There is the heterogeneous mixture of tall jackhammer men and squat real-estate agents, smooth-cheeked girls who have just come from cities and farms, and rough-faced women who must pry apart dour lips to force a smile. There is the dingy restaurant in which a skullcapped cook fries chops and hashed-browns amidst a sticky swirl of steam and smoke.

Intrinsically, the shack towns that look down on the enormous dam are of no significance. They are merely a shamble of human existence in the waste lands. But they show emphatically that there is still a frontier in the United States, and that man cannot penetrate that frontier without creating conditions akin to those which accompanied the first manifestations of organized society in the vast area west of the divide.

-5-

I am on a train. It is rolling swiftly through the Columbia basin, and the ridges twist and pass. I am in the day coach. It is more interesting there. I know what is taking place back in the observation car, where the men and women are talking about giving business a breathing spell. They are berating Roosevelt, and when the train crashes past Bonneville Dam, their hatred will become more pointed and more bitter. Up here in the crowded coach the people seem different. They look out with a different attitude at the wilderness hurtling by. Most of them have not made successes of their lives. Some of them are farmers going to Portland or Seattle for loans from the government. A few of them are dazed and bewildered refugees from the Dust Bowl. Others are men and women coming West to see if things are not just a little better than in the crowded East. Perhaps the frontier is the Promised Land of opportunity, after all!

On the other side of the car window, the hinterlands stretch away to the horizon. They appear to roll on forever. Surely there must be a chance in those limitless ranges for the weary people in the day coach. The train gathers speed. It rolls past the buttes where Lewis and Clark camped, and it thunders across a mountain creek that flows to the Columbia. I look around at the tired and wan faces in the long, air-conditioned car. A little boy toddles up the aisle. The brakeman calls out that Bonneville Dam is only two miles down the river. Faces are glued to the window. A stump rancher's uneven plot is passed, and he watches as the train becomes a dwindling speck along the river. I look around the car again. I gaze out at the wilderness. I see the faint smoke of a secluded lumber camp in the hills across the Columbia. And I think that here in the clattering, crowded day coach and out there in the hinterlands of the Northwest lies the future of America's Promised Land—that in the ability of these people who jam the railroad car to make the resources of the region serve them and others like them throughout the nation, rests the ultimate destiny of the great frontier beyond the Rockies.

15. Sundown Patrol

The Mediterranean era died with the discovery of America; the Atlantic era has reached the height of its development. The Pacific era, destined to be the greatest, is just at its dawn.

—THEODORE ROOSEVELT.

IT WAS Nyssa's greatest day. The President of the United States was coming. No President had ever visited Nyssa before. Why should the most important man in the country visit a little place far in the Oregon hinterlands—a place with fewer votes than one apartment house in Boston or Philadelphia? And this President coming to Nyssa was no ordinary President. He was Mr. Roosevelt, the famous "F. D. R." who built the big dams down the Columbia, who promised a new chance to the refugees from the Dust Bowl, who said the Indians should keep their ancient treaty rights, who sent the CCC boys into the wilderness, and who visioned one day a land of hope and promise on the last frontier.

The sun glared down from a cloudless sky. Off in the distance the ramparts of the Seven Devils marked the boisterous passage of the Snake through Idaho. Lower hills westward signaled the swift, downhill rush of the Columbia. Scattered farmhouses dotted the plain like dice on a gigantic gambling table. The people of the tiny hamlet waited impassively. Then—a swirl of dust on the macadam road, and Mr. Roosevelt was in sight! The grade-school band bravely started to struggle with the strong cadence of *King Cotton.* I saw a little Indian boy with puffed-out cheeks blowing at the cornet. Flags were gay splotches of color against the light green of poplar trees.

Behind motorcycle troopers of Oregon and Idaho, the President came. A golden-haired girl with a winsome smile held a sign, "Our President, Please Go Slow!" and he did. A cheer went up from the people converging on the narrow road that sounded like a hundred locomotives in a hundred echoing ravines. Mr. Roosevelt has had many enthusiastic receptions but, veteran Washington correspondents assured me, none more vociferous or warm-hearted than that given him by these people from the hinterland. Along the road I saw them: the citizens of the American backwoods. There they were—stoical, swarthy-faced Indians with braids of hair hanging over vividly plaided shirts; weary, gaunt-cheeked travelers from the burned-out States across the Rockies; smiling, devil-may-care cowpunchers in chaps and big sombreros; tall, slow-moving ranchers with half a century of range life behind most of them; impassive woodsmen and lumberjacks and trappers, down from the thick timber to get their first glimpse of a President of their country.

There was a reason for the whole-souled greeting the people on the frontier gave Mr. Roosevelt. To them he is not the average President. He is not merely the President of those legendary folks of the great cities far away. He is more than the President of the rich metropolises seen in the movies and Sunday rotogravure sections. To the inhabitants of the hinterland he is also *their* President, as honestly concerned about them as he is about the places with millions of people. What other President ever showed so great an interest in his constituents living beyond the final outposts of civilization?

An appraisal of the country's last frontier cannot be com-

plete without considering Mr. Roosevelt's part in the destiny
of the region. Profoundly and significantly though his policies have affected the rest of the nation, their greatest effect
has been on the wilderness areas.

From Jefferson, who sponsored Lewis and Clark, to the
present Roosevelt, no President displayed more than per-
functory interest in the spacious basin of the Columbia River.
All seven States wholly or partially encompassed by the
watershed have about as many electoral votes as Illinois.*
Why waste time on a hinterland eight or ten times as big as
New England, yet with less potency at the polls than New
York City?

Theodore Roosevelt loved to hunt in the Western fastnesses. He talked at length about conservation and reforestation, and he stopped the exploitation and waste of many
valuable resources. But he did nothing affirmative to develop
them, and nothing affirmative was done until his namesake
came along a generation later. Most Presidents concentrated
their attention on the centers of population, and glanced only
occasionally at the frontier between the upper forks of the
Missouri and the lower reaches of the Columbia. And an outlet westward was not necessary as long as the country was
booming and the economic machinery was functioning without unemployment. During the halcyon days of Coolidge prosperity, the country thought little about the irritating dilemma
of crowded rookeries in the East and uninhabited hinterlands
in the Far West.

Since 1933 the Promised Land dream has burst full anew
on the Pacific Northwest. The most massive dams of all time
have been built at Bonneville and Grand Coulee. Other barriers are contemplated on the Columbia, the Snake, the Wil-

---

* Montana, 4; Oregon, 5; Washington, 8; Nevada, 3; Wyoming, 3; Utah, 4;
Idaho, 4.

lamette, and the Skagit. CCC boys have begun an intensive program of soil and forest protection. Irrigation canals flow where only sagebrush grew before. Reclamation dams have transformed waste lands into orchards. The Farm Security Administration has helped thousands of Dust Bowl pilgrims become rehabilitated in the Far West. The Federal housing program may eventually turn into bungalows and apartment houses some of the lofty fir trees that blanket the slopes of the Cascades and Sierras.

With all these plans and undertakings, there are many imperfections; good ideas have been slovenly and carelessly carried out, as observe the financial confusion gripping the Bonneville public power districts. Yet the program of the New Deal, with all its faulty management, represents the first conscious attempt of the government to utilize for all the people the vast, untapped resources of the frontier. Whatever else Mr. Roosevelt may have done to or for the country, that much he has accomplished in the Columbia River basin. Never again can the natural riches of the hinterlands be left as undeveloped as they were in the years before the New Deal.

Mr. Roosevelt has a sort of personal affinity with the people of the frontier which cannot be disregarded. He likes them. He wants to help them. He makes small secret of the fact that he prefers them to the stuffy and artificial East. At Boise last year he called the national capital "one of the narrowest places in the world," and said that like Antaeus of old, he regained strength just by getting out in the country and meeting the people and touching the earth. And after his trip through the Columbia basin, the President quoted again Horace Greeley's admonition to "Go West!" and counseled on the New York *Herald-Tribune* Forum:

"Take a secondhand car, put on a flannel shirt, drive out to the Coast by the Northern route and come back by the

Southern route. Don't stop anywhere you have to pay more than two dollars for your room and bath. Don't talk to your banking friends or your chamber of commerce friends, but specialize on the gasoline station man, the small restaurant keeper and farmers you meet by the wayside and your fellow automobile travelers."

This friendly comradeship with the people of the back-woods, and with the people along the way to the backwoods, has prompted the President to devote much of his attention to the white spaces on the census map. He seeks to have the Western wilderness put to use. Not long ago this quest was carried on in the form of plans to conserve and increase the forest resources. And only recently Mr. Roosevelt proposed to Congress that the immense phosphate beds of Idaho, Montana, Wyoming, and Utah be developed for the farms of the whole nation.

His message in this respect dramatized sharply the way the natural wealth of the Columbia basin has been neglected and forgotten. The Northwest contains 91 per cent of all the phosphate rock in the country. Yet less than 3 per cent of the production takes place there. Florida and Tennessee have less than 10 per cent of the deposits, but furnish 97 per cent of the phosphate used. And phosphate is essential to farming. The President proposes that the vast Western sources of this agricultural prerequisite be tapped to some degree at least. Until he urged such action, the bulk of the country's most important stimulus to growth and plant life lay beneath the hills of the Columbia River country, almost as overlooked as it was before Captain Meriwether Lewis trod those hills and claimed them for the United States.

It is at Grand Coulee that the interest of Mr. Roosevelt in the hinterlands achieves its most spectacular and visible realization. The great river ponderously turns north in its rugged canyon, and beyond the brink of the cliffs the table-lands stretch away gaunt and barren. They are uninhabited now; but some day the vast dam down in the canyon will enable them to support countless Americans from the other side of the continent. Across the Columbia the enormous barrier sprawls. It stretches from precipice to precipice, a tangible manifestation of the President's hope of a Promised Land in the Northwest. The dam is only one-third finished now, but already it is larger than the Great Pyramid.

The President talked to an engineer about it the day he was there. They sat in his automobile and looked at maps and blue prints. Far below, pygmylike creatures moved about on the immense slab of concrete. Shadows slowly crept over the gorge. The President and the engineer looked now and then at the unbelievably large barrier in the canyon, and then bent again over the papers in the car. I felt I was seeing an American dream slowly take shape, as inch by inch the greatest structure on the planet rose above the pounding river, while from the heights above the President watched the dazzling fantasy.

Mr. Roosevelt munched the sandwich and sipped the coffee that constituted the bulk of his lunch, and over on the other side of the dusty road a dirt-streaked, helmeted worker from the dam did likewise. The President waved a hand at the worker, and the worker grinned back. They both were pushing back their country's frontier, weren't they?

-2-

"There are parts of this nation that are not as favored as the Northwest," Mr. Roosevelt declared in the Far West last year. "Mistakes have been made. They have cut off their timber. Their land is played out, or they plowed up prairie land which is now blowing away. I am thinking about those people as well as you people. You have got room for them here in the Northwest where they can make homes, where they can live happily and prosperously."

This is the President's vision—the vision of a Promised Land in the basin of the Columbia River.

Will it really come true?

I have a friend who is a Forest Service lookout on a mighty mountain peak in the hinterland of the State of Washington. Each year he spends four months on this lofty summit, watching for fires in the waves of timber far below. A narrow trail leads to his lonely tower. It is a day's climb to reach it, and the ascent nearly incapacitates an inexperienced climber.

One afternoon I sat with him in the little cabin that is anchored to the granite with bolts and cables to keep it from being blown away in the blizzards of winter. Night was coming on, and the sun had started to dip below the snow-capped pinnacles of the Cascades. Dusk was throwing a black coverlet on the frontier. We were riding the bowsprit of a great ship that plowed through a limitless ocean. As far as binoculars could reach, the wilderness seemed to stretch away to infinity. We might as well have been on a peak in the depths of Africa or Brazil. Yet through the little radio on the table came an orchestra from the East, and beyond the hinterland we knew there was the thin thread of Western civilization where timber interests and labor unions and power companies and politicians struggle and scramble greedily for power on the last frontier.

My friend looked out over the outpost land on which night was settling. "You know," he said, "I wonder if people ever will inhabit and settle all this territory. Do you think this will be a wilderness forever, or some day will there be cities and towns all through here just like in the East?"

I did not answer him. I just sat there, watching the darkness cover the last great frontier of the United States. But I wondered, too.

THE END